"Dr. Diane Poythress has writte[n] speaking world the significant [c...] man who, as a fountainhead of t[h...] widely known Protestant doctrine appealing to patristic support for [...] Greek New Testament of Desiderius Erasmus, interacted with luminaries like Martin Luther and Ulrich Zwingli, exerted significant influence on John Calvin and his reforming measures in Geneva, successfully confronted the corrupt Catholic Church of his day, and transformed Basel into a Reformed city (while restructuring the city government, schools, and university), interceded for the Anabaptists, and much more.

"So how does one describe a book that is in a category by itself? Definitive? Indispensible? Pioneering? Essential? Perhaps better than providing a description, let me offer thanks to Diane Poythress for her labor in preparing this unique gift. And let me urge all who love the Reformation and/or desire to know what has been up to now an overlooked theologian of that movement to read this exceptional, well-researched, and well-written book."

—Gregg R. Allison, *Professor of Christian Theology,*
The Southern Baptist Theological Seminary, and author of
Historical Theology: An Introduction to Christian Doctrine

"Those with a nodding acquaintance with the name and ministry of Johannes Oecolampadius have longed for a fuller introduction in English of this sixteenth-century Reformer's life and thought. This is what Dr. Diane Poythress's book provides. Usually associated with his contemporary German-Swiss Reformer Ulrich Zwingli, partly for his participation in the Marburg Colloquy of 1529 and partly for his death at age forty-nine just six weeks after Zwingli was killed in battle in 1531, Oecolampadius is shown here to have anticipated many of the reforming insights and activities of Martin Bucer and John Calvin. These appear in such areas as church discipline, the role of the elder, exegesis, and biblical theology. This scholarly and godly figure is one that twenty-first-century ministers and theologians can profit from knowing and emulating."

—William S. Barker, *Emeritus Professor of Church History,*
Westminster Theological Seminary

"Contemporary of Ulrich Zwingli and Protestant leader of Basel, Johannes Oecolampadius is arguably the most important of the forgotten first-generation Reformers. His numerous commentaries on Scripture and writings on the Lord's Supper and church discipline informed the leading lights of subsequent Reformers like Calvin, Bucer, and Melanchthon. Poythress artfully re-introduces Oecolampadius to twenty-first-century readers by leading them on a well-rounded tour of his life, reforming activities, hermeneutics, Reformed convictions, and commentaries. *Reformer of Basel* houses a wealth of historical and theological detail and will prove to be an important addition to Reformation studies. A must-read for all those who cherish their Reformation heritage."

—Robert Caldwell, *Assistant Professor of Church History,*
Southwestern Baptist Theological Seminary

"It is almost incredible that no book-length monograph has ever been published in English on this exceedingly important Reformer of the Basel church, Johannes Oecolampadius, who played such a decisive role in the formation of the later Presbyterian-Reformed church polity, especially in the inception and establishment of eldership among the church officers.

"This new book by Diane Poythress, thanks to her linguistic brilliance in the sixteenth- century Swiss German and Latin, sheds a new light on this Reformer, not just as an academic or a scholar but more as a pastor or, in German, a *Seelsorger* (caretaker of souls), by way of the autonomous discipline of excommunication, as John Calvin later named it. Through this book, the readers will learn that Oecolampadius's prayer was centered solely around the rediscovery and remedy of the lost sheep back to Christ's fold.

"I am convinced that this book will prove a great contribution to the Reformation research in English-speaking countries. It will be my great joy to see it enjoy an extensive circulation for years to come."

—Akira Demura, *Professor Emeritus of Church History,*
Tohoku Gakuin University, Sendai, Japan

"Recent years have witnessed the publication of many monographs and scholarly articles dedicated to serially neglected Reformed theologians of the sixteenth century. One such figure is Johannes Oecolampadius, a first-generation Reformed theologian and civic reformer who, when mentioned at all, is frequently depicted as a minor figure among better-known contemporaries such as Ulrich Zwingli and Martin Bucer. Diane Poythress has helpfully filled this lacuna with this new introduction to Oecolampadius's career and convictions. Her discussion of the Reformer's relationships with his more famous contemporaries, particularly his probable influence on Calvin himself, is particularly helpful. The sections on Oecolampadius's approach to biblical interpretation and the introduction to his core theological convictions are most welcome. Poythress's study will be the starting place for English-speaking students and scholars interested in studying the life and doctrine of this key early Reformed leader."

—Nathan A. Finn, *Associate Professor of Historical Theology,*
Southeastern Baptist Theological Seminary

"This scholarly book on Oecolampadius will be a necessary addition to any library of sixteenth-century works. Dr. Poythress has brought to life this lesser-known Reformer by painting a vivid picture of his life and contributions in the context of essential Protestant themes. She connects his theology to that of other Reformation personalities and provides a thorough review of all his published works. For Poythress, Oecolampadius is a model pastor-scholar who offered a fresh vision for renewing the church in his day and ours."

—S. Donald Fortson, *Professor of Church History,*
Reformed Theological Seminary (Charlotte)

"In *The Reformer of Basel: The Life, Thought, and Influence of Johannes Oecolampadius*, Diane Poythress provides a fresh reason to probe the lives and thinking of little-acknowledged figures of the Protestant Reformation. Oecolampadius, literally, the 'house lamp,' brought to light what became the distinguishing features of Reformed Christianity. In this excellent biographical and thematic study of the Reformer of Basel—one of the very few in English—Poythress probes his pioneering work in original languages, exegetical and historical studies, liturgy, church discipline, guidance to pastors, and balance of intellect and pious devotion. Commentator on over twenty biblical books, historian unpacking the labors of early fathers such as Chrysostom, John of Damascus, and Augustine, the Reformer of Basel foreshadowed what was best to be found in Bucer and Calvin. Zwingli had ample reason to call Oecolampadius's works a 'cornucopia.' An additional benefit of this fine work is Poythress's summaries of Oecolampadius's interaction with his contemporary Reformers and his influence on reformations occurring in other European countries."

—Andrew Hoffecker, *Emeritus Professor of Church History,*
Reformed Theological Seminary (Jackson)

"Thanks to Diane Poythress I must substantially modify my rather truncated lecture on Calvin's education in Strassburg under Martin Bucer. Poythress expands the Reformed axis by demonstrating a strong Basel-Strassburg and Genevan connection. The Reformer of Basel, Johannes Oecolampadius, was in fact the theologian behind many of the ideas Calvin embraced, including the relationship of church and state, church discipline, Reformed liturgy, and aspects of the Lord's Supper and union with Christ. Any subsequent study of the Lutheran and Reformed branch of the Reformation must include Oecolampadius. This book is the place to begin."

—Dale Walden *Johnson, Professor of Church History, Erskine Theological Seminary*

"In *Reformer of Basel* Diane Poythress introduces us to a generally overlooked early Reformer who was, in her apt metaphor, a 'funnel' who collected the wisdom of the past and poured it into his times. She documents the importance of Oecolampadius in the development of typological exegesis, his striving to reform the discipline of the church, and his remarkable capacity for friendship with other first-generation Reformers. As Dr. Poythress observes and ably demonstrates, if John Calvin is the father of the Reformed churches, he is also the son of Johannes Oecolampadius."

—John R. Muether, *Professor of Church History,*
Reformed Theological Seminary (Orlando)

"This work on Oecolampadius by Diane Poythress is an enchiridion on the Reformation. The life of the subject himself is a wonder of providence. His connections through personal contact or by theological and literary influence with the other major Reformers give an instructive picture of the organic relations of ideas in the development of Reformation thought and demonstrate the pivotal substantive nature of his influence on all aspects of the Reformation.

Poythress has done a masterful job of laying out the linguistic skills of the Basel Reformer as well as the more subtle and broadly demanding aspects of his full hermeneutical method. She has given a succinct yet sufficiently nuanced presentation of his Reformation theology and the relentless way in which he discussed all doctrine from a christocentric interpretation of the biblical text. Her presentation of Oecolampadius's instructions, and practice, about the importance of preaching is a sobering and encouraging word to any generation. In an immaculately scholarly and trustworthy presentation, Poythress has also managed to be highly accessible to readers, transparently devoted to Reformation theology, and seriously encouraging to biblical piety."

—Tom J. Nettles, *Professor of Historical Theology,*
The Southern Baptist Theological Seminary

"In his day, Oecolampadius attracted the likes of Erasmus and Luther. It's not too much of a stretch to claim that his exegetical and grammatical work in Hebrew and Greek stands behind the return to the Bible and the world-changing preaching of the Reformation. Yet he has become a forgotten soul today. This book corrects that. Thanks to the tireless and deft efforts of Dr. Diane Poythress, this great voice from the past once again speaks to the church with clarity and conviction. Oecolampadius and we too are in her debt."

—Stephen J. Nichols, *Research Professor of Christianity*
and Culture, Lancaster Bible College

"In this carefully researched study, Diane Poythress has opened for her readers the fascinating world of Johannes Oecolampadius, an important but often overlooked sixteenth-century pastor, teacher, and *Reformer. Reformer of Basel: The Life, Thought, and Influence of Johannes Oecolampadius* makes a valuable contribution to our understanding of the Protestant Reformation and one of its most interesting leaders."

—Garth M. Rosell, *Professor of Church History,*
Gordon-Conwell Theological Seminary

"Dr. Diane Poythress has produced a book that is both informative and inspiring. Informative because she brings needed data to our attention about a too-little-known figure of the Reformation in Basel, who not only influenced better-known Reformers but also did important theological work, especially in hermeneutics, ecclesiology, church polity, and even church and state. Inspiring because Oecolampadius was both learned and godly, and focus upon such a life is sure to encourage other pilgrims in their journey. Diane is to be thanked and congratulated for foregrounding Oecolampadius and translating some of his rarely read work so that we can all get to know him and the God that he sought to glorify better."

—Alan D. Strange, *Associate Professor of Church History,*
Mid-America Reformed Seminary

Reformer of Basel

THE LIFE, THOUGHT, AND INFLUENCE OF
JOHANNES OECOLAMPADIUS

Reformer of Basel

THE LIFE, THOUGHT, AND INFLUENCE OF JOHANNES OECOLAMPADIUS

Diane Poythress

Reformation Heritage Books
Grand Rapids, Michigan

Reformer of Basel
© 2011 by Diane Poythress

Reformation Heritage Books
2965 Leonard St. NE
Grand Rapids, MI 49525
616-977-0889 / Fax 616-285-3246
e-mail: orders@heritagebooks.org
website: www.heritagebooks.org

Printed in the United States of America
11 12 13 14 15 16/10 9 8 7 6 5 4 3 2 1

Library of Congress Cataloging-in-Publication Data

Poythress, Diane.
  Reformer of Basel : the life, thought, and influence of Johannes Oecolampadius / Diane Poythress.
      p. cm.
  Includes bibliographical references (p.   ) and index.
  ISBN 978-1-60178-150-5 (pbk. : alk. paper)
  1. Oecolampadius, Johann, 1482-1531. 2. Reformation. I. Title.
  BR350.O33P69 2011
  270.6092--dc23
  [B]
                              2011033846

For additional Reformed literature, both new and used, request a free book list from Reformation Heritage Books at the above address.

To my husband,

Dr. Vern S. Poythress,

the only person who has supported me through eleven years of a doctorate and twenty years of rewriting my dissertation. He has patiently read and reread paragraphs I've given him for inspection. He has helped me over translation difficulties. He has repeatedly fixed the obstreperous computer. And he has always prayed for and encouraged me. Besides this, he has always been the houselight in our home who explained the Bible, pointed to God, and lived a faithful and godly life. In all of this, he has loved me, which is the most overwhelming grace I have experienced apart from Christ Himself.

And to my parents,

Harold and Lucille Weisenborn,

and my sister,

Denise Weisenborn.

Contents

Observe here, whoever acts as a preacher, [the nature of] your office. For the task is, that with Isaiah you may first be a disciple rather than a teacher, and may be among those who have seen God, whom Scripture calls "theodidaktous" [taught by God]. May you also be called by God, as was Aaron, and not like Nadab and Abihu, and Korah and others. May the desire of Uzziah first die to you, who intruded into sacred things from his own audacity. [Such desire] dies, however, if you do not receive glory from people. For from arrogance is born in the mind the contagious disease of leprosy, which is a symbol of heresy. That you also may see, with Moses that earthly filthiness and dirtiness of passions, for you will not be fitting to them, in order that you may be sent or may teach. That you also may be a surety of election, the task is, that in you may be prostrated Saul, and may rise up Paul; that you may no longer seek the things which are of the flesh, the things which belong to pharisaical righteousness, the things which are yours, but those of Jesus Christ, and those of others [who are] in Jesus. Withdraw, you also, with Ezekiel to the river Chebar, lest you seek to be praised by people and to be called "rabbi." And when you know God and see how great is His majesty, beyond profound and inscrutable judgment, and how great is His goodness, then, if the vision be to that [such a calling], teach, lest you be among those who run but are not sent, and instead of the Word of God you offer the trash of your dreams. In Scripture, however, if you search them, you will see God.... As therefore the Seraph was sent to Isaiah, in order that he might be cleansed, might learn, and might teach; so Isaiah or another [is sent] to us, that we might be cleansed, might learn, and after that we might undertake the office of teacher.

—Johannes Oecolampadius, commenting on Isaiah 6:1

CHAPTER ONE

From Germany to Switzerland

THE LIFE OF JOHANNES OECOLAMPADIUS

"IT IS ONE OF SATAN'S most cunning and consistent strategies." That was my friend's remark when I showed him an extraordinary painting done by a little known Christian artist of the nineteenth century. Satan tries to bury in obscurity the stunning work by believers throughout history. Such is the case with Johannes Oecolampadius, the Reformer of Basel. His life of boldness, piety, and pathos alone should be read to inspire Christians today. A small glimpse of the pastor shepherding his own family, the faithful, the sick, the wayward, and the unbeliever should suffice to challenge all Christendom as a model. But such a limited portrait would ignore his historical significance as arguably the spiritual father of Calvin and the entire Reformed church. One particular aspect of his influence, soundly documented yet also forgotten, is his initiation of church discipline and reinstitution of the office of elder. His fluency in languages, exacting exegesis, and hermeneutics led scholars into proper biblical investigation. Personally, Oecolampadius's intimate love for God and understanding of His ways, as evidenced in his commentaries, have often sent me to my knees.

Oecolampadius drew words from the deep spiritual well of Scripture, words which have yet to be drunk by modern readers. None of his commentaries on Genesis, Job, Psalms, Isaiah, Jeremiah, Ezekiel, Daniel, Hosea, Joel, Amos, Obadiah, Jonah, Micah, Haggai, Zechariah, Malachi, Matthew, Romans, Colossians,

Hebrews, and 1 John have been translated into English. Perhaps one day this treasure box will be fully opened to modern readers. Until then, let us satisfy ourselves with this survey of the life and thought of this saintly man.

1482–1514

A great light in God's church shone through a baby, born in 1482, whose surname in God's providence meant "house lamp." Johannes Hausshein (or Oecolampadius in Greek) was born in Weinsberg, Germany. His father, Johannes, originally intended him to be a tradesman, but chose a law career for his son when the boy proved brilliant. His mother, Anna, encouraged her only surviving child in his studies and influenced him by her example of piety and practical charity, ministering to him until her death in 1528.

Young Johannes probably began his education at a local German school, then proceeded to a Latin school in Heilbronn where promising young men prepared for university. A typical day began at 5 a.m. with Latin. Atypically, his schoolmaster trained students in the humanist revival. This method involved a return to reading classical sources in original languages, covering grammar, logic, and rhetoric in a manner opposed to medieval Scholasticism.

At age seventeen, Johannes began university studies at Heidelberg. There he heard more humanist teaching from a forerunner of the Reformation, Jakob Wimpfeling, who passionately lectured on moral reform in the church. Young Johannes even wrote a Latin poem in honor of this teacher:

> To a youth, that he may begin to love God at the right time, the first effort of John Heusegen of Weinsberg: Love with your whole heart the word-bearing Christ, Who is the fount and garden of pious righteousness. Sweet marjoram must be sought in this Hyblaean field; For here lies the great grace of the almighty God.[1]

---

1. Ernst Staehelin, *Briefe und Akten zum Leben Oekolampads* (Leipzig: M. Heinsium Nachfolger, 1927; New York: Johnson Reprint Corp., 1971), 1:1–2, #2. See also Diane Poythress, "Johannes Oecolampadius' Exposition of Isaiah, Chapters 36–37," 2 vols. (PhD diss., Westminster Theological Seminary, 1992).

In 1501, at age nineteen, he received his B.A., followed by his M.A. after two more years of study. The latter came amid the complication of the entire university being removed to another city for a year because of the Plague (i.e. the bubonic plague, the Black Death). Then a family tragedy occurred. Sent by his father, Johannes went to study Roman law in Bologna. But the man entrusted with his tuition absconded with the money. However, God turned this seeming disaster into a great blessing, for Johannes returned to Heidelberg to pursue theology, with a small income acquired from teaching.

Upon graduation, a question presented itself: What does a late medieval major in theology do for work? As often happened at that time, he was hired by a nobleman to tutor four sons, ages twelve, eighteen, nineteen, and twenty. For four years, Oecolampadius trained these young men in deportment, higher education, languages, and how to maintain proper times of waking and retiring. But he especially prepared them for the church offices their father had purchased. One child had been a church prior since turning seven years old. So his charges had to practice daily prayers and church attendance.

The high social connections of this home brought Oecolampadius into contact with influential politicians and clerics. Occasionally he received offers to lecture at the nearby university, but he leaned toward a quiet pietism.

In 1510, he returned home to Weinsberg, where his family's influence brought him a preaching position, a new office at that time. This work required completing ordination regulations for the priesthood. Church positions were often bought for the mere profit of clerics, which meant that worship services and preaching frequently lay neglected. Poor young men could be hired cheaply to substitute. Karl Hammer sees this as the beginning of the centrality of preaching as practiced in the Protestant church today.[2] In God's plan that meant for the first time, fresh humanist graduates filled pulpits with a vigor for moral reform and biblical exposition.

---

2. Karl Hammer, "Der Reformator Oekolampad (1482–1531)," in *Reformiertes Erbe* (Zürich: Theologischer Verlag, 1993), 157–170, esp. 158–159.

Thus, foundations were laid on which later Reformation principles could be built. In fact, Oecolampadius himself was appointed to his preaching office by Duke Ulrich of Wurtemberg, who was methodically placing young humanists in positions throughout Germany.

Oecolampadius's significant sermon series from this time, "On the Passion of the Lord," found a printer in Strassburg in 1512. He first submitted the work to his old mentor, Wimpfeling, for approval. It contained some typical medieval divisions, yet it also held unusual insights into Christ as priest. For example, he compared Aaron's donning of priestly garments (which he said belonged to Jesus) to Christ's being stripped of His garments; he then contrasted that with the rich vestments of sixteenth-century priests. He spoke of the thief on the cross being justified by faith, as was Abraham, and of the thief being a sign in heaven that whoever believes in Christ will receive the same honor of being justified. This early emphasis on faith alone for salvation is noteworthy. Oecolampadius said that Christ's petition, "Father, forgive…," demonstrated His work as the God-man priest who offers Himself on behalf of humanity. Finally, he bound together these thoughts with a prayer to Christ for faith, knowledge of sin, forgiveness of sin, purity of understanding, holiness, and a view of Christ in His blessed glory. Many scholars mark this sermon as the sign of his true conversion. It also typified his future methodology of striking at human depravity, as Augustine had done, rather than attacking ecclesiastical authority, as other forerunners had done.[3]

Despite this auspicious beginning as preacher, Oecolampadius resigned his position in 1512, feeling unqualified for the responsibilities.[4] In spring 1513, he began studies at Tübingen, where he met Philip Melanchthon, fifteen years his junior, and Melanchthon's great uncle, Johann Reuchlin, one of the greatest humanists and finest Hebraists of the day. Now two streams joined to form a powerful

---

3. Hammer, "Der Reformator Oekolampad," 160. Hammer notes this was also a trait of Oecolampadius's "pupil," John Calvin.

4. Hammer, "Der Reformator Oekolampad," 161. Hammer quotes Wolfgang Capito as saying, "[Oecolampadius] considered himself not sufficiently mature for the office entrusted to him," which Hammer points out as rare humility of character.

river. The moral reform of Wimpfeling flowed into the original biblical language exposition of Reuchlin. Oecolampadius sped on into the implications of these two streams for the church.

The thrilling necessity of understanding the Bible as God spoke it evidently turned him back to Greek and Hebrew studies at Heidelberg in 1514. There he met Wolfgang Capito, who had also studied law along with theology and later became a significant German Reformer. With Capito, he shared books, manuscripts, and ideas like a brother. Neither could know the battles they would wage as comrades, their parallel roles as Reformers of two great European cities, or the events that would bring one to marry the widow of the other and raise his children.

At this time, Johannes, ever the teacher, also began lecturing in Greek, having written his own grammar, which saw significant use for almost a century. It is said that he spoke German, Greek, Latin, Aramaic, some Swiss German, Italian, French, and Hebrew, even rivaling Reuchlin.[5]

1515–1521

It appears that this fluency in languages elicited a call from Desiderius Erasmus for Oecolampadius to come labor with him in Basel, Switzerland, on a Greek New Testament. Erasmus, famous as a scholar and humanist even then, had chosen Basel to publish his work because of its reputation for beautiful fonts. By 1501, Basel had seventy printers, including Johann Froben, who published in both Latin and Greek, and Adam Petri, who printed mostly in German, including Luther's Bible. Erasmus did not have the capability in Hebrew to check Old Testament references, so he hired Oecolampadius to check the references, write theological annotations, proofread the print sheets, discard any heretical opinions, and write the postscript for *Novum Testamentum*, the printed Greek New Testament that was later the basis for the King James Bible. This was no small collaboration, since both men were risking their reputations

---

5. John T. McNeill, *The History and Character of Calvinism* (New York: Oxford University Press, 1954), 55.

and lives by correcting various corruptions carried into the church's traditional Latin texts. So it was through Erasmus that God introduced Oecolampadius to Basel in the summer of 1515. His ministry would change the city's history forever.

About ten thousand citizens lived in this center of learning in the early 1500s. Oecolampadius, age thirty-three, had come as Erasmus's aide, but he simultaneously began studies at the University of Basel for his first theological degree (*baccalaureus biblicus*). He studied intensively in order to receive his doctorate in three years rather than the normal twelve. The matriculation meant that he could begin lecturing at the university, which he did, beginning with Obadiah, followed the next week by Ephesians. At that point, he received a promotion (*baccalaureus sententiarius*), which allowed him to lecture on Peter Lombard's *Sentences*. His lectures on the first book of the *Sentences* ended in early 1516, at which time he received his next degree (*baccalaureus formatus*). The Greek New Testament work with Erasmus ended around the latter part of March that year.

From then until August 1516, he preached in his home town of Weinsberg and lectured on the other three books of Lombard's *Sentences*. This could be compared to seminary field work assignments today. Two months later, he sustained a battery of exams, including a disputation on the *Sentences* and a licensure exam, leading to his *licentiatus theologiae*. It appears he then returned to Weinsberg to continue preaching and to serve as penitentiary priest for the whole diocese. Alongside other duties, he managed to write the index to Erasmus's fifteen-volume edition of Jerome, in 1516. This tome, published in 1520, included a preface by Capito.

Apparently through Capito's arrangement, Oecolampadius came to Basel again in 1518 as penitentiary priest. He occasionally preached at the cathedral along with Capito.[6] While there, he completed his doctoral work, receiving his degree November 27, 1518, at the age of thirty-six.

Within a couple of weeks, the imperial city of Augsburg called him to be the cathedral preacher. Apparently Bernard Adelmann,

---

6. McNeill, *History*, 55.

who was canon of Augsburg and belonged to the Lutheran persuasion, influenced this hiring.[7] The cathedral position required presenting theological lectures as well as preaching. Through Reuchlin's urging, he had also applied to be Hebrew professor at Wittenberg. However, the institution cut him from its short list, and he was rejected because of his humanist ties.

Association with the humanist movement did not embarrass him. Rather, almost immediately upon being installed at Ausgburg, he published a treatise, for which Capito wrote the preface, that attacked the common practice of preaching a humorous sermon the Sunday after Easter. In this treatise, he also noted how current practices of penance had only a slim basis. Then, in 1519, he stated in a pamphlet that Roman Catholic theologian Johann Eck's argumentation was untenable, that Luther came closer to the gospel, and that indulgences were wrong.[8]

In 1520, he translated and published with comments a manuscript, provided through Adelmann, by John of Damascus: "How Much Do the Good Works of the Living Benefit the Dead." The article dealt with prayers for the dead. Along with John of Damascus, Oecolampadius asserted that any works done on behalf of the deceased are done in vain, including prayers.[9] The Reformer's booklet proved so popular that it was published five times in thirty-four years.

---

7. Adelmann and Oecolampadius were declared to be friends and supporters of Martin Luther in a letter from Guy Bild to Luther, dated April 16, 1520. Guy Bild, "Bild an Luther," *Zeitschrift des Historischen Vereins für Schwaben und Neuberg*, vol. 20, #160 (Augsburg: Ludwig Schulze, 1893), 221–222. Accessed at http://periodika.digitale-sammlungen.de/schwaben/Band_bsb00010266.html, Aug.19, 2010.

8. Olaf Kuhr (*Die Macht des Bannes und der Busse: Kirchenzucht und Erneuerung der Kirche bei Johannes Oekolampad, 1482–1531* [Bern: Peter Lang, 1999]) seems to ignore Oecolampadius's independent Reformed stance prior to 1520, which was even acknowledged by peers Adelmann and the university at Wittenberg.

9. The Latin title is "Quantum defunctis prosint viventium bona opera sermo Ioannis Damasceni, Ioanne Oecolampadio interprete." The thesis of Irena Backus (in "What Prayers for the Dead in the Tridentine Period?" in *Reformiertes Erbe* [Zürich: Theologisher Verlag, 1993], 13–24) is flawed in that 1) the word *only* is actually implied in the Greek; 2) Oecolampadius would not *pragmatically* risk his reputation as a scholar nor his integrity before God by adding words not existent in his manuscript; 3) his scholarship was precise, not sloppy, as she herself admits (p. 22); 4) without a manuscript, the entire argument is merely speculative; 5) she ignores his similar meticulous gathering without revision of Patristics on the Eucharist; and 6)

Oecolampadius held the exalted position of cathedral preacher in the imperial city of Augsburg less than two years. A mysterious interlude followed. Oecolampadius entered a German monastery in Altomunster on April 23, 1520. No one knows why.[10] Did it perhaps have something to do with the counsel he gave a young woman about entering a convent for holiness? Did he feel confused by the political winds blowing through the church doors concerning reformation? Did he long for a less public, more pietistic life? Did he think he could change the church more effectively by scholarly writing and research?

Another possibility is that he felt threatened by an impending condemnation of his position. He had anonymously edited a reply supposedly by Adelmann to Eck after the latter's debate with Luther. This led Eck to place both Luther and Adelmann on Pope Leo's list of accused. Oecolampadius later confessed to Melanchthon that he had personally accepted Eck's challenge for someone to refute him and had authored the defense of Luther's position. In it, he used a sermon by Basil the Great (Basilius) against usury and several other translations of the Fathers.[11] Eck was so infuriated that he wanted the authors and supporters burned. But Wittenberg's rector and their senate interceded, along with Reuchlin. When Eck later discovered the true author, he urged Oecolampadius to nullify the publication. When Oecolampadius refused, Eck in 1522 denounced the Reformer to Rome as more dangerous than

---

Oecolampadius's quote on p. 14 does not require tampering with evidence, but rather underlines the applicability of ancient evidence. That quote is "But in order that the ungodly should be rebuked by this sermon, so the inventions of superstitious people are not approved." Staehelin, *Briefe und Akten*, 1:132–133, #90.

10. Hans Guggisberg suggests that Oecolampadius was torn between Reformation idealism and pragmatic realism, desiring a quiet retreat where he could study the issues more carefully. See Guggisberg. "Johannes Oekolampad," in *Die Reformationzeit*, vol. 1, Martin Greschat, ed. (Stuttgart: W. Kohlhammer, 1981), 117–128, esp. 120. Hammer concurs that he needed to think through Luther's ideas and the implications of reformation. Hammer, "Der Reformator Oekolampad," 162.

11. Hammer notes that in contradiction to the sociologists who see the Reformation as originating in society, this publication of Oecolampadius in particular, with its discussion of usury, proves a religious foundation and origin. "Der Reformator Oekolampad," 164.

Luther. Oecolampadius may have seen the writing on the wall and moved into the cloister fortress.

Capito wrote to Melanchthon concerning Oecolampadius's decision to enter the monastery: "A man otherwise cautious and prudent, who burdened a melancholy spirit with unaccustomed labors in the cause of religion, acted indiscreetly...it must be endured since it cannot be changed."[12] In the end, only God knows how He was moving on the nascent Reformer's heart at that time.

The Augustinian monastery he entered fell into the more Lutheran outlook, but Oecolampadius argued for greater reforms. A special agreement allowed him privileges: to leave the convent to preach, to obey only those convent rules that did not contradict the gospel, to live freely according to God's Word, to miss convent prayers and worship, and to be given a study area. Hammer writes that on his part, he agreed to be a confessor priest at the convent.[13] Adelmann brought him reading glasses so he could study by candlelight and write. Here he wrote a 120-page treatise on confession, proposing confession only to God, the church, and one another, but not to a priest alone. He wrote, "If it is not liberating, it is not Christian confession."[14] This publication contained mature theological formulations. For example, he defined sin as not loving God or man, with the conclusion that there is never a moment we do not sin. He argued that every deed done in unbelief is a mortal sin. Among Reformers, he was unique in ordering confession along the same lines as Augustine, i.e. public confession for public sin, brotherly confession when sin is against a brother, and private confessions to God for private sin.

Ever the scholar, he also began a lifelong work of translating John Chrysostom's homilies while completing several translations of works by John of Damascus. In addition, he finished other

---

12. Akira Demura, "Church Discipline According to Johannes Oecolampadius in the Setting of His Life and Thought," (PhD diss., Princeton Theological Seminary, 1964), 36. See also James M. Kittelson, *Wolfgang Capito: From Humanist to Reformer* (Leiden: E.J. Brill, 1975), 55–56.

13. Hammer, "Der Reformator Oekolampad," 162.

14. Bernd Moeller, *Imperial Cities and the Reformation* (Philadelphia: Fortress, 1972), 51.

sermons, papers, and translations, composed a verdict on Luther's teaching, and wrote about the Eucharist. He exchanged letters with those beyond the monastery walls, such as Erasmus, Melanchthon, Veit Bild, Adelmann, Nikolaus Ellenbog, Konrad Peutinger, and others. In August 1520, Oecolampadius wrote to Bernard Adelmann concerning Luther:

> Now concerning Martin, I speak freely as always before that he approaches nearer to Gospel truth than his adversaries.... Bishops may see whether they damn me or stop condemning me. I do not speak concerning everything Martin has written, for I have not read everything. But what I have read is falsely rejected, so that injury is done to sacred Scriptures which he sincerely expounds. And many of the things said by him are so certain to me that, even if heavenly angels contradicted them, they would not change my convictions.[15]

Given this espousal of support, it must have been a shock when, in May 1521, Luther was declared to be cut off from the church. No one was allowed to buy his books, and all adherents were to be treated as outcasts and their property confiscated. By implication, Oecolampadius thus became severed from the church. His possessions technically already belonged to the monastery. Rumors arose that the local prince might have him arrested. Therefore, for what appear to have been prudent political reasons, he remained in the monastery most of this tense time, while Luther hid in a castle (May 1521–March 1522).

If Oecolampadius thought he would be safe in the monastery, he misjudged. God did not want him comfortable but crucified. Oecolampadius came to see that the ruling against Luther had placed him outside the church, as well. No longer could reform take place from within the church. Therefore, he determined to leave the monastery. Suddenly and somewhat secretly, the bishop gave him permission to leave. Therefore, he did not violate his vows by leaving. Still, in one sense, he had been banished by the church itself. But what would it mean to leave: dishonor or death? He left on

---

15. Staehelin, *Briefe und Akten*, 1:134, #91.

January 23, 1522, writing to Pellican, "To enter a monastery is not so serious; but to go out, to be ridiculed as apostate and heretic, to have no sure home or employment—that is not without pain."[16]

Outside the monastery, he found himself stripped of home, job, reputation, respectability, credibility, his beloved church, and even his books and reading glasses. All he had was God and His Word. But that was all he needed to embolden him to face warfare, since now he had nothing left to lose except life itself.

1522–1525

Oecolampadius learned that safety did not exist anywhere outside the refuge of Christ Himself. For a few months, cathedral preacher Caspar Hedio hid him in Mainz, where Capito resided. He was offered a professorial position in Ingoltstadt if he would distance himself from the Lutheran position, but he declined. Then, in April, he was named resident chaplain at a castle in Ebernberg. The castle belonged to Franz von Sickingen, who was leading the German knights in preparing for a revolt and was himself under a papal ban. Here Oecolampadius led a daily Reformed chapel service, reading from the Gospel and Epistle lessons in German. He reformulated the liturgy, and the Mass in particular, in a way that was "seen widely as revolutionary."[17] It was published as "The testament of Jesus Christ formerly called the Mass brought into German by Oecolampadius." He also took the time to translate a codex given him in Mainz by Capito containing 150 sermons by Chrysostom.

Martin Bucer hid simultaneously in the same castle, while Luther continued to hide at a castle in Wartburg. However, Luther returned to Wittenberg in March without repercussion. So in November 1522, Oecolampadius also ventured out, hoping to return to Augsburg and his publisher, Sigmund Grimm. This attempt proved unwise. However, in God's providence the outcast turned to Basel. Still, his safety could not be guaranteed there either, since just that year St. Albans priest, Wilhelm Roubli, was expelled from the city

---

16. Staehelin, *Briefe und Akten*, 1:167, #118.
17. Hammer, "Der Reformator Oekolampad," 165.

when he protested the Mass and purgatory, broke lent, and carried the Bible instead of the Eucharist in the Corpus Christi procession.

Doctor Johannes Oecolampadius was an acclaimed scholar, an expert in the Patristics, a renowned linguist, and a former imperial city preacher and university lecturer, but at forty years of age he was alone, with no job and no social position, shunned by the church, and a German refugee. Thus, he came as a beggar to his former publisher, Andreas Cratander. His old friend offered a room in his home on Petergasse and a job proofreading at the presses.

The Basel printing presses carried great esteem. Erasmus had chosen to live and publish there because of the Basel printers' beautiful fonts. Luther's German translation of the New Testament had just come off the presses in Basel two months previously, to be followed the next year by his Old Testament translation. The city bore an enviable reputation as a center for humanist and Reformation publications. Beginning in 1522, Cratander published Oecolampadius's translations of Chrysostom, which included notes on contemporary applications such as rejection of papal succession, since Christ is the only foundation of the church; the importance of clergy being servants, not rulers; church and civil orders; caring for the poor; rejection of any use of force to produce faith; separation of church and civil rule; excommunication understood not as anathema but as a curative discipline by the church body; and the difference between the true and false church.

Before November passed, another employment opportunity presented itself. The congregation of St. Martin's Church in Basel unanimously called Oecolampadius to be its vicar, replacing an ailing preacher. Assuming he applied in Basel the same reforms instituted at Ebernberg—an altered meter, a canon read aloud, the Gospel and Epistle lessons read in German, and a non-sacrificial Eucharist—it is possible that the earliest Reformed liturgy was practiced in Basel. There is no evidence that Oecolampadius presented Mass as a sacrifice. We know an assistant performed this task at an early stage. Oecolampadius had written to William Farel to encourage him about changing the words spoken publicly at the

Eucharist.[18] Luther also had urged the omission of words that called the Eucharist a sacrifice during worship.[19] Thus, it seems likely that Oecolampadius instituted these reforms at St. Martins, making it the earliest Protestant liturgy.

Before the end of December, Oecolampadius began lecturing, without a professorial post, at the University of Basel on Isaiah and Jeremiah in German, Latin, Greek, and Hebrew. Speaking often in the common language of the populace, he included discreet attacks on the errors of the church. Within two months, his presentations drew as many as four hundred listeners at one time. "Hundreds flocked to Oecolampadius's lecture theater and his devotees wished to risk body and soul for him, when respected citizens demanded daily Bible studies in the Franciscan Church. Everywhere it was a matter of fellowship with spiritual power which knew no compulsion, a free-will rallying around the word of the preacher."[20] The powerful university sophists tried to get his lectures banned, as they had Pellican's. But no one could stop the mighty work God initiated through this instrument refined through the fires of affliction.

By January 1523, Pope Hadrian VI pronounced that the Reformed "heresy" must be eradicated, Luther's books burned, and all Lutheran preachers banished. This did not sit well with the Baslers, whose town was the main source for Lutheran and Reformed publications. In addition, they had enjoyed the freedom and dignity of living in an imperial city with a bishop's seat for centuries. Through God's grace, Baslers were being revived along with all structures of basic life: church, university, government, marriage, and family. So they refused to acquiesce to Rome.

Undaunted by threats, Oecolampadius preached a controversial Easter series from Isaiah, some of which is found in this book. Opponents pulled in outsiders to validate their more Catholic positions.

---

18. Aime Louis Herminjard, ed., *Correspondence des Reformateurs dans les pays de langue francaise*, 9 vols. (reprint; Nieuwkoop: DeGraaf, 1965–66), 1:335. Previously printed in Geneva, 1878.

19. Martin Luther, *Luthers Sämmtliche Schriften*, ed. John Georg Walch (St. Louis: Lutherischer Concordia Verlag, 1890), vol. 20, column 80.

20. Rudolf Wackernagel, *Humanismus und Reformation in Basel* (Basel: Helbing und Lichtenhahn, 1924), 346.

However, in April, the City Council took a decided stand for the Reformation by opposing the pope's pronouncement. Instead of banishing their "Lutheran" preacher, the City Council appointed him as teacher of theology and professor of biblical exegesis at the university—but not under the auspices of the university.

In a matter of five months, Oecolampadius had been raised by God from the status of a transient pauper to the exalted rank of head theological professor, city preacher, and leader of the Reformation in Basel. His fiery but seasoned sermons led other preachers to turn pulpits into propaganda platforms.

The city churches, university, and Council each divided over Reformed versus traditional ideas. Without consensus, the City Council could only order that preaching should be scriptural and no one should call another man "heretic" without biblical basis.

The ailing priest at St. Martin's grew so disabled by the spring of 1523 that Oecolampadius took over the entire parish preaching. This work joined other tasks, such as lectures on Isaiah (interrupted for a Christmas series on 1 John), a published commentary on Isaiah, translation projects, proofreading, sermons, and professorial duties that lay heavily on his shoulders. In fact, his physical and spiritual stature stood in strong contradiction. According to one report, he appeared emaciated, with a yellow face, big nose, babbling falsetto, and retiring behavior.[21] In addition to the burden of momentous issues, he dealt with personal distractions. His two friends and co-Reformers, Hedio and Capito, broke fellowship with one another because Hedio received an appointment to the Strassburg cathedral that Capito had coveted. Evidently Oecolampadius scolded Capito for pouting.[22]

Beginning the same year of 1523, the priest at St. Ulrich's in Basel celebrated Mass with a new liturgy, offering Communion in both elements. Oecolampadius was the first to receive such Communion from him. Others followed this example, so by July of the following year, Oecolampadius himself offered the chalice to believers.

---

21. Kittelson, *Capito*, 95–96.
22. Kittelson, *Capito*, 95–96.

By 1524, the Reformation picked up speed in Basel. In his Latin and German lectures at the university, Oecolampadius concentrated on Romans. His ideas quickly spread through publications. He attacked church accretions more pointedly and strongly opposed free will in a sermon. Ever after, a rift grew between him and Erasmus, who had argued with Luther in print in favor of free will. Printers who were arrested for publishing a tract attacking Luther's view of consubstantiation appealed to the fact that Oecolampadius, who had been the publisher's reader, found nothing amiss. By November, it became known that Oecolampadius and Ulrich Zwingli shared similar views on the Eucharist. Also this year, a married priest in Basel posted five theses against clerical celibacy, which no one refuted.

Basel, being a university center, was characterized by a studied approach to every issue. This city on the Rhine had been the eleventh covenant member of the Swiss Confederacy, not joining until 1501. Prior to that, the town's identity had been wrapped around the prestige of being an imperial city with kingly privileges, even boasting a bishop's chair from the time of Roman settlement. An imperial city in the Holy Roman Empire subjected itself to no authority except the emperor himself. Now, as the empire declined, the Baslers faced the question of whether to define themselves as an imperial city or a Swiss city. The answer would decide their ecclesiastical stance. Remaining with the empire meant maintaining traditional allegiance to the Roman Catholic Church; becoming independently Swiss probably meant yielding to the popular Reformation. The City Council judiciously and irenically sat on the fence as long as possible. Every Swiss canton held debates. When, in January 1525, six traditional Swiss cantons sent a delegation to Basel requesting help to quell a rebellion, Basel characteristically urged them to make peace, refusing any overt alignment. The Council replied to inquiries concerning its Swiss allegiance by saying that it believed questions of belief should be decided internally by each city, with each pulpit preaching the Scriptures. In effect, the Council supported the Reformation by not censoring it.

In the meantime, Oecolampadius continued the work of reforming. In 1525, he produced one of the earliest German Protestant liturgies, remolding the missal to state, "May those be excommunicated from us who...will not let the Word judge in the matter of faith."[23] In addition, he refused to have Communion at St. Martin's Church when no communicants presented themselves. He took the position of people's priest with the proviso that he be given freedom in preaching. Previously, he had established two worship services: an evangelical morning service at which he presided and a traditional evening one led by an assistant. The Council members agreed to such changes as long as he first presented new ideas to them for approval. He also refused to say Mass for the dead; in one case, the Mass had already been paid for by a brother and sister, but the Council merely transferred the money and responsibility to a papist church in town.

A new Catholic preacher, Augustinus Marius, took up the challenge of defending the papist position that year. After the priest's first sermon, Oecolampadius visited him with an irenic letter urging that they might confer amicably together. Marius refused, claiming he could not associate with heretics. He then began such a virulent campaign that it brought protests even from his own supporters.

The year 1525 brought more Council concessions. Oecolampadius and Pellican received promotions to empty theological chairs at the university. This aided the credibility of Oecolampadius's arguments concerning the Eucharist. His exhaustive written work on Communion, *De Genuina Verborum Domini,* published in Strassburg, circulated widely that summer of 1525. But the Council, after consulting two lawyers, Erasmus and Ludwig Bar, confiscated the work within Basel.

What caused this strong reaction? Perhaps it was the condemnation of the work by the University of Paris. Yet with many other inflammatory publications coming off the presses, why the censure? Within this heavy volume, Oecolampadius compiled all the Patristic citations concerning the Lord's Supper, thereby proving the papist position to be an erroneous innovation. Every orthodox father could be called to witness the truth of the Reformed position. These

---

23. Demura, "Church Discipline," 55.

included Chrysostom, Cyril, Hilary, Epiphanius, and Ambrose, with the only possible exception being John of Damascus.[24] Eventually the convincing arguments of the book even put a wedge between Luther and Melanchthon.

Despite the forbidden sale of this book in Basel, others rolled off the presses. That summer saw the publication of Oecolampadius's sixty-six translated sermons of Chrysostom on Genesis. Appended to this were four of his views proffered for public debate: the prime authority of Christ and His Word (*sola Scriptura*); justification by faith (*sola fide*); no invocation of saints; and the liberty of Christians as brothers. Following this, the papist champion, Eck, challenged the Swiss cantons to a debate, specifically mentioning Oecolampadius and Zwingli.

Earlier in 1525, the Reformer had written a letter concerning liturgical changes he wanted and which he probably had begun implementing. His worship order included confession, preaching and prayers, hymns, the Trisagion ("holy, holy holy"), silent meditation, the Lord's Prayer said together, a call to participate in Communion, a deacon's warning to test the conscience (anyone admonished two to three times who remained unrepentant was denounced and denied the Lord's Supper unless he repented and was reconciled), then the Lord's Supper, followed by a commendation to aid the poor and do charity, then dismissal.[25]

In the summer, while preaching sermons, he spoke of the Anabaptists as a sect. Several adherents met with him the first week in August.[26] Oecolampadius thought that since Scripture did not com-

---

24. See Jaroslav Pelikan, *Reformation of Church and Dogma (1300–1700)*, vol. 4 in *The Christiam Tradition: A History in the Development of Doctrine* (Chicago: University of Chicago Press, 1984), 198. See also Eric W. Northway, "Patrisic Reception and Eucharistic Theology in Johannes Oecolampadius (1482–1531), with Special Reference to the *Adversus Haereses* of Irenaeus of Lyons" (PhD diss., University of Durham, 2009), and his forthcoming critical edition of *De Genuina Verborum Domini*.

25. Staehelin, *Briefe und Akten*, 1:345, #239.

26. Despite the similarity of nomenclature, Anabaptists are not the forefathers of the Baptists, but rather of the Hutterites and Mennonites. Their confession refused oath-taking, so that they could not swear to the defense of the city nor to obedience to its laws. They also refused all participation in government. Baptists are more closely related to English Puritans.

pellingly forbid or command infant baptism that both paedobaptism and believer's baptism could exist within the church, particularly for the sake of church unity in love. Summarily, Anabaptists wanted church purity by means of baptism and Oecolampadius wanted it by means of Communion. He pointed out that adult baptism did not make one more pure or morally better, and that no one could see into the heart of an infant or an adult. Both sides agreed that one is not saved by baptism. In addition, Oecolampadius argued that the soul of a child could not properly be cared for outside the church. A church child should be cared for differently than a child of the world. In conjunction with this discussion, he set forth three criteria for abandoning a traditional church practice: 1) the Bible forbids the practice; 2) the practice is disputed throughout church history; and 3) the practice is against love and faith.[27]

Many connections may be traced between Oecolampadius and the Anabaptists. In fact, the Reformer had to defend himself in a 1525 letter to Wilibald Pirkheimer concerning his friendly relation to Thomas Muntzer.[28] Most notably, he was a friend of Hans Denck, who had been a student of Oecolampadius, attending his lectures on Isaiah in 1523.[29] Probably Denck's idea that an unbeliever received further condemnation by hearing Scripture came from the Reformer's stance on fencing the Scripture.[30] Some peers also contended that Denck's concept of the inner word derived from Oecolampadius's Isaiah lectures.[31] The student evidently had had several private, non-theological discussions with Oecolampadius.[32] Oecolampadius had recommended Denck for

---

27. See Edmund Pries, "Anabaptist Oath Refusal: Basel, Bern and Strasbourg, 1525–1538" (PhD diss., University of Waterloo, 1995), esp. 56, 80–84. Pries exaggerates similarities between Oecolampadius and Karlin, and seems to agree with Anabaptists that the goal of church membership is purity, so the weak must not be admitted (78).

28. Staehelin, *Briefe und Akten*, 1:364f.

29. Staehelin, *Briefe und Akten*, 1:364f.

30. Jan J. Kweit, "The Life of Hans Denck (ca. 1500–1527)," *Mennonite Quarterly Review* 31, no. 4 (October 1957): 227–259, esp. 240.

31. John Horsch, "The Faith of the Swiss Brethren (2)," *Mennonite Quarterly Review* 5, no.1 (January 1931), 17n115.

32. Staehelin, *Briefe und Akten*, 1:364.

appointment as headmaster at a Nuremberg school. At the end of Denck's life, he wrote to ask his former teacher to intercede for him to be allowed to live in Basel. Upon coming to Basel, in 1527, he wrote a confession and recantation of his Anabaptist beliefs given to Oecolampadius and attested by the Reformer.[33]

A debate arranged by Oecolampadius for June 25, 1527, concerning Anabaptist tenets did not happen. The discussion would have included the imprisoned Karlin (a.k.a. Karl Brennwald) on one side with Oecolampadius and his assistant, and the Catholic priest Marius and his assistant on the other side. Marius refused to participate. Papers, however, were presented to the Council, with Oecolampadius's being published by Cratander during the same year.[34]

1526–1528

By 1526, the Eucharist discussion moved to center stage. Johann Brenz wrote *Syngramma Suevicum*, defending the Lutheran position. Undaunted, Oecolampadius replied with thirty-nine chapters in *Antisyngramma*, arguing that someone who honors an "imbreaded" god does not remain free from false religion, since God committed Himself to no other creature than the flesh of Christ.[35] Earlier that year, he had published a booklet in Augsburg on conducting a biblical baptism and Lord's Supper, and ministering to the sick.

At about this time, God honored Oecolampadius and his church with something spectacular. Normally a choir gave short responses in Latin at various prescribed liturgical moments in the worship service. However, on Easter Sunday, the congregation of St. Martin's spontaneously broke out in German singing during the service. Nothing like this had happened anywhere. The Council immediately forbade such

---

33. Staehelin, *Briefe und Akten*, 2:111–112. Also Huldreich Zwingli, *Huldreich Zwinglis sämtliche Werke*, vol. 8. Ed. Emil Egli et al. (Leipzig: M. Heinsius Nachfolger, 1914). [CR 95], 9:318.

34. Pries, "Anabaptist Oath Refusal," 70–74. Oecolampadius also replied to Balthasar Hubmaier's retort in 1527. See Staehelin, *Briefe und Akten*, 1:356, #243.

35. Gottfried Locher, *Zwingli und die schweizerische Reformation* (Gottingen: Vandenhoeck und Ruprecht, 1982), 303.

singing.[36] The congregation responded by continuing to do it. Oeco-lampadius, who had approved of congregational singing of psalms and spiritual songs in his preaching the previous summer,[37] then petitioned the Council, which relented, making Basel the first city in Switzerland with an evangelical profession.[38] The German singing found an ordered place just after the meditation on the Psalms.

This and other innovations began to be adopted by most of the Reformed churches in southern Germany. Changes included alternative rites for marriage, baptism, and Communion, plus a

---

36. Willem van 't Spijker, "Der kirchengeschichtliche Kontext des Genfer Psalters," in *Genfer Psalter und seine Rezeption in Deutschland, der Schweiz und den Niederlanden* (Tübingen: Niemeyer, 2004), 45–60. He says people were already singing in their homes.

37. In the summer of 1525 Oecolampadius preached a sermon on Psalm 77, in which he described a congregation singing psalms together: "The singing was not in the manner of our priests who sing for pay or out of custom without spirit and understanding like parrots sing or cry, like donkeys who say what they do not understand" (van 't Spijker, "Genfer Psalters," 55, quoting from the later published version of the sermon, Oecolampadius, *In Psalmos LXXIII LXXIIII, etc. conciones* [Basel: Robert Winter, 1544], 139 [ad loc. Ps. 77:1]). In a speech delivered before the City Council in 1526, Oecolampadius included a reference to Numbers 11:29 as a call to all Christians to praise God and nourish the soul. Van 't Spijker also gives the Reformer's points of petition to the Council: God is always praised through singing; it enlivens a burdened spirit; it draws men to prayer who otherwise would turn away; and it increases the value of God's Word and the sweetness of divine things while avoiding pride and frivolousness. He pastorally added that people's consciences were marred by singing when they thought it was against the law ("Genfer Psalters," 56, referencing "Gesuch Oekolampads beim Rat um die Erlaubnis für deutschen Kirchengesang," in *Aktensammlung zur Geschichte der Basler Reformation in den Jahren 1519 bis Anfang 1534*, hg. v. Emil Dürr/Paul Roth, Bd. II: *Juli 1525 bis Ende 1527* (Basel: 1933), 374–376; Staehelin, *Das Buch der Basler Reformation: zu ihrem vierhundertjährigen Jubiläum im Namen der evangelischen Kirchen von Stadt und Landschaft Basel* [Basel: Helbing & Lichtenhahn, 1929], 133–136.).

38. Olaf Kuhr seems unaware of this incident and the ensuing action. He thinks that Geneva copied the Strassburg Psalm-singing of 1526 (27), which technically is probably true, although Oecolampadius had sent a liturgical form to Martin Bucer earlier, which may have included this element in worship. The hymnals in rhymed German, which were used in Basel in the summer of 1526, came from Strassburg. The Constance songbook was used in Basel and Zurich from 1540 to 1573. Calvin's congregation sang for the first time in 1538. See van 't Spijker, "Genfer Psalters." In general, Kuhr looks too much at secondary secular causes and political, psychological motivations. In so doing, he omits God as the primary cause and the godly honoring of Christ as a primary motivation. Oecolampadius shows himself to be far more spiritual than Kuhr allows.

new catechism for children. All this flowed from Oecolampadius's heart and pen.

Disappointingly, the Council did not as yet accept his proposal for the excommunication of unrepentant sinners. But Basel was the first city where excommunication became a standard part of the Communion liturgy. Excommunication was incurred primarily through public breaking of one of the Ten Commandments and being unrepentant. Oecolampadius elucidated this practice in his 1526 sermon and liturgy. He explained in an exhortation from the pulpit that all who did not have faith thereby mocked God in taking Communion, yet they could repent and begin a new life. During the proposed service, which included excommunication, the pastor was to encourage people from the pulpit to test their consciences, then together people were to profess the Apostles' Creed. Afterward, an announcement of excommunication could be made, with an explanation as to how to treat such a person. Sins of disobedience were to be listed, and then the pastor was to come to the table to dispense the Lord's Supper.[39]

Throughout the empire, the Reformation gathered impetus. In response to Eck's *Commonplaces*, which accused Lutheranism of heresy, the Swiss scheduled a disputation at Baden from May to June 1526. Baden was situated in a more papist region, making travel for the Reformed there so dangerous that the Zurich Council forbade Zwingli to go. So Oecolampadius, as the main Reformed proponent, led the argument concerning intercession of the saints against one hundred papists. On the first day, he opened with a three-hour lecture that adhered to the prescribed agenda of eighteen rounds over a sixteen-day period. The result of this convocation merely confirmed all the cantons in their preconceived positions. Within the next three months, five Reformed cities swore allegiance to one another. This alliance was countered in December when seven papist cities refused to continue allegiance to the cities that had allowed a Reformed liturgy, including Basel. However, the Basel Council protested that it

---

39. Olaf Kuhr, *Die Macht des Bannes und der Busse*, 10. See entire book for a detailed development.

upheld neither the Reformed nor the papist view, since both adherents practiced faith in its jurisdiction. But the papist cities refused to separate political allegiance from tolerated religious practices, and so separated themselves politically.

In May 1527, the City Council ordered Oecolampadius to submit arguments favoring the Reformed stance and Marius to present the papist position. As was typical of the Council, its final judgment proclaimed evangelicals could worship at three designated city churches, while traditionalists could worship at the remaining churches. It added an amendment stating that anyone could join or abstain from the Mass. A citizen could choose his church rather than report to the one in his district. As a result, Oecolampadius's congregation at St. Martin's grew. The increasingly powerful guilds snubbed the Catholic priests by sending invitations to their annual feasts only to the Reformed priests. The following month, four hundred citizens presented a petition requesting that Basel tolerate only Reformed preaching. Clearly the Council lagged behind the populace at this time.

Around this time, Oecolampadius's parents apparently came to live with him, evidently after the destruction of their home along with all of Weinsberg during the Peasant Revolt. His mother kept house, cooked, and entertained Oecolampadius's many guests and visiting dignitaries. However, five days after he returned from delivering nine sermons at a disputation in Bern at the beginning of 1528, she died. Not unlike Isaac after his mother's death, he found comfort in marriage. Correspondence reveals he had wrestled with this possibility as much as four years previously. In that year, Capito, who had just married, wrote: "Accordingly, there are those who approve and those who disapprove. But what is it to us, who depend upon the Lord?... Marriage is an honest and holy thing, especially in a Christian and a bishop. Besides celibacy has its vices and dangers."[40] Difficult questions arose for Oecolampadius concerning matrimony: Would he be killed and leave a widow? lose his income? bring disgrace to God's

---

40. Kittelson, *Capito*, 109. See also Ernst Staehelin, *Frau Wibrandis* (Bern/Leipzig: Gotthelf Verlag, 1934), 13.

cause? neglect God's workload in favor of his own pleasure? overburden a helpmate? Would anyone want him? Finally, affirming his call to marriage at the age of forty-six, he wed Wibrandis Rosenblatt, a twenty-four-year-old widow with one child.

Wibrandis became one of the most outstanding women of the Reformation.[41] God blessed them with three children during the next three years: Eusebius ("Godliness"), Irene ("Peace"), and Aletheia ("Truth").

The meek Reformer now became the bold Reformer. "His outspoken references to public matters, to usury, to bribery and corruption were worthy of a Zwingli or a Latimer, and led to frequent consultation with the Council, before whom he was respectful but firm, as when he refused to give the authorities the names of those whose crimes he had denounced."[42]

Conceding too little too late, the city governors had again affirmed "that every man should abide by his own faith."[43] This incited a shameful incident the following month. On Good Friday, April 10, 1528, a band from the spinners' guild took matters into its own hands. The "Small Iconoclastic Tumult" happened. Five men removed and destroyed images at two churches. The next Monday, citizens broke into another church, desecrating images. So the Council decreed the official, orderly removal of images at four churches. But restless citizens in December again petitioned for the abolition of the Mass and cessation of divisive preaching.

1529–1531

Worse followed. On January 5, 1529, the Council met with representatives from both ecclesiastical persuasions while three thousand

---

41. When Wolfgang Capito became a widower with children, he married widowed Wibrandis and took in Oecolampadius's children. When Capito died, widower Bucer, who had children of his own, married Wibrandis, taking in the children of Oecolampadius and Capito. When Bucer died, Wibrandis returned to Basel, where the plague took her at age sixty in 1564 and where she was buried with Oecolampadius. Ernest Gordon Rupp says, "Her offspring represent a history of the Reformation in several volumes." *Patterns of Reformation* (London: Epworth Press, 1969), 8n3.

42. Rupp, *Patterns*, 32.

43. Rupp, *Patterns*, 31.

armed reformed-minded citizens met at one church opposed by 350 papists meeting at another church. The next day, officials declared that anyone wishing to leave the city could do so; that a June disputation would be held; and that until June, the Mass would be suspended at all but three churches. Patience reached its limit.

The next month, Baslers sent a delegation requesting that all Catholic Council members be dismissed, including the burgomeister (mayor); that all images be removed and Catholic preachers be replaced by Reformed preachers; and that guild representatives and masters be chosen by guild members and that Councilmen be chosen by consulting guild representatives. Immediately the mayor and another Council member left town secretly. The remaining Council members merely conceded that one Catholic pulpit be supplied by a Reformed preacher. This paltry condescension so angered citizens that two days of rioting ensued, with three hundred armed men crushing all images in four churches. Erasmus described the scene in letters:

> Smiths and carpenters were sent to remove the images from the churches. The roods and the unfortunate saints were cruelly handled. Strange that none of them worked a miracle to avenge their dignity, when before they had worked so many at the slightest invitation. Not a statue was left in church, niche, or monastery. The paintings on the wall were whitewashed. Everything combustible was burnt. What would not burn was broken to pieces. Nothing was spared, however precious or beautiful; and Mass was prohibited even in private houses.
>
> The affair was less violent than we feared it might be. No houses were broken into, and none was hurt. They would have hanged my neighbour, the Consul, if they had caught him, but he slipped off in the night; not unlike St. Paul in a basket, but down the river in a boat. His crime had been that he had so long obstructed the Gospel. As it was, no blood was shed; but there was a cruel assault on altars, images, and pictures.[44]

With revolution forcing its hand, the Basel Council declared the city to be Reformed. This effected the dismissal of twelve

---

44. Desiderius Erasmus, cited in James A. Froude, *Life and Letters of Erasmus* (New York: Scribners, 1895), 359–360.

Council members, the abolition of the Mass, removal of all images, the promise of a new political structure, union with the Christliche Burgrecht (Protestant Swiss cities), and promotion of Oecolampadius to cathedral preacher. Although Oecolampadius never participated in the riots, his words, empowered by the Spirit, had long ago engendered a radical thirst for biblical truth. When a lay commission met to draw up new ordinances, many memos with biblical advice left his desk to aid the newly reformed civil order. These suggested changes included a restructuring of the University of Basel. The opposition professors had left their classrooms, causing the school to be temporarily closed.

Erasmus, feeling unprotected, also left town after visiting Oecolampadius. It is ironic that the work of Erasmus had brought the Reformer to Basel, while the latter's work forced Erasmus's departure. Despite their theological differences, their Christian love for one another remained strong through the years. Oecolampadius even framed a letter from his old friend that hung on his study wall until it was stolen. Erasmus finished some printed work of Oecolampadius, while relinquishing the final translation of fifty-five Chrysostom homilies to the Reformer. When Oecolampadius received printed criticism from Germanus Brixius of Notre Dame, Erasmus defended his old friend. Neither did Erasmus concede to Tunstall's plea to keep Oecolampadius's name out of further translations. After Oecolampadius's death, Erasmus returned to Basel to live out the last year of his life.

The bloodless revolution increased, rather than lessened, Oecolampadius's workload. By spring 1529, he formulated one of the earliest Protestant ecclesiastical ordinances, including a directory for church discipline. It had become necessary not only to set aside errors, but also to set up proper practices. In many ways, though, the proposed ordinance merely restated his earlier document, *Agende*, submitted in 1526. The opening sentence quoted Romans 1:16: "For I am not ashamed of the Gospel of Christ." After this, the first section of the document established God's Word as the highest authority, while the second part dealt with methods of control. Only Scripture was to be proclaimed, with Scripture authoritatively interpreting Scripture. Deacons and ministers had to be examined biennially at a synod as to their piety of life and orthodoxy. Baptisms administered to infants needed to be in German, with no manmade additions.[45] Communion administered in German would rotate each Sunday among four churches that comprised four parishes. Public, punishable sins were listed along with penalties. Fines were imposed for bars remaining open after the designated hour chimed by the cathedral clock. Only Easter, Ascension, Pentecost, and Christmas were to be recognized as holy days. Spiritual education would take place in both schools and universities. Parish children seven to fourteen years of age would attend classes at church four times yearly to learn catechism before partaking in the Lord's Supper. Oecolampadius's catechism, which centered on the Apostles' Creed, the Lord's Prayer, the Ten Commandments, sacraments, and the formation of faith, was published in 1537. The 1534 Basel Confession of Faith lists other changes initiated at this time, such as dropping requirements for observing certain practices: auricular confession, Lenten and other fastings, certain holidays, clerical celibacy, and worship of saints and images.[46]

Church restructuring, which actually bore fruit in 1531, as explained later, included weekly exegesis of Scripture, alternating between the Old and New Testaments. This exegesis involved a technical explanation of the Word, a biblical-theological exegesis expounded by Oecolampadius, and a pragmatic exhortation in the common language. Usually Oecolampadius himself preached at the Munster Cathedral on the Lord's Day at eight, twelve, and four o'clock. In addition, he was visiting the sick and directing the restructuring of the city government, churches, schools, and the university—all while adjusting to married life and a new baby. In God's providence, as spoken in Matthew 19:29–30, He graciously made the last first: the once-forlorn beggar and scorn of the university became the architect of the city church, government, and academy.

---

45. Apparently Oecolampadius wanted freedom in the question of baptism, but the Council insisted on imprisonment of any parent who did not baptize his child.

46. Bernd Moeller, *Imperial Cities and the Reformation* (Philadelphia: Fortress Press, 1972), 157.

One historian envisions a scene as follows: "We glimpse the bearded scholar with pendulous nose, peering through his spectacles at some propped-up codex by candlelight (he would do very well for Rembrandt's 'The Philosopher'); the cathedral preacher making the best of a poor voice, but taking fire beneath the burden of his message—like the baritone bell in his sermon, he was 'gravis et sonora'—moving the hearts of his great audience."[47]

Instead of a theological department at the university, Oecolampadius substituted a biblical department, where theology would arise from Scripture itself. He added Hebrew and Greek as means for knowing God's Word in truth. Since the Word nurtured both doctrine and morality while producing faith in God, it took the central position. His task was to create a blueprint for modern Christian education.

Another controversy of eventually world-shaking proportions arose about this time. In 1525, Oecolampadius had defended Tertullian's interpretation of the Eucharistic "body" to mean "symbol of the body."[48] Now Philip of Hesse called for a meeting of Reformers at the Marburg Colloquy, in October 1529, to attempt reconciliation between two main Protestant views concerning Communion. One side, led by Luther and Melanchthon, upheld consubstantiation, which asserted that the physical body of Christ was with and under the bread and wine. Oecolampadius and Zwingli maintained a spiritual eating, eschewing cannibalism. The Swiss declared that believers did not eat the physical body of Christ, but spiritually partook of His spiritual body. This did not imply Christ's absence, however, as Oecolampadius explained: "I grant that there are not only signs in the Lord's Supper, but also the real body of Christ through faith."[49] The colloquy organizer knew that Oecolampadius and Melanchthon were more gracious and gentle, while Luther and Zwingli were more fiery. In addition, honor was given in this way

---

47. Rupp, *Patterns*, 45–46.

48. Staehelin, *Briefe und Akten*, 1:123, #235; Walther Kohler, *Das marburger Religionsgesprach 1529: Versuch einer Rekonstruction* (Leipzig: M. Heinsius Nachfolger Eger & Sievers, 1929), 7–38.

49. Oecolampadius, cited in *Great Debates of the Reformation*, ed. Donald Ziegler (New York: Random House, 1969), 104.

to Luther and Oecolampadius, who had their doctorates. So for the opening exchange, Luther was paired with Oecolampadius and Zwingli with Melanchthon.

Appropriating Scripture, Oecolampadius demonstrated to Luther that some verses such as "I am the vine" were metaphoric. Other Scripture passages, such as John 6:48–63, supported this hermeneutic. Luther agreed. Oecolampadius proceeded into John 3, Romans 8, and Matthew 16 and 26, wherein Luther conceded that a spiritual as well as a physical eating took place. Finally, Luther admitted Christ was in heaven, but insisted He must be in the bread as well. At this point, Oecolampadius accused Luther of an innovation, deviating from the Church Fathers. Luther protested that God would decide.

Agreement uniting all Protestants almost was reached, as Luther and his party "were prepared to repudiate all of their previous works against Zwingli and Oekolampadius as irrelevant because they were based on misunderstanding."[50] However, Zwingli's entrance into the room and ensuing words sent sparks flying again. To the disappointment of all, agreement could not be reached. The recorded transcript of closing remarks reveals the men's strong personalities:

> Luther: I commend you to God and to his judgment. My thanks to you, Herr Oecolampadius, for presenting your case, not in a spirit of bitterness, but with friendliness. Also to you, Herr Zwingli, I express my thanks despite your expressions of bitterness. Please forgive me if I have spoken harshly to you. I am after all only flesh and blood. I should like to have had the matter settled to our mutual satisfaction.

> Oecolampadius: I call upon the will of God to protect the poor church.

> Zwingli: I call upon you, Doctor Luther, to forgive my bitterness, I have always desired your friendship a great deal, and I want it still (With tears in his eyes.) There are no others in Italy and France whom I would rather see.

> Luther: Call upon God that you may receive understanding.

---

50. Roland Bainton, *Studies on the Reformation* (Boston: Beacon Press, 1963), 48.

Oecolampadius: Call upon him yourself, for you need it just as much as we![51]

Each Marburg participant returned home to burgeoning duties. Oecolampadius met for discussions with the French Waldensians. A new baby arrived in his home. He had to intercede for some thirty Anabaptists who faced execution in Basel after an imperial mandate decreed they should be killed.

In 1526, the Council had issued a softer edict concerning the sect, threatening exile to all rebaptizers. By 1527, the position had hardened to the point that anyone sheltering an Anabaptist would suffer corporal punishment and confiscation of property. Any Anabaptist would be dunked in the Rhine and exiled for a first offense. Second offenders were to be executed. After the imperial decree, however, all Anabaptists within the district found themselves imprisoned. A disputation before the Council and city preachers concerning the matter occurred on December 29, 1529. Oecolampadius spent many hours pleading with Anabaptist prisoners, getting one sentence commuted to a fine and, after a moving appeal in the Council chamber, securing the release of Jacob Treyer.[52] In fact, he counseled these prisoners and dramatically pleaded on his knees before the Council for their lives, with the result that apparently only one was executed. Oecolampadius's charity toward the sect can be seen in the fact that the theologue-turned-Anabaptist-proponent, Andreas Karlstadt, had dared to visit the city incognito in the winter of 1524–25, at which time Oecolampadius treated him kindly, although wisely he advised the Council not to permit publication of Karlstadt's pamphlet.

The cathedral church duties weighed heavily on Oecolampadius's conscientious shoulders. It was not an institution but the children of Christ whom he sought to nurture, visiting in their homes as well as preaching four times a week. All his various labors fit together in God's plan for building His kingdom. "Pursued by enemies and surrounded by hatred, fighting against sophists and

---

51. Cited in Ziegler, *Great Debates of the Reformation*, 104–105.
52. Rupp, *Patterns*, 40–41 and 40n1.

papists and also against Luther when his convictions led him, he trained the life and character of this church, led her from her beginning to maturity, to independence."[53]

By May 1530, the Council commissioned Oecolampadius to draft a paper on church discipline. Many at that time believed excommunication to be a civil duty, whereas the Reformer placed it squarely under ecclesiastical jurisdiction. He outlined this process in a presentation for the clergy's spring synod, where he argued for reinstituting lay elders to make decisions along with ministers and councilmen.[54] This would offset political or ecclesiastical tyranny. Walther Kohler remarks that this practice had been neglected since the apostles' time.[55] Prior to this time in Basel, the Council alone had handled all church discipline. Oecolampadius advised: "This power cannot be handed to the congregation, which includes women and children. The true representatives of the Church ought to be as in the early Church, Elders, 'whose judgment, as of the more prudent, expresses the mind of the Church'" concerning offenses in purity of life and doctrine.[56] Despite Oecolampadius's advice, the government officials decided to maintain their own control.

During this synod, complaints were voiced that many were not coming forward for Communion, including several city officials. Yet no one was being punished for despising the sacrament. This synod authorized Oecolampadius and three others to present the problem to the Council.[57]

Another tome from Oecolampadius's pen circulated at this time, the *Dialogue*. This compilation of Patristic literature proved the

53. Wackernagel, *Humanismus*, 344.

54. Oecolampadius, *Oratio de reducenda excommunicatione*, 1530.

55. Kohler, *Das Marburger Religionsgesprach*, 284, cited in Demura, "Church Discipline," 86.

56. Rupp, *Patterns*, 39.

57. See Kuhr, *Die Macht des Bannes*, for a more detailed discussion of the practical applications and effects. For example, an excommunicated bookbinder evidently threatened Oecolampadius with a sword. Guggisberg says this establishment of elders and synods found expression in Bucer's Strassburg and Calvin's Geneva. "Johannes Oekolampad," 126.

Reformed view of the Eucharist, demonstrating that the spiritual presence of Christ in Communion was the historic, faithful view of the church. This work, when added to the previous *De Genuina Verborum Domini,* carried such weighty argumentation that Melanchthon never again gave wholehearted consent to the Lutheran view, but eventually moved closer to the Reformed perspective.

That same year saw the Diet of Augsburg, lasting six months, where the emperor offered to accept an evangelical confession if the Protestant cities provided troops to fight the Turks. Basel chose not to send a representative. The Diet commanded Oecolampadius to give a written reply. The Basel leaders restrained him as they quietly waited for the dust to settle.

Melanchthon offered the Augsburg Confession, which Bucer and Capito rejected by objecting to the Lutheran wording concerning the bodily presence of Christ in the elements in Communion. So Capito composed an alternative, a Strassburg confession, which he delivered to the Basel Council. The officials accepted it, thereby aligning themselves with Strassburg, and then commissioned Capito and Oecolampadius to travel to Zurich to seek Zwingli's approval. After four days, no agreement ensued. From a human perspective, this failure appeared enormous, for it meant a lack of union with the Schmalkald League, a defense covenant among Protestants in Germany. Bucer spent October 14 and 15 in Basel, where he and Oecolampadius discussed excommunication. Bucer thought a church court was possible only if the civil government were Christian. But this discussion laid the foundation for Bucer's later view and all the structures of church and state that he influenced.

Returning to Basel from Zurich, Oecolampadius packed for another conference, a meeting of government officials in Aarau. There he proposed a church-directed approach to excommunication, asking that Basel be granted permission to tentatively implement the plan. His zeal for discipline found impetus in the fact that eighty Basel citizens now refused to take the Reformed Communion. Permission was granted, but Basel officials balked until censors (men who oversaw cases of excommunication) could be appointed as well. Apparently the Reformer's arguments convinced Ambrosius

Blaurer, Berchtold Haller, Joachim Vadian, Martin Bucer, Wolfgang Capito, and Ulrich Zwingli of the plan's worthiness.[58] The
cities of Bern, Ulm, Memmingen, Biberach, Lindauer, Constance,
and Ziegenhain also concurred.

By early 1531, with another baby coming at home, Oecolampadius found politics ever impinging on his calling. Bucer brought
to Basel another confessional wording on the Lord's Supper. Each
city refused to agree with the other, producing a constant stalemate.
Oecolampadius proposed that synods be regularly held to facilitate
discussion and hopefully resolution. The city of Ulm requested
that he, Bucer, and Blaurer come in order to draw up a Reformation ordinance for their city and church. This project alone busied
Oecolampadius from May until July. Meanwhile, he still worked on
restructuring the university, lecturing there on the Old Testament
every other week. On Sundays, he presented a series of 131 sermons
on Mark at the cathedral, while on weekdays he began a series on
Colossians. With the newly gained permission from the Council,
he also rode around the district of Basel visiting, examining, and
exhorting parishioners.

During the year of 1531, the heretic Michael Servetus settled in
Basel. At first, Oecolampadius patiently bore with him. But finally
the Reformer made quite clear to Servetus that if he were to call
himself a Christian he must confess that Jesus is God.[59] Servetus
was kicked out of Basel in 1531, the Council forbidding the sale of
his anti-Trinitarian books. When Servetus finally faced trial much
later in Geneva, Oecolampadius's letters were brought in as con-
demning evidence.

At the September Basel synod, Oecolampadius gave the opening
speech to about forty members of the ministerium. He expounded
the biblical history of elders, the necessity of the civil government

---

58. Rupp, *Patterns*, 42. See especially the whole of Demura, "Church Discipline," 97–112. There is evidence that Calvin's idea of the *consistoire*, or elders, with
their involvement in excommunication, was taken directly from Oecolampadius by
Calvin after a sojourn in Basel in 1536. See Demura, "Church Discipline," 161–180.

59. Ernst Staehelin, *Das theologische Lebenswerk Johannes Oekolampads* (Leipzig: M.
Heinsius Nachfolger Eger und Sievers, 1939), 537–538.

being a protective arm of the church, yearly examination of elders, the faith that the church confesses, and how excommunication is a means of salvific repentance. Discussion at the synod revolved around unenforced rules.

In Zurich, politics turned to warfare. Zwingli accompanied the troops as a chaplain when the Catholic cantons attacked. He died on October 11, 1531. Afterward, the Zurich City Council commissioned Leo Jud to invite Oecolampadius to come as Zwingli's replacement. Oecolampadius declined saying, "My post is here."[60] The Basel Reformer barely had time to pray and send his refusal before he joined Zwingli before Christ's throne. At the age of forty-nine, he sickened with either a tumor of the breastbone or blood poisoning.

His last days reflected His peaceful trust in God. Looking into tearful faces, he said, "Rejoice! I am going to a place of everlasting joy.... My brethren, the Lord is there; He calls me away."[61] He warned colleagues, "Oh, my brethren, what a black cloud is appearing on the horizon—what a tempest is approaching! Be steadfast: the Lord will preserve His own."[62]

On the evening of 21 November he called his children to his bedside to give them his blessing. Wibrandis stood by the little group of rather frightened infants, her cheerful face now pale and anxious. He spoke to them one by one, Eusebius, Irene, Alethia, and the babes answered his questions with stammered promises they could hardly have understood. Next morning his brethren hastened silent through the streets to gather at his side. Now he could speak but faintly and had not strength to take Communion. Only once, when somebody asked if the light were too strong, if they should draw the blind, did he strike his breast and murmur with a smile (perhaps remembering his name): *"Abunde lucis est"*—"here's light enough within."[63]

---

60. Jean-Henri Merle d'Aubigné, *History of the Reformation of the Sixteenth Century*, H. White, trans. (New York: American Tract Society, 1836), vol. 4, bk. 16, ch. 10, 465–468, esp. 466.

61. d'Aubigné, *History of the Reformation of the Sixteenth Century*, vol. 4, bk. 16, ch. 10, 466.

62. d'Aubigné, *History of the Reformation of the Sixteenth Century*, vol. 4, bk. 16, ch. 10, 466.

63. Rupp, *Patterns*, 44.

The day began to break; he repeated in a feeble voice the 51st Psalm: *Have mercy upon me, O Lord, according to thy loving kindness.* Then remaining silent, as if he wished to recover strength, he said, "Lord Jesus, help me!" The ten pastors fell to their knees around his bed with uplifted hands; at this moment the sun rose, and darted his earliest rays on a scene of sorrow so great and so afflicting with which the Church of God was again stricken.[64]

Early in the morning of 23 November he entered God's presence; a wife and three babies under the age of three were suddenly bereft. His epitaph may be found inscribed on the Reformation Tablet on the wall of the Munster Cathedral in Basel, under which he is buried along with his wife. It reads: "Dr. Johannes Oecolampadius, theologian by profession, most skilled in three languages, the primary author of the evangelical teaching in this city and true bishop of its Church. As in doctrine, so in the holiness of his life he was highly esteemed; he lies buried beneath this small stone."

Basel, also orphaned after his sudden death, turned to Capito for help in reestablishing the churches. Politically, the city defended Zurich in 1535 with troops during a religious skirmish. However, Basel increasingly tied itself to Bern and Strassburg, where Capito and Bucer led the Reformation. Christian lives began burning brighter and God's glory shone more brilliantly because of Oecolampadius, Christ's house-lamp in Basel.

---

64. d'Aubigné. *History of the Reformation of the Sixteenth Century*, vol. 4, bk. 16, ch. 10, 467.

TIMELINE FOR JOHANNES OECOLAMPADIUS

1482—Born in Weinsberg, Germany, to Johannes and Anna Hausshein

1499—Enters Heidelberg University

1501—Receives his B.A.

1503—Receives his M.A.; enters Bologna Law School; returns to Heidelberg University; tutors

1510—Assumes preaching position in Weinsberg

1512—Publishes "On the Passion of the Lord"; resigns pastorate

1513—Enters Tübingen University for theological studies

1515—Begins New Testament Greek Bible collaboration with Erasmus in Basel; enters University of Basel; receives *baccalaureus biblicus* and *baccalaureus sententiarus*

1516—Receives *baccalaureus formatus*; interns at Weinsberg; receives *licentiatus theologiae*

1518—Receives doctorate from University of Basel; becomes Augsburg cathedral preacher

1520—Leaves pastorate and enters Altomunster monastery

1522—January—leaves monastery and hides in Ebernberg castle; November—refugee, proofreader for Cratander's press in Basel, vicar at St. Martin's Church

1523—Lectures on Isaiah at University of Basel; draws hundreds; Basel Council opposes Pope Hadrian's declaration to ban "Lutheran" preachers and appoints Oecolampadius as theology teacher at University of Basel; Oecolampadius becomes chief priest at St. Martin's; publishes *Isaiah Commentary*

1524—Offers Communion cup to believers; lectures on Romans at University of Basel; clearly agrees with Zwingli about Eucharist

1525—Produces earliest German Protestant liturgy; refuses to say Mass for dead; preaches only evangelical sermons; receives theological chair at University of Basel; publishes *De Genuina Verborum Domini* in Strassburg and *66 Sermons by Chrysostom* with his own comments on *sola Scriptura, sola fide,* and invocation of saints

1526—Publishes *Antisyngramma*; congregation sings, which is approved by Council, making Basel the first Swiss city with an evangelical profession; Baden Disputation, first proposal of *Agende* to Council (earliest Protestant church ordinance, including church discipline)

1527—Basel Council allows people to choose their own church and whether they will take Communion

1528—Bern Disputation; mother dies; marries Wibrandis Rosenblatt; son Eusebius born; Small Iconoclastic Tumult; Council orders images removed from four churches

1529—Basel Iconoclast revolt; Oecolampadius restructures University of Basel; Basel enters Federation of Reformed Swiss Cantons; *Reformationsordnung* (constitution of Reformed church) based on earlier *Agende* accepted by the Council; Oecolampadius becomes head pastor at Munster Cathedral and is over Basel clergy; Marburg Colloquy; daughter Irene born; emperor issues decree against Anabaptists

1530—Publishes *Dialogue*; outlines plan for lay elders and church discipline; Diet of Augsburg; Augsburg and Strassburg Confessions; Aarau Conference

1531—Assists in restructuring of Ulm; daughter Aletheia born; Servetus exiled from Basel; Zwingli dies October 11; Oecolampadius refuses Zurich leadership; dies November 23

CHAPTER TWO

Colleagues in the Kingdom

THE BASEL REFORMER had influenced most of the Reformers of his time, even unknown gospel laborers in other countries. By God's grace he had become a funnel for collecting past faithful doctrine, pouring it into his generation and beyond. In this chapter, we will look at some of Johannes Oecolampadius's colleagues and the influence he had in the efforts of reforming the church.

Wolfgang Capito

Church purification never comes without opposition. In any controversy, people take sides, painting opponents with one brush and supporters with another. So it was with Johannes Oecolampadius, who spawned detractors as well as loyalists. Some admired his early humanist attacks on immorality, but later abhorred his interpretation of Communion. One, however, remained a faithful friend and cohort from the moment of their first meeting: Wolfgang Capito.

We know that Oecolampadius and Capito shared classes, books, and ideas at university, and often corresponded with exhortations and counsel for one another. Capito preached in Basel for several years, laying the groundwork for his friend's arrival there. When Oecolampadius began lecturing on Isaiah, Capito requested the notes immediately. They traveled to Zurich together to confer with Ulrich Zwingli and attended disputations. When Oecolampadius died, Capito carried on his friend's work in Basel, edited posthumous commentaries on Ezekiel and Jeremiah, wrote the Basler's biography, and married his widow, adopting his children. Probably at Capito and Martin Bucer's instigation, the Strassburg Magistrate furnished copies of all Oecolampadius's biblical commentaries to every pastor in Strassburg. Capito boldly defended a Reformed Lord's Supper in a treatise, stating that "none other than Zwingli and Oecolampadius in his own presence had declared this [that 'is' means 'signifies.']."[1] These Eucharistic arguments were taken over from the Basel Reformer by Capito as early as 1525.[2]

Did they differ in any respect? The writings of both men appear equally irenic, but not equally firm. Both taught election, but Capito minimized its importance to the point of deleting it from the articles at the Synod of Bern in 1532. Capito tended to define the covenant more in terms of law, repentance being at the heart of the obligations. In contrast, Oecolampadius emphasized the mercy of God in binding a people to Himself out of His great love. Both men agreed about the continuity of the covenant, but Capito developed a further distinction. He spoke of an external covenant by which Israel was cut off and an internal covenant made with the elect for all eternity. Ultimately, the writings of both concentrated on love for God and love from God.

Martin Bucer

Another Reformer, Bucer, became a good friend of Oecolampadius and a coworker. He traveled to Ulm with Oecolampadius in order to establish a Reformed government and church. They fought as comrades at the Marburg Colloquy, often exchanged letters, and read one another's publications. As previously mentioned, Bucer, along with Capito, apparently encouraged the dissemination of Oecolampadius's commentaries in Strassburg. He married Oecolampadius's wife after Capito's death, raising both Oecolampadius's children and Capito's along with his own after the Plague's devastating attack.

---

1. Julia Gauss, "Basels politisches dilemma in der Reformationzeit," *Zwingliana* 15 (1979–82): 519.

2. Kittelson, *Capito*, 150.

As early as 1525, Bucer espoused ideas about the Eucharist derived from Oecolampadius.[3] He repeated the Basler's ideas on church discipline (excommunication), even proclaiming, "Where there is no discipline and excommunication there is no Christian community."[4] Bucer imitated Oecolampadius in organizing the elders as an official body to minister to souls and to examine regularly the conduct and teaching of pastors. According to Henry Strohl, Bucer "recovered and developed Oecolampadius's theory of the visible Church, mother of the faithful."[5]

Oecolampadius also led Bucer to embrace a "clear distinction between the purpose of the State and that of the group [church]," so that the magistrate's limited authority over the state was distinctly separate from the elder's rule in the church.[6] Both men construed the relation of church and state as one wherein the church constrained evil by persuasion (particularly through the means of grace) and the state constrained evil by force. Both perceived that the gospel, made effective through the Holy Spirit, was the power of God to establish the local Reformation, as well as the universal kingdom. The force of arms was not the means for establishing the kingdom of God.

These cohorts believed in covenant unity, that is, that circumcision before Christ and baptism after the coming of Christ granted entrance to the covenant. Both believed God gave His Name and Himself in covenant to Israel and the church, with elements of continuity and discontinuity. The eternal covenant was the law of love. This pact held true eternally since God guaranteed it through His Holy Spirit in the elect. Law intertwined with faith demonstrated through love. "The covenant is composed of the Holy Spirit's work on the man of faith's heart causing him to keep God's law through love. In fact, it would not be too strong to assert that the whole

---

3. François Wendel, *Calvin, sources et evolution de sa pensée religieuse* (Paris: Presses Universitaires de France, 1950), 265n148. Also, Martin Bucer, *Common Places*, trans. D. F. Wright (Appleford: Sutton Courtenay, 1972), 33.

4. McNeill, *History*, 80–81.

5. Henry Strohl, *La Pensée de la Réforme* (Neuchatel/Paris: Delachaux et Niestle, 1951), 14.

6. Strohl, *Pensée*, 193. See also J. Wayne Baker, *Heinrich Bullinger and the Covenant* (Athens, Ohio: Ohio University Press, 1980), 168.

rationale for the covenant is to create those who will love God and neighbor by the Spirit's law."[7]

Both men held the authority of Scripture to be above the church. The body of Christ bore the task of making the Bible's authority effective. But the Holy Spirit, as God, knowing the intent of Scripture, interpreted it directly into the heart of believers. The law of God became written on the Christian's heart. So law and gospel were not antithetical, as with Martin Luther.

Bucer's personality, being less irenic, placed slight differences in a more stark contrast. For example, whereas Oecolampadius stressed that baptism signified regeneration, Bucer emphasized the sign itself. They agreed that baptismal water did not magically regenerate, but Oecolampadius underlined that real grace that aided regeneration was administered through the faith of the parents. Bucer took the perspective that since Old Testament babies received the advantages of the covenant community after circumcision, New Testament babies should receive as much advantage through baptism. But while God did not tie His grace to things, He did tie it to the covenant promise. Or, to put it another way, Oecolampadius repeated that God instituted the sacraments to strengthen the believer's faith, whereas Bucer considered baptism more a legal incorporation into the covenant.

Despite slight differences, Oecolampadius, Capito, and Bucer held the same main tenets of the Reformation: *sola Scriptura*, *sola gratia*, *sola fide*, and *soli Deo gloria*. All three agreed on the spiritual presence of Christ in the Lord's Supper. Further, in the mysterious sovereignty of God, each one nurtured the spiritual and, in some instances, physical offspring of the others.

Ulrich Zwingli

Zwingli proved a more distant friend to Oecolampadius, though an established relation dated from 1522. Both men studied at the University of Basel. They agreed on Communion despite occasional

---

7. Peter A. Lillback, *The Binding of God: Calvin's Role in the Development of Covenant Theology* (Grand Rapids: Baker, 2001), 143.

disunity over exact wording; although some might see more spiritual content in the Basel Reformer's view. They fought side by side at the Marburg Colloquy for "est" to mean "signifies." Concerning the Basel Reformer's work of 1525, *De Genuina Verborum Dei*, Zwingli wrote, "The learned and pious Oecolampadius has already published a most Christian book in which he has proved this interpretation at great length out of the early Fathers."[8] In 1558, Zwingli's successor, Heinrich Bullinger, equated the Eucharistic views of the two men, mentioning only the name of Oecolampadius in his *De Testamento*.[9]

Zwingli read with approval other works by the Basler, as may be seen in this comment: "[Oecolampadius], a man in every way more perfect than in the opinion of the multitudes, has given us, after these things, Isaiah, accompanied by commentary, which set forth the sense and text; no other work has gone out which more fittingly could be called a cornucopia."[10]

Although Zurich handled the Anabaptist controversy differently from Basel, both cities and their Reformers held similar views on paedobaptism. Zwingli and Oecolampadius maintained that infant baptism provided a New Testament expression of circumcision; one covenant existed for all people at all times; election was integral to the covenant; unity existed between promises and fulfillment; and the covenant was unilateral on God's part, with faith being the sign of election and the moral law being the eternal law and will of God.

In the area of justification, both championed salvation by faith alone through Christ's work alone. However, while still in the Reformed camp, they seemed headed toward divergent paths in one area, had they continued living. Oecolampadius, as a proponent of

---

8. Geoffrey W. Bromiley, ed. and trans, *Zwingli and Bullinger: Selected Translations with Introductions and Notes* (Philadelphia: Westminster, 1953), 231.

9. Gauss, "Basels politisches Dilemma," 540. "John Oecolampadius was the only authority whom Bullinger cited who seemed to support the unity of the covenant in the sense of a contractual agreement." J. Wayne Baker, "Covenant and Society: The *Republica Christiana* in the Thought of Heinrich Bullinger" (PhD diss., University of Iowa, 1970), 204.

10. Ulrich Zwingli, in *Corpus Reformatorum*, vol. 101, *Huldreich Zwinglis Samtliche Werke*, Band 14 (Zurich: Verlag Bericht Haus, 1959), 87–88. In the same place, Zwingli calls Jerome and Oecolampadius "most holy men of God" and says he himself used the LXX, Jerome, and Oecolampadius.

elders' involvement in excommunication, leaned toward a greater separation of church and state. Zwingli apparently conceived of a Christian state that would play a greater role in the establishment of God's kingdom. Only implications and nuances of application may be drawn. In the fall of 1530, at a meeting of theologues in Zurich, Zwingli attempted to persuade his city government to incorporate Oecolampadius's idea of excommunication and hoped other cities would join in the same regulations. When Zwingli died, Oecolampadius commented, "Alas, that Zwingle, whom I have so long regarded as my right arm, has fallen under the blows of cruel enemies!"[11]

Martin Luther

While everyone knows about Luther's involvement in the Reformation, few know of his frequent interaction with Oecolampadius. It could not be said that the men were friends, but they were acquaintances. Luther's concern revolved around how a sinner might be made just before a holy God. The Basel Reformer concerned himself more with how a Christian might be filled with love for God and enjoy God. Yet the two men bore many outward similarities. They were born in Germany one year apart, attended law school, received theological doctorates, functioned as priests, belonged to Augustinian monasteries, hid as outlaws of the church in castles in 1522, married and had children, and became great Reformers. Both read the Scriptures in the original languages, facilitating a common journey toward biblical truth under the Spirit's guidance.

Yet although each man read the other's publications, neither shows direct evidence of having been influenced by the other. On June 10, 1521, Luther wrote to George Spalatin: "I marvel at the spirit of Oecolampadius, not because he has hit upon the same line of argument as I have, but because he is so outspoken, so confident, so Christian. May the Lord preserve him and make him great. Amen." Then, on July 13, 1521, he noted to Melanchthon, "I greatly wish that Oecolampadius's book *On Confession* would be

---

11. d'Aubigné, *History of the Reformation of the Sixteenth Century*, vol. 4, bk. 16, ch. 10, 465.

translated at Wittenberg in the same way, so that the papists would be blown apart."[12]

Letters carried between the two remain to be investigated. From as early as 1519, Oecolampadius demonstrated his support for Luther by anonymously editing a treatise in defense of the Wittenberg Reformer. Interestingly, Oecolampadius chastised Luther in one letter concerning his caustic tone, which never changed. The friendly correspondence was ended by Luther after he incorrectly supposed Oecolampadius to belong to the "false brethren" in Andreas Karlstadt's camp. Oecolampadius denied this in his "A Reasonable Answer to D. Martin Luther's Report" in 1526. Nevertheless, despite disagreements, Oecolampadius described Luther as "our faithful coworker and preacher of the inexpressible majesty and praise of God."[13]

Manifestly, both displayed concern for salvation by faith in the accomplished work of Christ alone, and that having been saved by grace alone, men should walk in appropriate daily paths of faith. However, Luther saw himself as teaching justification without fulfillment of the law, and falsely caricatured Oecolampadius as teaching justification by faith evidenced through the fulfillment of the law of love. The Basel Reformer also spoke of differences with Luther: "It is true that I do not ascribe as much to the external word…as Luther for 'the external word does not bring me resurrection' nor was it 'the object of faith.'"[14]

Both Reformers believed that the moral law is binding, that the Old Testament law bears witness to Christ, and that the law shows us our sins and provides an expression of God's unilateral covenant. But the Basler attributed more life to the law, stating frequently that there remained a sense in which the law still held sway. He declared more specifically the inseparable relationship between God's Word

---

12. Martin Luther, *D. Martin Luther's Werke*, vol. 48 (Weimar: H. Böhlaus, 1912–30), 255, 258.

13. Pelikan, *Reformation of Church and Dogma*, 184–185.

14. Pelikan, *Reformation of Church and Dogma*, 188, citing Johannes Oecolampadius, *Das der misverstand D. Martin Luthers uff die ewigbestendige wort Das ist mein leib nit beston mag* (Basel: Cratander, 1527), 16, and Johannes Oecolampadius, *Antisyngramma* (Basel: [unknown printer],1525/Zurich: Froschauer, 1526).

and His Spirit. In general, his hermeneutical approach made wider use of the Scriptures in a less issue-oriented manner than Luther. Their difference over Communion is commonly known. While both believed in a spiritual presence of Christ in the Lord's Supper, Luther stressed a bodily presence as well. Oecolampadius stressed Christ's bodily ascension, which precluded a physical Communion.[15]

Both held that excommunication did not include temporal punishment, that the power of the keys in absolution belonged to clergy and laymen, and that unbelief was the real mortal sin. However, Luther did not want to eliminate secret confession and did not campaign for public church confession as did Oecolampadius.

Both conceived of two kingdoms: an inner spiritual one and an outer civil one. Both concluded that the church had been entrusted with no outer force, but only God's Word; however, because of sin, the outward civil force is necessary for protection, peace, and binding of evil. The state cannot rule the conscience. Oecolampadius published these ideas in 1521, two years before Luther's treatise on government.

In spite of earlier antagonistic remarks, Luther was very moved by Oecolampadius's and Zwingli's deaths. "The blow inflicted on

---

15. David Law misunderstands the significance of a spiritual presence. Reformed Christians, descendants of Oecolampadius and Calvin, understand this to be an intensified presence of Christ accompanied by grace for the believer. It is not a mere remembrance. See David R. Law, "Descent into Hell, Ascension, and Luther's Doctrine of Ubiquitarianism," *Theology* 107, no. 838 (July–August 2004): 250–256. Luther incorrectly grouped together Oecolampadius, Zwingli, and Karlstadt in the Lord's Supper issue, even implying a connection with Marcion. Ironically, however, it is Luther's ubiquitous body that treats Christ in a more docetic manner. See Wolfgang A. Bienert, "Marcion in Werk Martin Luthers," in *Rezeption und Reform: Festschrift für Hans Schneider zu seinem 60 Geburtstag*, Wolfgang Breul-Kunkel, Lothar Vogel, Hans Schneider, and Donald F. Durnbaugh, eds. (Darmstadt, Germany: Verlag der Hessichen Kirchengeschichtlichen Vereinigung, 2001), 19–34. Katharina Greschat also argues that Luther is the Marcionite in the Eucharsitic argument, but she minimizes Oecolampadius's spiritual presence interpretation, which goes beyond the symbolic. Katharina Greschat, "'Dann sind gottwilkommen Marcion und Marciönin': Marcion in den reformatorischen Auseinandersetzungen um das Abendmahl." In *Marcion und seine kirchengeschichtliche Wirkung*, vol. 150. Gerhard May, Katharina Greschat, and Martin Meiser, eds. (Berlin/New York: Walter de Gruyter, 2002), 235–251. ["'Then Marcion and the Marcionites are acceptable to God': Marcion in the Reformation Disputations over the Lord's Supper." In *Marcion and His Impact on Church History*.]

him by their sudden decease was such, that many years after he said
to Bullinger: 'Their death filled me with such intense sorrow, that I
was near dying myself.'"[16]

Philip Melanchthon

Ironically, it was Luther's successor, Philip Melanchthon, who bore
the imprint of Oecolampadius's teaching. At the University of
Tübingen, he served as the fifteen-year-old researcher for the thirty-
year-old Oecolampadius. They worked on production of an original
Greek edition of Aristotle, reading Erasmus along with Ambrosius
Blaurer. The older man became a mentor to the younger, bestow-
ing a set of Agricola's *Dialectics* as a gift. Melanchthon testified that
"with a fellow student, Oecolampadius, he read Hesiod and other
Greek works, and later said that no one did more for him in his
youth than Oecolampadius."[17]

Clearly, as early as 1522, Melanchthon changed his view on the
law from that of the previous year. He no longer viewed the New
Testament as a complete annulment of the Old Testament law, but
rather saw the New Testament as a change in law. He explained
that the law must be looked at by way of the soteriological unity of
the testaments.

The most obvious and well–documented example of Oecolampadius's influence on Melanchthon concerns the Lord's Supper.
After reading the Basel Reformer's *De Genuina Verborum Domini*,
which argued that the Patriarchs taught "this signifies My body,"
he began to change. By 1529, he penned an open letter to Oecolampadius, confessing that the Patriarchs did not really teach the same
meaning of "est" as did Luther.[18] By 1559, he concluded that Luther
contradicted Clement of Alexandria, Origen, Tertullian, and Augus-

---

16. d'Aubigné, *History of the Reformation of the Sixteenth Century*, vol. 4, bk. 16,
ch. 10, 468.

17. Clyde Leonard Manschreck, *Melanchthon: The Quiet Reformer* (New York:
Abingdon Press, 1958), 39.

18. Peter Fraenkel, "Ten Questions Concerning Melanchthon, the Fathers and
the Eucharist," in *Luther and Melanchthon*, ed. Vilmos Vajta (Philadelphia: Muhlenberg, 1961), 157.

tine. Other implications ensued. For example, Melanchthon moved toward the Basel Reformer's view that a close association existed between Christ's efficacy and His benefits. That is to say, union with Christ, not simply forgiveness, is the benefit received in Communion.

Erasmus and Others

Other cobelligerents disagreed more extensively with Oecolampadius and yet fought alongside him. One, a personal acquaintance, was Desiderius Erasmus. His stance defined him as a more-distant forerunner of the Reformation. Erasmus agreed with Oecolampadius that the church should have public confession and should not wield political authority. But he emphasized the pragmatic more than the doctrinal issues, which hinders a precise comparison of the two men.

Additional colleagues included Conrad Pellican, who had overseen the Basel Franciscan monastery and who labored with the Reformer at the University of Basel; Duke Ulrich (later Frederick II), who, by God's grace, was converted through Oecolampadius during his exile in Basel in 1523;[19] Johann Froben, who worked for reform through the Basel presses, as did Johann Dent, along with Andreas Cratander, who first took the nascent Reformer into his home; and Caspar Hedio, who ministered the Word with him at St. Martin's Church.

John Calvin

A far-flung "colleague," challenging time and the Basler's physical death, appears in John Calvin. In God's plan, the two men never met personally. Just four years after Oecolampadius's death, Calvin came to live in Basel for a year, beginning in 1535. The entire city still reflected the doctrine, praxis, and structure of Oecolampadius. Here the Frenchman wrote parts of his *Institutes of the Christian Religion*, including the preface. Calvin dedicated his commentary on Romans to Simon Grynaeus, Oecolampadius's successor in Basel, whom he befriended along with Sebastian Munster during his stay there. Clearly, he could not have been unaware of the Basel

---

19. Locher, *Zwingli und die schweizerische Reformation*, 487.

Reformer's ideas. Afterward, he lived under Oecolampadius's influence in Strassburg, 1538–1541, where Capito and Bucer espoused his teachings and where each pastor was given a set of Oecolampadius's commentaries. At times, Calvin echoed the Basel Reformer's very words. For example, Calvin repeats Oecolampadius's words, published in *Paradoxon* in 1521, that a believer is taken up into heaven to meet Christ in Communion.[20] Concerning the Lord's Supper, Calvin wrote, "Hitherto, indeed, I have intentionally not dealt with the matter [of the Lord's Supper] because I was unwilling to do what has been done already. This was first performed with accuracy and skill by Oecolampadius, who clearly showed that the figment of a local presence was unknown to the ancient Church."[21] In fact, the final accord between Geneva and Zurich concerning Communion (*Consensus Tigurinus*, 1549) merely repeated the Basel Reformer's earlier thoughts. Theodore Beza concluded that Oecolampadius and Calvin agreed on the Eucharist.[22]

The *Articles on the Organization of the Church and its Worship at Geneva*, submitted to the Genevan city council in 1537, repeated Oecolampadius's practices established in Basel: 1) more frequent Communion—in fact, the regulation exactly replicated Basel's arrangement, set up by Oecolampadius, of weekly communion, rotating among the main parish churches; 2) excommunication; 3) congregational psalm-singing, which had been employed since 1526 in Basel; 4) catechism studies required for youth, as set out in Basel's 1529 Ordinance; 5) a secular court for marriage difficulties; 6) and a requirement for all Geneva citizens to sign a confession of faith, as was done by all Council members and guildsmen beginning in 1534 in Basel.

More exact imitation can be seen in the practice of excommunication, as handled by the Genevan Articles of 1537 and Basel's

---

20. Staehelin, *Lebenswerk*, 144. For a more complete comparison of Calvin and Oecolampadius, see Poythress, "Johannes Oecolampadius' Exposition of Isaiah," 133–147.

21. John Calvin, "Partaking of the Flesh and Blood," in *Calvin: Theological Treatises*, trans. with notes by J. K. S. Reid (Philadelphia: Westminster Press, 1954), 292.

22. Jill Raitt, *The Eucharistic Theology of Theodore Beza* (Chambersburg, Pa.: American Academy of Religion, 1973), 38.

Discipline Ordinance, proposed by Oecolampadius to the Basel Council in May 1530. Both documents assert that 1) ministers and laymen from the congregation should be on the disciplinary board; 2) lay *censores*/commissioners should represent the congregation, meeting weekly on Thursdays (*censores* became "elders" in the Genevan *Ordonnances Ecclésiastiques* of 1541); 3) a public offender should be privately exhorted before being reported to a *censore*/commissioner/elder; 4) the minister should publicly announce the name of any unrepentant offender; 5) an ecclesiastical court was to be established in the city of Geneva (in each parish in Basel); 6) offenses would include doctrinal issues such as blasphemy, as well as missing Sunday worship and contempt for the sacraments; 7) *censores*/elders were to admonish the offender in the presence of all elders (this was established in Ulm in 1531 by Oecolampadius and Bucer when the latter became convinced that this was the correct arrangement); 8) and excommunication was to have no legal implications outside the church.[23] All eight of these Genevan practices under Calvin reiterate the Basel practices proposed by Oecolampadius. Olaf Kuhr observes: "The fundamental ideals of Oecolampadius concerning ecclesiastical discipline had been realized by the *Ordonnances Ecclesiastiques*. Here one only has to point to the institution of the Consistory. While for political reasons Oecolampadius was unable to establish a central disciplinary court for the whole church (instead each city parish had its own), Calvin did succeed."[24]

Both men held to justification by faith alone through grace alone as found in the authority of Scripture alone. But they concurred in even more finely delineated areas. Calvin's emphasis on covenant theology was preceded by Basel. Oecolampadius held a thoroughly

23. Olaf Kuhr, "Calvin and Basel: The Significance of Oecolampadius and the Basel Discipline Ordinance for the Institution of Ecclesiastical Discipline in Geneva," *Scottish Bulletin of Evangelical Theology* 16 (Spring 1998): 19–33, esp. 23, 33. Kuhr seems unclear as to the public dimension of announcing the offender. See 24, 29, and 30. This may be because at an earlier time, the unrepentant was to be denounced before the Magistry, then in the late 1540s was to make a public apology before the congregation. *Registers of the Consistory of Geneva in the Time of Calvin, 1542–1544*, vol. 1, ed. Robert M. Kingdon (Grand Rapids: Eerdmans, 2000), xxx and 420.

24. Kuhr, "Calvin and Basel," 30.

mature and highly developed doctrine of the covenant. In fact, he might be considered the father of covenant theology, after Paul and Augustine. Even Bullinger, in his famous work on the covenant, *de Testamento*, cited only Oecolampadius for formulating the covenant as a contractual agreement. Both Calvin and Oecolampadius could speak in the same breath of the covenant signs of circumcision and baptism for the elect. Each referred to the church as being in the Old and New Testaments. Similarly, both emphasized the unilateral quality of the covenant, the existence of only one covenant of grace for all time, and the Old Testament covenant being confirmed by ceremonies that prefigured Christ. Together they believed Scripture to teach that God had always bound His people to Himself in covenant through the binding cord of Christ's death and resurrection.[25]

Oecolampadius was also a predecessor of Calvin in his fully developed use of election within the covenant plan. Calvin echoes the idea that grace is neither equally offered nor received by all. Oecolampadius not only wrote about this election, but thoroughly integrated it into his biblical-theological framework, as can be seen in his commentaries. He wrote that God zealously pursued His children with mercy. "Perfectly, however, He will immediately console the humble and those hoping in Him, such as whom He selects, from whom He does not draw away His mercy."[26] He saw election as an outcome of God's mercy. This included His choice to protect His children and punish their enemies; love the elect and speak tenderly to them as to a child; embrace them as a husband his bride; redeem, remember, guard, and sanctify them; deliver them from unbearable temptation; liberate, feed, prune, and pardon them; rescue them from hell; reward them; empathize with them; carry them; give them wisdom; open Scripture to them; answer their prayers; console and deliver them; incorporate them into His body; forgive,

---

25. Poythress, "Johannes Oecolampadius' Exposition of Isaiah," 490–664 has more detailed discussion of bilateral and unilateral covenant and other aspects of Oecolampadius's covenant theology.

26. Johannes Oecolampadius, *In Iesaiam prophetam Hypomnematon, hoc est, Commentariorum* (Basel: Cratander, 1525), 6r (ad loc. Isa. 1:1). Henceforth, the notation "r" for recto refers to the front side of a numbered page. The "v" stands for verso, the back side of the page.

revive, and grant eternal mercy to them; strengthen, honor, cleanse, and grant authority to them; call, intercede for, and heal them; and lay down His life for them.[27] God's plan not only accomplished salvation, but also effected it for each saved believer. This eternal covenant, where man saw God's mercy, was a source for strengthening faith. It confirmed God's plan for the glorious exaltation of Christ and the vindication of all His people for eternity.

One passage from Oecolampadius's Isaiah commentary even mentions the covenant of redemption, which Calvin also discusses:

> Hear then also the larger promises, for there will be with you an everlasting covenant, because God has given His law in your heart: for He will be your God, and you will be His temple and of His people. And just as He entered into a pact with His Son, our Lord Jesus Christ, as David describes in many places, and raised Him from death, so also by the highest faith His mercy will be to you, and also He will not suffer you to suffer above what you are able to bear.[28]

No question remains as to Calvin's source for establishing elders and a consistory. Clearly, while sojourning in Basel, the Frenchman revised his *Institutes* on church order and discipline to reflect Oecolampadius's ideas. François Wendel, J. Wayne Baker, and Akira Demura concur. Demura traces this absorption of the concept from Basel through Strassburg, where Calvin witnessed a more perfect application of excommunication. While in Germany, he drafted *Traité de la sainte Cene*. This incorporates the doctrine of church discipline, where Calvin emphasized, along with Oecolampadius, that being a member of Christ's body implied a necessary purity in that union.[29] Bucer himself gained an understanding in

---

27. Poythress, "Johannes Oecolampadius' Exposition of Isaiah," 490–664.

28. Oecolampadius, *In Iesaiam*, 268r, (ad loc Isa. 55:3). See also Lillback, *Binding*, 140–148.

29. Kuhr ("Calvin and Basel," 26) sets statements by Calvin and Oecolampadius in parallel. For example, Calvin: "It seems to me, that we shall not have a lasting church unless the old, that is apostolic, church discipline is in its totality reinstated–which is needed in many respects among us." Oecolampadius: "As far as I can see, it shall never be well with us unless excommunication is maintained according to the apostolic and evangelical rule in the churches."

Ulm of Oecolampadius's concept that excommunication and the distribution of sacraments marked the true church. At the very least, through Bucer, this concept was transmitted to Calvin.

Calvin apparently also learned from Oecolampadius, via Bucer, the relation of church and state.[30] From his passion for church purity, Oecolampadius developed the biblical application of elders administering excommunication, as opposed to excommunication being the sole domain of the civil government. This was new. Never had a European city removed state authority over excommunication and given it to the church in this way. Bucer developed the idea. Calvin imitated it. "In the first place, Calvin recovered from Bucer the affirmation that ecclesiastical institutions are not submitted to human arbitrariness but that they have divine right since they have been dictated by the Holy Spirit."[31] "It [church discipline] had to be exercised independently.... Church and state were two separate entities. Calvin had finally secured what Oecolampadius had always envisaged but could not realize."[32] "The two swords [church and state] should not be fused.... The views of Oecolampadius found fertile soil at Geneva and Strasbourg." In essence, Oecolampadius was redefining 'Christian,' 'the nature of the church,' and the possibility of a 'Christian society.'"[33]

Calvin patterned his worship service after William Farel's "La Manière et Fasson" from 1533, which found roots in Bucer's Strassburg liturgy of 1530. Strassburg, in turn, reflected Oecolampadius's liturgy of 1525, which eventually included congregational singing. Calvin, too, requested congregational singing. The track shows clearly that Oecolampadius's views, copied by Bucer, were passed

---

30. Strohl, *Pensée*, 221n3, states that Calvin's view on the church and state are the thesis of Oecolampadius. The stream of influence, however, is somewhat muddied by all the footsteps back and forth between Basel and Strassburg, as in the case of congregational singing. For example see van 't Spijker, "Genfer Psalters."

31. Wendel, *Calvin*, 104, and 104n103.

32. Kuhr, "Calvin and Basel," 32.

33. T. A. Fudge, "Icarus of Basel?" *The Journal of Religious History* 21, no. 3, 268–284, and J. Wayne Baker, "Church Discipline or Civil Punishment: On the Origins of the Reformed Schism, 1528–1531," *Andrews University Seminary Studies* 23, no. 1 (Spring 1985): 3–18, esp. 17–18.

to Calvin. Even Calvin's Eucharistic liturgy, especially in its list of those candidates for excommunication, "reveals exactly the same structure as we find in the Basel communion ordinance."[34]

Calvin's idea about knowing God through knowing his own sin reflects Oecolampadius's new interpretation of the Samaritan woman story. Medieval writers framed her interview with Jesus as saintly. However, the Basler saw her as a woman who knew her sin before acknowledging Christ. This self-knowledge, he insists, could come only through Christ revealing Himself to her, not through any human effort.[35]

But how do we know for sure that Calvin read the Basler's commentaries or appropriated them? We know that all of Oecolampadius's Old Testament commentaries were printed in Geneva in 1558, which would not have been done without the recommendation of Calvin. The Genevan Reformer wrote to Pierre Viret, May 19, 1540, commending Oecolampadius's Isaiah commentary. He conceded, "No one, therefore so far has engaged more diligently in this work [of writing a commentary on Isaiah] than Oecolampadius."[36] Similarities between the two Reformers' commentaries touch even unique interpretations, such as their comments on the Samaritan woman, although differences also emerge.[37] This reliance of Geneva on Basel becomes apparent not only by comparing ideas verse by verse, but also by comparing exact wording. The fact is that Calvin constantly interacted with the Basler's materials and occasionally quoted them almost verbatim without citation. In one place, he even copied Oecolampadius's notes about two Old Testament cities so quickly, he reversed the names. By looking at both men's commentaries on

---

34. Kuhr, "Calvin and Basel," 26.

35. Craig S. Farmer, "Changing Images of the Samaritan Woman in Early Reformed Commentaries on John," *Church History* 65, no. 3 (September 1996): 373. Farmer's own later interpretation contradicts this statement by overlaying an enlightenment approach, ignoring the emphasis on salvation by grace alone as a gift from God (374). He also unfairly equates exploring new scriptural meaning with personal bias (375).

36. John Calvin, cited in *Corpus Reformatorum* (henceforth CR), ed. William Baum, Edward Cunitz, and Edward Reuss (Brunsvigae: C. A. Schwetschke and Sons, 1872), vol. 39, no. 217, 36.

37. Farmer, "Samaritan Woman," 372–373.

Isaiah 36:19, a copying mistake appears. Oecolampadius relates: "They wish Hemath to be the Antioch mentioned by the ancients. Sepharvaim is in the region of the Assyrians, whence colonists came to Samaria. Jerome attests that Arpad was a city in Damascus." Compare this with Calvin on the same verse: "It is supposed that Hamath was Antioch in Syria, that Arpad was that city from which colonies were brought to Damascus, and that Sepharvaim was a city situated in the country of Damascus." Quoting Oecolampadius nearly verbatim, Calvin retains the same order of description, but reverses the city names of Sepharvaim and Arpad. The statement in Calvin's commentary is incorrect.[38] Other parallels in idea, phraseology, theology, or vocabulary become obvious when a verse-by-verse comparison is undertaken in other commentaries, too.[39]

It is not surprising that Calvin leaned heavily on the older Reformer's work. What was more natural than for Calvin to make use of the best tools available to him? If Oecolampadius's commentaries were the best source, why not plumb them for insight?

But the above misquote and apparent similarities in commentaries are not the only evidence of Calvin's reliance on the Basel scholar. In Calvin's own published work on Isaiah, he puzzled in print over Oecolampadius's translation of *excelsa*.[40] This again proved his familiarity with the Basel Reformer's earlier commentary, as well as the fact that he seriously meditated on it. In addition, Calvin cites Oecolampadius by name as a source in his Daniel commentary.[41] Like other Reformers, Calvin rushed through available material in order to defend positions and instruct the faithful. Often he used reliable resources from published scholarly editions,

---

38. An exact quote where city names are switched in haste, making the statement false in Calvin, can be seen by comparing Oecolampadius, *In Iesaiam*, 187v (ad loc. Isa. 36:19) with Calvin's at the same place. See Poythress, "Johannes Oecolampadius' Exposition of Isaiah," 133–147, 462–463.

39. Akira Demura, "Two Commentaries on The Epistle to the Romans: Calvin and Oecolampadius," in *Calvinus sincerioris religionis vindex*, ed. Wilhelm H. Neuser and Brian G. Armstrong. (Kirksville, MO: *Sixteenth Century Journal*, 1997), 165–188.

40. Calvin, in CR, 65:262.

41. John Calvin, *New Testament Commentaries*, Thomas H.L. Parker, ed. (Grand Rapids: Eerdmans, 1959–65), 87.

producing his own papers and commentaries quickly. Citations were less of a requirement then. So Calvin's commentary material drew on Oecolampadius's previous work, just as his *Institutes* drew on Bucer's *Enarrationes.* Oecolampadius's impeccable historical research and pious commentary, thereby, has come down to many preachers today through Calvin.

Oecolampadius surpassed Calvin in Christocentric exegesis. This may surprise some, but a close comparison shows the truth of this observation. For example, commenting on Isaiah 37:36, Calvin pointed out that Isaiah had to be confirmed as a credible prophet. Concerning the same verse, Oecolampadius commented, "This is that remarkable miracle that has been touched upon frequently throughout this book, that Jerusalem will be freed from her cruelest enemies, not by a human, but by a divine hand [Christ's redemption]." Calvin ignored the parallel between Hezekiah's temptation and Christ's, which the Basel Reformer eagerly pointed out. Again in Isaiah 37, Oecolampadius referred to the importance of prayer in trials, presenting Jesus' example in the Garden of Gethsemane. Calvin lacked this parallel. Calvin concentrated more on what man should do than on who God was. Or, more bluntly, Calvin exhorted while Oecolampadius praised. For example, Calvin commented on Isaiah 37:5, "Instructed by this example, if we seek relief from him by pouring our cares and anxieties into the bosom of God, our hope shall never be disappointed." Oecolampadius wrote, "Nor indeed do they pray for their own advantage, but for the glory of God and thus almost always do the saints." The difference is subtle but symptomatic. Another example comes from Isaiah 37:35, where Calvin appropriated promises for the Christian, but Oecolampadius displayed Christ. Calvin wrote, "But we ought to look directly to God, and embrace His promises, by which we are defended as by a shield...for God affirms that He will be the guardian and protector of the city" Oecolampadius wrote, "We have, moreover, the stronger promise given to us in Christ who was God's Beloved and He Himself is the poor and wise one through whom God delivered the city." The Genevan Reformer sought rules or principles by which God operated, while the Basel Reformer sought the character of

God Himself. In a caricature of the two, it could be said that Calvin spoke about Christ for the sake of the elect, while Oecolampadius breathed out the image of Christ.

Other aspects of imitation included fencing the table, a dialogue format for the catechism, an emphasis on education, a study of the Patristics, the primacy of scriptural preaching, the initiated but not perfected character of man, creation, and the kingdom, and biblical-theological exegesis. They both believed in the third use of the law, seeing Mosaic law as complementary to the gospel, not antagonistic.

Scholars who concur that Calvin was influenced by Oecolampadius include Paul Wernle, Uwe Plath, Akira Demura, J. Wayne Baker, Thomas A. Fudge, Olaf Kuhr, Karl Hammer, and, to a lesser degree, Bernard Roussel and Henry Strohl.[42] By God's gracious union of these two Reformers in Christ, Calvin became both a brother and a son to Oecolampadius. The implication is clear that although Calvin is perceived as the father of the Reformed church, he is actually the son of Oecolampadius. Demura states, "The true founder of the later Presbyterian-Reformed churches is Johannes Oecolampadius of Basel."[43]

Influence on France

Many others among the French found their way to Basel, including William Farel. This fiery evangelist spent six months preaching to French refugees, dining with Oecolampadius, and debating before the faculty. While in Basel, Farel received a greeting from Jacques LeFèvre, which he conveyed to Oecolampadius. Also through Farel, Gerard Roussel from LeFèvre's Meaux Circle became acquainted with Oecolampadius's writings. Alternately, the Basel Reformer came into contact through Farel with Anemone de Coct, and Morelet du Museau (son of the French ambassador). He influenced these

---

42. Fudge, "Icarus," 279; Strohl, *Pensée*, 192; Hammer, "Der Reformator Oekolampad," 160, who says Calvin was Oecolampadius's indirect pupil, successor, and consummator, 167.

43. Akira Demura, "Calvin's and Oecolampadius' Concept of Church Discipline," in *Calvinus ecclesiae Genevensis custos* (Frankfurt: Verlag Peter Lang, 1984), 187–189, esp. 180.

two Frenchmen tremendously. Apparently, again, Farel provided the connection between Oecolampadius and the Waldensians. These brave believers, at their own peril, sent ambassadors to the Reformer of Basel in 1530. Later the Waldensians chose Basel, Lausanne, and Geneva as the cities where their pastors would train. The Frenchman Jacob Faber (Jacques LeFèvre), who fought for scriptural authority, salvation by faith alone, and rescission of clerical celibacy, also befriended Oecolampadius. In fact, his work was published together with Oecolampadius's in 1535. As mentioned previously, Oecolampadius wrote a tract for Jacobus (Masson) Latomus; a letter between them from about 1524 exists concerning secret confession. Ten years later, Ruchat translated into French a *Method [of] Theological Catechism* by Oecolampadius. The two-sided Pierre Toussaint courted Oecolampadius during his stay in Basel in 1524–1525. Two French refugees in Basel, Elie Couraud and Claude de Feray, after learning from Oecolampadius, became Calvin's coworkers in Geneva.

Influence on Italy and Bohemia

Although Italy stood against the Reformation, even there some received Oecolampadius's writings. A certain Giovanni della Casa became classified as a Zwinglian, supposedly holding a position between Hus and Oecolampadius.[44] Other Italians also connected with the Basel Reformer's teachings over distance and time. The most famous Italian refugee, Peter Martyr Vermigli, fled to Strassburg in 1542. There he lived with Bucer, who had married Oecolampadius's widow by that time. His theological positions, particularly on Communion, distinctly reflect the Basel Reformer's thought.

Further afield, Johannes Dubcansky, who helped compose the Bohemian constitution, patterned it after texts written by Oecolampadius, Zwingli, and Bucer.[45] An unexplored connection existed with Poland's Caspar Schwenckfeld, since Oecolampadius wrote a one page introduction to his short work in 1527.

---

44. Locher, *Zwingli und die schweizerische Reformation*, 665.
45. Locher, *Zwingli und die schweizerische Reformation*, 655–656.

Influence on Britain

The British Isles did not remain isolated from Oecolampadius's influence. John Foxe and John Frith lived in Basel for a while, after which Frith wrote a treatise on the Eucharist reflecting Oecolampadius's position. George Wishart traveled to Switzerland and was exposed to the Basler's precepts. Thomas Bilney confesses that his conversion came through reading the Erasmus-Oecolampadius Greek text of 1519. Nicholas Ridley attributes his understanding of the Lord's Supper to a tract either translated or edited by Oecolampadius. Miles Coverdale read the Basler's works and then influenced John Knox and William Tyndale. An entire Society of Christian Brethren smuggled Reformed writings into England beginning in 1520, which made their way to Cambridge and Oxford students. "They did not press for a vernacular Bible, for they delighted in the new linguistic tools, and the book lists of proscribed books which they bought show that they were mainly after the new Latin biblical commentaries of the 1520s as they stemmed from that remarkable German, Rhineland, Swiss ferment, the commentaries of Luther, Melanchthon, Oecolampadius, Bucer, Zwingli, Hedio, and Lambert of Avignon."[46] In fact, some of Oecolampadius's works were published in England itself at Ipswich and later Worcester through John Oswen's press. Also, his books found refuge in Scottish libraries, such as those of Clement Little, Adam Bothwell, or Ninian Winzett.

Several English authorities vigorously opposed Oecolampadius's writings, as did men in other countries. The bishop of London, John Fisher, and an Oxford professor, Richard Smith, both wrote works arguing against his tenets. The archbishop of Canterbury forbade Oecolampadius's books in 1526 and 1531. This edict may have been driven by the fact that Oecolampadius opposed Henry VIII's divorce, citing Leviticus 18:16.

---

46. Ernest Gordon Rupp, *Six Makers of English Religion, 1500–1700* (London: Hodder and Stoughton, 1957), 15.

John Chrysostom

Another type of colleague in the kingdom, one whose relation spanned a thousand previous years, lived in the fourth century. He was John Chrysostom, AD 345–407. Oecolampadius made it his lifetime work to translate the homilies of this Patriarch, seventeen of which sustained him in his 1522 castle exile. By 1525, sixty-six of his translated Chrysostom sermons on Genesis found a publisher. When Erasmus's 1530 edition on Chrysostom appeared, fifty-five of the sermons on Acts acknowledged Oecolampadius as translator. Chrysostom interpreted Scripture grammatically-historically, minimizing allegory and speculation. Yet he embraced sober typological exegesis, as did Oecolampadius. Scripture always interpreted Scripture. This early saint specifically avoided fanciful or philosophical entanglements in his fourth homily on Genesis, warning others, "I mean, if these people accepted the teachings from Sacred Scripture with the proper dispositions and didn't invent their own from their own reasoning, they would never have been caught in such folly."[47] Oecolampadius followed this approach, yet eschewed the view of free will, made little use of the attachment to Aristotle, and rejected earned grace.

With a strong use of metaphor and personal pronouns, an integration of the text with current events, a scholarly analysis, and a knowledge of Scripture and of man's heart, Oecolampadius reflected the renowned ancient preacher in approach, substance, and form. They both understood Scripture as an integration of Christ-centered history and salvation. In other words, biblical history contains theological meaning that is found only in Christ. They both targeted the heart. "These practical moral applications of the Gospel were given with great moral earnestness. He [Chrysostom] taught that there must be no divorce of morals and religion;

---

47. John Chrysostom, *Saint John Chrysostom Homilies on Genesis 1–17*, trans. Robert C. Hill (Washington, D.C.: Catholic University of America Press, 1986), 59–60. See also on Chrysostom, John Robert Walchenbach, "John Calvin as Biblical Commentator: An Investigation into Calvin's Use of John Chrysostom as an Exegetical Tutor" (PhD diss., University of Pittsburgh, 1974), 51–52. See also John Chrysostom, *Patrologiae cursus completus*, J. P. Migne, ed. (Paris: Garnier Fratres, 1879), 55:126–127.

the Cross and ethics must go hand in hand."[48] Similarly, the Basel Reformer preached that godly virtues should accompany true faith. Both initiated teachings in the pulpit for the sake of laymen, teachings that later were published.

A comparison of Chrysostom's homilies on the books of Genesis, Isaiah, and Romans with Oecolampadius's writings uncovers identical themes of mercy, strengthening of faith, divesting of Jews through unbelief, Christocentricity, humility, and God's love.[49] Both men placed God's binding love for believers within covenant continuity. However, some differences in substance distinguish the two. Chrysostom believed that Adam passed on nature and punishment, but that descendants did not share his sin and guilt, whereas Oecolampadius believed Adam passed on original sin with its guilt and necessity of redemption. In addition, they differed theologically on the sovereignty of God and nature of man, where Oecolampadius stood closer to Augustine.

Even the written format of the two men demonstrates parallels, as the Patriarch and Reformer both open their Isaiah commentaries by extolling the excellencies of the prophet's clarity, boldness, and godliness. Both refer in their introductions to the same Romans 10 verse. Even wording is reminiscent, as Chrysostom begins Genesis with an invitation to a feast and Oecolampadius begins Isaiah with a poem inviting readers to a feast. Characterized by scholarly study of Scripture and eloquent communication to the common man, both left remarkable tomes of Christian exhortation. Apparently Oecolampadius thoroughly, yet discerningly, imbibed his tutor's example in exegesis.

---

48. Earle E. Cairns, *Christianity through the Centuries* (Grand Rapids: Zondervan, 1954), 152. Even their life stories and temperament mimicked one another. Chrysostom had a kindly, affectionate nature, was ascetic with an emaciated face, had begun to study law, became a monk at twenty-three, became a preacher in Antioch, fought immorality, was made patriarch of Constantinople at age fifty-three, cared for three thousand poor there, sent out missionaries, and died in exile for criticizing the empress's forging of a silver statue of herself.

49. Peter Gorday, *Principles of Patristic Exegesis, Romans 9–11 in Origen, John Chrysostom, and Augustine* (New York: Edwin Mellen, 1983), 129. Chrysostom: "The event of Christ and the New Covenant for the Gentiles have divested the Jews as a people of any special standing before God."

When the waters poured out by the Holy Spirit merge into mighty rivers of truth, it is difficult to separate various strains. We can only note that Chrysostom influenced Oecolampadius who then diversely affected Captio, Bucer, Zwingli, Luther, Melanchthon, Erasmus, Calvin, believers in France, Italy, Bohemia, and Britain. Together, Oecolampadius, along with the aforementioned army of colleagues anointed by God through the centuries, nourished the kingdom faithful and fought off ravaging wolves.

CHAPTER THREE

Scriptural Study
EXEGESIS AND HERMENEUTICS

THE LIFE AND INFLUENCE of Johannes Oecolampadius are startling in their expanse, considering his short life and history's obscuring of his name. Apparently the powerful effect of his ministry was produced by a pious life joined with scriptural insight. His approach to the Bible drew out remarkably edifying truths which sent the hearer to his knees in worship. This chapter examines his exegetical and hermeneutical foundations, along with applications.

Sources

Johannes Oecolampadius's exegesis was influenced primarily by two main Patristic sources—John Chrysostom and Augustine.[1] His hermeneutics present a mature critical synthesis of these two Patristic streams. From Chrysostom issued his concentration on salvation history, Christ's humanity, Old Testament symbolic types pointing to consummation, the continuity of covenants, the centrality of

---

1. Origen employed grammatical-historical, spiritual, and symbolic meaning. Oecolampadius used some of these but also criticized some of Origen's conclusions. Donald Fairbairn argues convincingly against categorizing early Fathers into Antiochene versus Alexandrian schools. His theory that theology drives exegesis takes into account the VanTilian idea of presuppositions that do not leave an interpreter neutral concerning Scripture. However, in postmodern culture, we must necessarily also affirm the perspicuity of Scripture. Donald Fairbairn, "Patristic Exegesis and Theology: The Cart and the Horse," *Westminster Theological Journal* 69, no. 1 (Spring 2007): 1–19.

Christ, close examination of the original text, Scripture interpreting Scripture, avoidance of speculation or philosophizing, moral applications, and emphasis on the necessity for true piety. Oecolampadius turned to Chrysostom in particular for his major theme of God's mercy and man's faith. From Augustine came strong doctrine and logical exposition, including his doctrines of the sovereignty of God, the nature of man, election, anti-Pelagian bondage of the will, mercy in Christ, the consummation, love's motivation, and *sola gratia,* as well as a distinction between sign and reality. His Eucharistic arguments used significant material from Augustine.

One example of his blending of these fourth- and fifth-century Patriarchs' hermeneutical methodologies may be observed by looking at how he dealt with the doctrine of sin. According to Walchenbach, Chrysostom believed that "While Adam's posterity inherit Adam's nature and punishment, they do not share in Adam's sin and guilt."[2] Augustine believed original sin to be inherent in all men since Adam. Following Augustine's doctrine and Chrysostom's salvation emphasis, Oecolampadius asserted, "Not only from original sin, but from all sins He freed us, and so reconciled us to the Father."[3] Thus he mined Chrysostom for philology, historical background, and subject matter, but preferred Augustine for theology and argumentation. His methodology employed the best of both Church Fathers while avoiding scholasticism, mysticism, and Platonism.

Like a bridge, he spanned the Patriarchs' time with the Reformation, ushering in modern hermeneutics.[4] For example, such medieval

---

2. Walchenbach, "Calvin," 43. He quotes Chrysostom: "But how does it follow that from his [Adam's] disobedience another would become a sinner? For at this rate, a man of this sort will not even deserve punishment if, that is, it was not from his own self that he became a sinner," 44 in *Epist. ad Rom*, ch.10. Migne, ed., *Patriologia Graece*, 60:477.

3. Oecolampadius, *In Iesaiam*, 263v (ad loc. Isa. 53:5).

4. See also Esther Chung-Kim, "Consent of the Ancients: Role of the Fathers in Sixteenth Century Debates over the Lord's Supper" (PhD diss., Duke University, 2005). Also discussing the reliance of the Reformers on the Patriarchs in the Marburg Colloquy, esp. Oecolampadius's use of Augustine, see Hermann Gottfried Hoffman, "Sententia Patrum: Das Patristiche Argument in der Abendsmahlskontroverse zwischen Oekolampad, Zwingli, Luther und Melanchthon" (PhD diss., Ruprecht-Karl Universitat zu Heidelberg, 1971).

interpreters as Theophylact of Bulgaria saw the Samaritan woman as a sweet lady. Oecolampadius contradicted this saccharin image, setting a precedent for all subsequent Reformed commentators.[5] More importantly, through the work of the Holy Spirit, he connected the scholarly world of textual analysis and of historical research with the heart of a believer.

Faith

When it came to hermeneutics and exegesis, Oecolampadius began at the heart. The beginning of all interpretation for him was knowing God, the Interpreter. He alone guides to what He "wants us either to imitate, or to raise up."[6] Without knowing the Interpreter, hermeneutical analysis is vain. We cannot delve into Scripture independently, since "no one is touched or receives worthily, except by faith."[7] Therefore, "The sense of Scripture is opened to none except those who seek Christ, and to whom Christ reveals Himself. For He has the key of David, He closes and no one opens, He opens and no one closes, Revelation [3:7]. Indeed also, if you say that the Holy Spirit is the door-keeper, He opens to no one except the one who enters through the door which is Christ."[8] This stance parallels John Calvin's similar observation in his commentary on Romans 1:16: "Because God does not work efficaciously in all men, but only when the Spirit shines in our hearts as the inward teacher, he adds 'to everyone that believeth.'"[9] Both Reformers understood the Word of God to be more than intellectual facts, more than mere words of man, but what it really is, God's speech, which can be understood only through the action of God Himself on the heart (see 1 Thess. 2:13). Therefore, every biblical scholar must first lay

---

5. Oecolampadius said the Samaritan woman rejected Christ as a Jew and was almost joking with Him. See Farmer, "Samaritan Woman," esp. 371.

6. Oecolampadius, *In Iesaiam*, 5v (ad loc. Isa. 1:1).

7. Oecolampadius, *In Iesaiam*, 60v (ad loc. Isa. 6:7).

8. Oecolampadius, *In Iesaiam*, 2r (preface).

9. John Calvin, *Johannes Calvini in Epistolam Pauli ad Romanos*, ed. Thomas H. L. Parker (Leiden: E. J. Brill, 1960), 27.

down his intellectual pride and seek the Creator of his mind and the author of the Word. Any attempt to circumvent this initial step results in vanity.[10]

Oecolampadius understood that all believers hear their Master's voice in Scripture. By contrast, none who are apart from Christ, in any age, can hear it. The primary foundation for all interpretation lay in the cross, in Christ, as the Paraclete of history.[11] History would not even exist without the cross. Mankind in Adam would have been destroyed instantly. Continued life without the cross would have been only a sinner's meaningless activity, proving God's just glory in humanity's own destruction. So past generations, as well as present ones, had to find the historical setting significant for interpretation because it is contained and sustained by Christ alone. He is the center and meaning of all history. This historical context embraced the original languages and setting.

If a scholar knows God by faith, then he may begin the first step in exegesis, knowing the language. The Word of God in the purity of its original language was rediscovered in the sixteenth century. The Reformation and its forerunners often spoke of *ad fontes*, "back to the sources." This led to the upsurge in philology and study of biblical languages that characterized this period. In fact, Ulrich Zwingli's commentaries consist almost entirely of explanations concerning his choice of a word for translation, with only limited applications. Biblical languages were axiomatic prerequisites to interpretation. Many, including Desiderius Erasmus, acknowledged Oecolampadius's unique competence in Latin, Greek, and Hebrew. Oecolampadius was honored by most of his peers as the best linguist of his day. Truly this gift from God formed the first step for

---

10. Oecolampadius writes: "But those who are true members of the church and are illuminated can be teachers of others, and have no need of an external teacher, as have the ignorant. I speak here of the knowledge of the truth as it pertains to salvation. He who had the fountain of all knowledge, the Holy Spirit, can He be ignorant of that which is needful to know?" Oecolampdius, *Demegoriae*, fol. 42a, cited in John Horsch, "The Faith of the Swiss Brethren," part two, *The Mennonite Quarterly Review* 5, no. 1 (January 1931): 7–27, esp. 17n115.

11. Oecolampdius, *Demegoriae*, fol. 42a, cited in John Horsch, "The Faith of the Swiss Brethren," part two, 17.

the Basel Reformer in his pre-eminent exegesis. As Henry Strohl observes, "In order to be sure to find that which the text originally says and not to be influenced by the traditional artifices of allegory and typology, Oecolampadius began by consulting the best Jewish lexicographers and exegetes before interpreting a Hebrew text."[12] Oecolampadius himself confessed, "If I had not been capable of reading Hebrew and consulting commentaries of the Hebrews, I would not have undertaken this work at all."[13] Oecolampadius believed that since God had condescended to communicate with man in common words, then each inspired letter held significance. For him, the words themselves exemplified God's mercy through accommodation and lent force to the idea of a *sensus literalis*.

Language

Although Oecolampadius consulted the Septuagint (Greek), the *Targum of Jonathan* (Aramaic), and the *Vulgate* (Latin), his final authority for Old Testament study remained the Hebrew text. Why? "[Hebrew] ought most to be consulted and respected in the Old Testament. But let me not disparage on account of these things what is written by Jerome and LXX. But when I am able to drink from the source, what work would it be to descend to the stream."[14] He criticized Jerome's dependence on the Septuagint, which produced incorrect translations in the *Vulgate*. For example, in Isaiah 13:4, Jerome and the Septuagint translate the word *mepaqqed* as "he commanded," but Oecolampadius explains that the underlying Hebrew root *pqd* means "he visited" or "he mustered."[15] Logically, he also objected to other variant *Septuagint* renderings, even going so far as to call one a "paraphrase."[16]

---

12. Strohl, *Pensée*, 13.
13. Staehelin, *Briefe und Akten*, 1:346, #241, which he cites from Oecolampadius's commentary on Isaiah.
14. Oecolampadius, *In Iesaiam*, 3r (preface).
15. Oecolampadius, *In Iesaiam*, 105v (ad loc. Isa. 13:4).
16. Oecolampadius, *In Iesaiam*, 56v (ad loc. Isa. 6:1). Oecolampadius's meticulous scholarship and critical use of primary resources provided a boon to researchers of St. Cyril of Alexandria's *Contra Julianum*. The original Greek manuscript belonging to Johann Reuchlin apparently burned in 1648 in a French attack. Oecolampadius's

He was adamant about staying close to the original text. He even restored the orthography of proper names to a more Hebraic original in order to underline their authenticity. But he was no prejudiced novice. Where an underlying word insisted on being ambiguous, he left it so. Such meticulous word study led to some variants from tradition in interpretation, crucial to a church exploring its roots. Newly awakened laymen, as well as scholars, insisted on knowing the truth of God's Word, as opposed to what tradition had taught. In this, the Basel scholar remained sensitive to an audience less familiar with academics. Cognizant of his less linguistically inclined readers, Oecolampadius in his commentaries always immediately translated for them any Hebrew or Aramaic word being scrutinized.

Grammar

Along with foundational word studies in the original languages, Oecolampadius stressed syntactical studies. He appears to have been so concerned for this pursuit that he wrote his own Greek grammar. It was used in classrooms in several countries for more than a century. In his commentaries, he drew the reader's attention to the significance of grammatical structures. He sometimes noted a certain subordinate clause begun by "that" or a sentence in the declarative form. Here he would demonstrate how each grammatical requirement particularized its interpretive point. Each detail bore relevance to the meaning, since the text was understood to be inspired. For the aid of those less familiar with Hebrew, Aramaic, or Greek, he carefully noted any idioms as well.[17] For example, in Isaiah 1, Oecolampadius complained that a plural word, often mistranslated, should be rendered in the singular form because of a Hebraism as well as because of a parallel singular word. He defended his overall literal translation saying, "In many places I have not avoided plain and inexcusable barbarisms and solecisms,

---

1528 Latin translation, with codex of different readings, helped reconstruct the text. William J. Maley, "*Contra Julianum* of St. Cyril of Alexandria and St. Peter Canisius," *Theological Studies* 25, no. 1 (March, 1964): 70–74.

17. In his practice of explaining idioms and syntactical points, he was similar to Luther, one of the other few Reformers with a doctorate.

in order that before the eyes I may put the phrases that the prophet has made use of which, although it is harsh among us, nevertheless in the holy language is exceedingly beautiful."[18]

These language peculiarities were not the only points of grammar in which he instructed scholars. His commentaries reflected on plural collectives, tropes, metaphors, similes, allegories, accommodation, pronoun referents, the Latin *persona*, synecdoche, cohortatives, hyperbole, personification, metonymy, etc. For Oecolampadius, the syntax had to be seriously examined since it provided an inherent guide to the correct interpretation.

Resources

Although the Basel Reformer never outlined his full exegetical procedure, it is clear that research into ancient sources had an integral role in the interpretation process.[19] He not only probed into the languages, but also investigated all relevant materials about historical background. Unlike some modern exegetes, he believed neither that scriptural interpretation must be confined to the book's historical setting, nor that it must be only a contemporary application. Rather, Oecolampadius advised interpreters to pay attention to the historical setting, since God's Word was presented to ancient

---

18. Oecolampadius, *In Iesaiam*, 3r (preface).

19. After publication of my dissertaion, another scholar noted similarities of exegesis among men from the "Rhenish School," 1525–1540. These included Oecolampadius, Zwingli, Bucer, Capito, Sebastian Munster, Conrad Pellikan, Simon Grynaeus, Sebastian Mayer, John/Jean Rabus, and eventually Peter Martyr Vermigli and Calvin. He points to both personal as well as exegetical similarities. The men wrote to one another, read one another's works, were of similar ages, married, fought for Reformed Communion, were against distinctive Anabaptist beliefs, respected magistrates, and had been priests before becoming prominent preachers. Capito posthumously published Oecolampadius's works. Bucer disseminated these works. Exegetically, they were marked by similar approaches to grammar, style, interpretation of the Old Testament, emphasis on moral life, the place of the law, respect for the historical, the sufficiency, authority and unity of Scripture, faith as the key, their use of Jewish tradition, their emphasis on typology over allegory, their regard for the importance of Hebrew and Greek, skepticism of Jerome's translation, and a Christ-centered and gospel-centered interpretation. Bernard Roussel notes these are also all hallmarks of Paul Fagius, Peter Martyr, and Calvin. Bernard Roussel, "De Strasbourg à Bâle et Zurich: une `école Rhénane' d'exégèse (ca 1525–ca 1540)," *Revue d'Histoire et de Philosophie Religieuses* 68 (1988): 19–39.

peoples. But, in addition, current believers have to apply the Word today. Scripture as the eternal, living Word of God speaks in a lively power to all listeners at all times. This is why he could write, "And also Isaiah did not write so much concerning his own times, but ours, which are called the end of the ages [1 Cor. 10:11]: not to one race of men, but to all."[20]

In the opening of his commentaries, Oecolampadius often established the specific date of a book, followed by geographic details derived from historical data. In establishing the time and chronology of Isaiah, he came to a minority opinion. Counter to several commentators, he concluded after studying the kings that the Isaiah 6 vision did not precede all other prophecies. He believed Isaiah had already begun prophesying while Uzziah reigned, prior to the vision. He then used this historical timeline of kings to mark the divisional sections in his commentary on Isaiah: Uzziah, Jotham, Ahaz, Hezekiah, Cyrus, and Christ.

Author

The discussion of a book's author necessarily touches on the doctrine of inspiration. Oecolampadius understood the biblical author to be inspired by God and yet having his mind guided along the lines of familiar grammatical devices that would have been understood by him. He neatly addressed this issue by writing a speech that he imagined Isaiah saying: "I have the words of the Lord, which He spoke to me: I speak nothing that the Lord has not said before, let me invent nothing out of my head: not from other men or counselors let me take commands, but greater and greatest commands, which the Lord ineffably showed."[21] Here, the Basel scholar clearly aligned himself with the historic, orthodox doctrine of inspiration.

Knowing that God was the Author of all inspired Scripture, Oecolampadius also considered whether a particular human author was inspired. Had God spoken through this specific man? Was this book canonical? The human author had to be tested by certain

---

20. Oecolampadius, *In Iesaiam*, 4v (ad loc. Isa. 1:1).
21. Oecolampadius, *In Iesaiam*, 6v (ad loc. Isa. 1:2).

criteria. The Reformer's argument in establishing the credibility of Isaiah appealed to other Scripture passages, extra-biblical sources, fulfilled prophecy, Isaiah's piety, the similarity of his words with Moses', the witness of other inspired men, and, finally, the testimony of Jesus Christ Himself. Why did he spend so much time in establishing the author's credentials? It was not so that the prophet would receive glory, but rather that he would be seen as a true glory-giver. Had he been anointed with the very word of the Creator Himself? If so, then the reader must recognize the gravity of hearing or rejecting his book. Oecolampadius concluded that Isaiah, the Christ-bearing prophet whose very name meant "salvation," should be received with reverence.[22]

Historical Background

In establishing the author and historical content, Oecolampadius referenced an amazing catalog of resources. These included the geographers Strabo and Ptolemy, the historians Herodotus and Josephus, the philosopher Plato, the conqueror Alexander the Great, the poet Homer, theologians Jerome, Chrysostom, Augustine, Tertullian, and Origen, the rabbinical *Targum of Jonathan*, Saadja, Salomen ben Isaac, Abulwalid Merwan ben Gannach, Abraham ibn Esra, Mose Kimchi, Jesus ben Sidrach, Dionysius, the Septuagint, Onkelos, Gregory of Nyssa's *Life of Moses*, the history of Queen Semiramis, Marcion, Pliny, Pomponius Mela, Pelagius, Suetonius, Mercury, Ambrosius, Berosus, Sybil, and the Greeks. All of these came into play in just seven chapters of his Isaiah commentary. Oecolampadius's use of them was sophisticated. He would not say that all sources weighed equally, but that greater attention should be paid to the most illustrious and most ancient. Sometimes he quoted a source merely to provide information. For example, referring to Josephus, he stated in Isaiah 37 that the area of Lobnam indicated Lachish. But sometimes he quoted an ancient source because it especially strengthened a believer's faith. Thus, the murder of Crassus during the battle of Carrhae by the Parthian commander Surena in 53 BC was referenced

---

22. Oecolampadius, *In Iesaiam*, 3r (preface).

from Plutarch along with Ptolemy's identification of Carrhae with Gozan. This last historical reference was included in order to reassure the reader of the authenticity of Gozan's existence and location.[23] The opening defense of Isaiah as God's chosen prophet was partly for the purpose of strengthening faith as well. Amazingly, Oecolampadius not only had all these resources available but also read them, knowing their content well enough to reference each. When you add to this the Reformer's encyclopedic knowledge and his renowned mastery of three classical languages, the picture of an astounding scholar emerges.

Included in the Basel Reformer's research was information about customs and social habits. For example, while discussing Christ's reading of the synagogue scroll, he noted that the book of Isaiah was so obscure that the common man would scarce attempt to explain it. The Nazarenes, thinking Jesus was an ordinary hometown boy, were astonished that Jesus would explain this passage. The hardness of their hearts was made more heinous by the fact that they could see that Jesus discerned its meaning. Oecolampadius also noted that Christ's sermon did not evoke the customary hissing in the synagogue that indicated minor irritation over an unsatisfactory exposition. Rather, His exegesis was completely rejected.

While studying a different Old Testament passage, Oecolampadius again referenced a custom. This time it was the wearing of sackcloth as one of several traditions for disciplining the body.[24] But although he consulted historical mores, ancient culture never occupied a domineering role in his interpretation. They merely reinforced his exegetically established understanding of a text.

Oecolampadius commonly harnessed the power of historical data for the purpose of driving faith higher. For instance, he detailed the magnificence of Babylon by referencing Strabo, Herodotus, Jerome, the *Targum of Jonathan,* contemporary Jewish exposition, and the Septuagint. The goal was to magnify God's destruction of the mighty city by Alexander the Great. This demonstrated God's

---

23. Oecolampadius, *In Iesaiam*, 200v (ad loc. Isa. 37:12).
24. Oecolampadius, *In Iesaiam*, 199r (ad loc. Isa. 37:1).

rule above the greatest powers of men. Similarly, when discussing King Uzziah's reign, the Basel commentator began by relating the repeated rebellion of Israel's kings and people against the Lord, as catalogued in Scripture. Then he pointed to how God persistently warned His people through the prophets. From these observations, he derived a principle directed at the reader's heart: "Therefore God threatens no less evils through these…than to his contemporaries. Since we sin no less than they…the same justice of God is for all ages, the same mercy also."[25] Occasionally, though, historical background served merely to help the reader grasp a situation, as when he explained a war strategy. However, researched facts were always subservient to Scripture itself. They never took precedence in interpretation over the Bible's primary purposes.

Some of the other Reformers emulated Oecolampadius's approach to historical background in their commentaries. Some did not. Martin Luther utilized contemporary references more frequently, whereas the Basler confined himself more to information from historical research. In fact, Oecolampadius's scholarship was so thorough and precise that Calvin often used it as a reliable source, as mentioned previously. Unknowingly, many present-day scholars and pastors are standing on the shoulders of Basel.

Scripture Interprets Scripture

The primary research tool for Oecolampadius's interpretation was always Scripture itself. The principle of *sola Scriptura* lay at the heart of the Reformation movement. By necessity, this interpretive approach to exposition began with the immediate context of a passage. "The proper meaning of the words [should] be first elucidated with appropriate attention to the preceding and following words, namely in the right context in which the particular vocabulary stand; then, and only then, the soteriological significance of that word can be made manifest to the glory of the Father and Christ."[26]

---

25. Oecolampadius, *In Iesaiam*, 6r (ad loc. Isa. 1:1).
26. Oecolampadius, *In Iesaiam*, 201r (ad loc. Isa. 37:15).

Looking through the immediate context as well as the larger context of Scripture brought out fuller implications. For example, Oecolampadius mentioned that upon examining all the instances of the tetragrammaton in Scripture, it could be concluded that when it was placed alongside "Elohe Israel," it normally signifies God as judge and liberator. Parallel Scripture passages could enrich the understanding of a text or untangle a difficult phrase. So in Isaiah 1, the sentence "Sons I have nourished and raised" leaves "sons" ambiguous. Are these the children born of the flesh or of the Spirit? Turning to Matthew 15:26, Oecolampadius found it could refer to both believing and non-believing Jews. With this clarification, the theological point could be made that God was so merciful that He could call the Jews "sons" even in the midst of their unbelief. Oecolampadius taught that these parallel passages were included by God intentionally to aid us in our understanding: "[The interpreter is] helped in this [exegesis] by the diligent comparison of Scriptures. For it cannot be denied, everything that is written, is written for our instruction, 1 Cor. 10."[27]

The whole of Scripture, from Genesis to Revelation, had to be scoured for parallel words or phrases. So, for example, the peculiar use of the word *drip* in Isaiah 52:15 found its explanation in Ezekiel 20 and Amos 7. The strange use of the word *spirit* in Isaiah 40:7 was explained by Isaiah 12 and 4:4, which teach that the appropriate meaning entails the wrath of God and His judgment. The phrase "wail, for it is near" in Luke 21:28 is amplified by Genesis 15:16, Zephaniah 1, Matthew 22:32, Romans 2, and Revelation 18:2. Plumbing the phrase "the Word of God endures forever" in Isaiah 40 provides another example of Scripture interpreting Scripture. Oecolampadius let verses in Jeremiah 7 and 17, Matthew 5, Luke 21, John 1, and 1 John 1 comment on these words, showing the affinity of Christ, His kingdom, His words, and divine law.

The advantage of this approach was that the interpreter discovered a fuller or more exact meaning in accord with the mind of God. The Basel Reformer used parallels to define, reinforce, clarify,

---

27. Oecolampadius, *In Iesaiam*, 5r (ad loc. Isa. 1:1).

deepen, or intensify meanings, and to untangle difficulties, ultimately for the enhancement of God's glory. Where probable interpretations by other scholars vied with the Basler's own, he cited those as well. Nevertheless, Scripture alone commanded final authority in all hermeneutics.

The integrity and unity of the Bible established the foundation for Oecolampadius's interpretation. He poured Scripture from every book into the passage being exposited. For instance, he incorporated no less than ten verses from across the Bible to explain one verse in Isaiah 37:15. He often disdained to write his own words when commenting on a passage. Rather, he let Scripture itself speak as the ultimate interpreter of Scripture. When we compare him with Calvin, we find that Calvin tended to speak more principially. For example, concerning Isaiah 36, Calvin wrote, "When Christ calls us to Heaven, Satan endeavors to keep us still on the earth." But Oecolampadius at the same place quoted Matthew 16:26, "But what exchange will a man be able to accept for his own soul?"[28] By allowing Scripture to interpret Scripture, he submitted his own views to those of the Author. It was a matter of God being heard, not man. "The aim of the entire Scripture is to vindicate the glory of God, so that God might reign in all, chiefly in the hearts of men."[29]

Oecolampadius's commentaries overwhelm the reader with Scripture references, all focused on the one verse being studied. It defies understanding how, without modern research tools, he extensively quoted verses. Themes converged from the entirety of the Bible onto one pericope. For example, in discussing the coal taken from the altar in Isaiah 6, he referenced redemption, the sacraments, faith, justification, preservation, sanctification, absolution, God's glory, and man's calling; he consulted 1 Kings 7, Psalm 119, Luke 24, and Revelation 2 and 6. Instead of the usual mere prooftexting of positions, he quoted Scripture without citation in

---

28. Oecolampadius, *In Iesaiam*, 198r (ad loc. Isa. 36:16).
29. Jaroslav Pelikan, *Reformation of Church and Dogma*, 207. Here he quotes Johannes Oecolampadius, *In Epistolam B. Pauli Apost. ad Rhomanos Adnotationes* (Basel: Cratander, 1526), preface 2r. The 1525 edition that I regularly reference in other footnotes has no pagination in the preface.

his commentaries, combining phrase after phrase from the whole gamut of the Bible. If we look at a comment in Isaiah 36, we can see that he alluded to Philippians 3:8, Galatians 6:14 and 2:20, 1 John 2:16–17, and 1 Corinthians 2:14 in the following exhortation: "the world considers as dung all the glorious things of the Christians, such as the Word of God, the cross, and the sacraments. On the other hand, Paul and the Christians for the sake of Christ no less despise all the glories of the world. Thus the pious are crucified to the world and the world to the pious." Apparently, not only was Oecolampadius fluent in Hebrew, Greek, and Latin, but also in Scripture itself. He truly thought God's thoughts after Him. This ability derived not merely from knowledge, but from a life of piety lived in faith before his Lord.

Genre

Exegetes today promote attention to genre as if this were a new phenomenon. But five centuries ago, Oecolampadius not only used genre but also gave guidelines for how it should be approached. In 1527,

> Oecolampadius called it a "rule" that "in dealing with sign, sacraments, pictures, parables, and interpretations, one should and must, in accordance with the principle of signs or sacraments, understand the words figuratively, and not understand the language simply." The first chapter of the Book of Genesis and the first chapter of the Gospel of John are "historical, without any ceremonies, and they will not tolerate my using the word 'sign,'" while the words of institution in the Lord's Supper "are expository (*ausslegende*) words, and not simply historical ones."[30]

Visions had to be examined for accommodating anthropomorphic language as well as literal speech, such as in the description of the faces of the seraphim, which connoted intelligence. As with modern exegetes, Oecolampadius recognized the various genres of history,

---

30. Pelikan, *Reformation of Church and Dogma*, 194, from Oecolampadius's *Missverstand*, 3 (1527:C1r) and 206, from Oecolampadius's *Missverstand*, 3 (1527:C4v–D1r). Interestingly, while he and Luther both mention God's provision of signs to confirm the Word, they diverge in the particular application of sign to the Eucharist.

prophecy, hymns, visions, poems, epistles, didactic and expository forms, accommodation, and even a sophisticated *persona* or role device understood by Ambrosius.

The Reformer attended to genre within a phrase as well as within a book. For example, within the vision of Isaiah 1, he understood that there was a personification of creation that figuratively pictured man's impiety. Within the oracle of Isaiah 13, a metaphorical understanding of "on a high mount" led to the meaning "those of high status." He proved this interpretation by citing the Septuagint, *Targum of Jonathan*, and contemporary Jewish exegesis, as well as by demonstrating its common usage by the extrabiblical authors Pliny, Strabo, Pomponius Mela, and Herodotus. Within a historical context, a detail might confirm the historicity of a passage. For instance, concerning Hezekiah's reign, he observed that the "carefulness of the number shows the certainty of the history."[31] Or a phrase within an historical genre might prove symbolic, such as the bronze serpent in the wilderness: "And although now history clearly is being narrated, it is nevertheless itself also a type pregnant with great mysteries, but as the history of the bronze serpent which Moses lifted up is true, and we are not able to confess but that the serpent itself also was no less a figure of Christ."[32]

Oecolampadius's view of the historical genre in Scripture was complicated. He did not see it as brute facts related to unavoidable events of a mechanical universe. Rather, each detail was scripted for the purpose of communicating theological meaning, a visual speaking of God's glory and plan.

> It is the case that histories, which are true in themselves, also prefigure the mysteries either of Christ or of the antichrist, by a certain hidden type. Therefore the diligent interpreter overlooks neither. But, in order [to do so], he may first compose the history, then he may also uncover the coverings of the mysteries, mentioned by the Apostles, and [he may show] what the Spirit wants us either to imitate or raise up.[33]

---

31. Oecolampadius, *In Iesaiam*, 194r (ad loc. Isa. 36:1).
32. Oecolampadius, *In Iesaiam*, 194r (ad loc. Isa. 36:1). See also John 3:14–15.
33. Oecolampadius, *In Iesaiam*, 5v (ad loc. Isa. 1:1).

God governed the past specifically in a way that would reflect the advent, parousia, and consummation in Christ, so the scriptural genre of history must never be interpreted simplistically.

Oecolampadius also weighed the implications of the genre of Hebrew poetry. He understood, for example, that Hebrew poetry uses parallelism. For example, he finds in Isaiah 40:3 these parallel lines,

> in the wilderness prepare the way of the Lord,
> make straight in the desert a highway for our God.

Oecolampadius understood this parallelism, and used it to interpret the coming of John the Baptist: "According to the Hebrew there is a separation, 'In the wilderness prepare the way.' And this accords with the elegance of the passage, because afterward he adds, 'Make straight in the desert.'"[34] As a result, Oecolampadius interpreted the coming of John the Baptist in Luke 3:4 differently. John the Baptist is not "a voice crying in the wilderness, 'Prepare the way of the Lord,'" but rather "a voice crying, 'In the wilderness prepare the way of the Lord.'" Respecting the character of each genre leads to a richer, more precise interpretation.

The prophetic genre had its own complexities. Prophetic proclamations found their obvious meaning in later scriptural fulfillment. But at the same time, fulfillments could shed light on previous, more subtle prophecies. For example, the foretelling of Sennacherib's reign could be seen in hindsight in Isaiah 7, 8, 17, 20, 28, and 33. According to Oecolampadius, prophecy could not be understood as narrowly foretelling the future. Since prophecies were revelations of God's mercy, fondly warning His children, they should apply to their historical context as well as to future generations: "For what love would it be to set forth strictly future things after many ages, and to flatter those walking about before the eyes?"[35] After all, judgment falls on all mankind, since all have sinned and fallen short of the glory of God. Therefore, the warnings in prophecy were for all men.

Actually, in Oecolampadius's view, prophecy's main focus was Christ. According to the Basel Reformer's hermeneutic, prophetic

---

34. Oecolampadius, *In Iesaiam*, 211r (ad loc. Isa. 40:3).
35. Oecolampadius, *In Iesaiam*, 5r (ad loc. Isa. 1:1).

visions often held both a literal and a symbolic dimension. This approach led the interpreter to see Christ in the prophecy, revealing Him to the eyes of faith. By seeing Him and His gracious warnings, sinners were pointed to Jesus. Interpretation of prophecy, therefore, made use of history and typology as it merged in Christ. So, for example, the prophecy of a harvest in Isaiah 37:30 applied to all hearers. Just as the crop would be full in three years, so Christ's resurrection on the third day would bear full fruit. This revealed Christ as the true food who preserved His people with His own body. The prophecy was as true then as it was for later readers, whose faith grew by seeing God's faithfulness to His children.

Typology

At this point, we should look at Oecolampadius's use of typology more closely. Previously, commentators such as Dante Alighieri followed a fourfold medieval approach. This methodology included interpretive elements of the grammatical-historical (simple facts), allegorical (symbols of Christ), moral (ethical applications), and anagogical (eschatological themes).[36] What Dante called "allegorical" was often an expression of typology, but medieval interpretation was not always sufficiently anchored in grammatical-historical study to keep interpreters from drifting. The practice sometimes led to contrived conclusions. Oecolampadius warned, "You should beware either of despising [allegories] universally, or inopportunely bringing [them] forward. For both alike are unworthy of Scripture."[37] Typology could be addressed, but only after studying the grammati-

---

36. "Which method of treatment, that it may be clearer, can be considered through these words: 'When Israel went out of Egypt, the house of Jacob from a barbarous people, Judea was made his sanctuary, Israel his dominion' (Douay-Rheims, Ps. 113.1–2). If we look at it from the letter alone, it means to us the exit of the Children of Israel from Egypt at the time of Moses; if from allegory, it means for us our redemption done by Christ; if from the moral sense, it means to us the conversion of the soul from the struggle and misery of sin to the status of grace; if from the anagogical, it means the leave taking of the blessed soul from the slavery of this corruption to the freedom of eternal glory." Dante Alighieri, *Epistle to Can Grande della Scala*, trans. James Marchand, in *Dante to Cangrande: English Version*, from http://ccat.sas.upenn.edu/jod/cangrande.english.html, accessed on Feb. 14, 2009.

37. Oecolampadius, *In Iesaiam*, 5r (ad loc. Isa. 1:1).

cal-historical basis: "For unless rightly they first place the things for a foundation, whatever they build on top would fall down."[38]

Typological understanding was endorsed by Christ Himself in John 3, where He referred to the bronze serpent, and in Matthew 12, where He referred to the sign of Jonah.[39] Jesus also provided a general principle while on the road to Emmaus. He commended all of Scripture to be examined for how it pointed to Himself. Therefore, appropriate typology, fitted to the whole of scriptural revelation, uncovers the shadows of Christ, especially in the Old Testament. For example, Oecolampadius demonstrated how Christ fulfilled the meaning of manna, bread, fruit, the bronze serpent, the hen with chicks, David, Moses, Isaiah, Cyrus, the good shepherd, the poor and wise one, the servant, the Red Sea, baptism, blood sacrifices, king, son, door, key of David, mediator, legislator, the altar, prophet, sons of Adam, root, shoot from dry ground, Holy of Holies, a grain of wheat dying, a rich man, a poor man, a wise man, the temple, and the mercy seat. Indeed, even seraphs image Christ, who incarnately became both the Messenger and the Message. In discussing the meaning of all these symbols, Oecolampadius always appealed to parallel Scripture passages. Meaning was circumscribed by Scripture as a whole and guided by the Spirit through the study of parallel passages.

Because typology could be governed by the Reformation principle of *sola Scriptura,* many Reformers developed it. Some of Oecolampadius's use of typology was repeated in Calvin, where Jerusalem was seen as a type of the church and Sennacherib a type of Satan. Zwingli also replaced allegory with typology, as in his interpretation of Cyrus as a foreshadowing of Christ. Luther employed it as well, and, like Oecolampadius, saw the root of faith in Isaiah 37 as springing from the stump of the saints/Jerusalem. In short, Oecolampadius, as well as others, used typology so that the full meaning of God's Word would be displayed. But he was also wary of the temptation for pride in man's intellect: "Now truly

---

38. Oecolampadius, *In Iesaiam*, 5r (ad loc. Isa. 1:1).
39. Oecolampadius, *In Iesaiam*, 203r (ad loc. Isa. 37:30).

while we treat the historical sense, I should like to notice also the allegory, lest for the pious there be missing something by which they might engage the eyes of the mind; and exaggerations in words much please this [the mind], for they appear to require more subtle intelligence."[40] The warning is against being proud of one's typological insight, which might penetrate deeper than the usual superficial interpretation.

Style

Briefly, as an aside from Oecolampadius's methodology, let us look at his writing style. He believed that nothing should interfere with hearing God's voice in Scripture. Therefore, brevity, conciseness, and clarity marked his writing. That meant not refuting errant views unnecessarily, engaging in speculative philosophical argument, psychologizing motives, or veering into tangents.[41] His public lectures were often given in the common German language. His published scholarship pointed readers back to the original language, the most basic source. He therefore rejected the typical translation of "Isaiah" (Esaias) and substituted "Iesaias," which both underlined the Hebrew root meaning, "salvation is of the Lord," and also pointed to Isaiah as a shadow of Christ.[42] His style of argumentation was a beautiful yet precise Ciceronian Latin, discussing broader issues, then narrowing to the intensity of the point, perhaps in just a one-word conclusion. The biblical Word had to be made clear, for by it came the knowledge of God.

To this end, he often used a literary device of epexegetical dialog. It occurred when a point was reworded in a paraphrase or an imagined quote. The usual introduction to the quote was "as if he were to say" or a similar expression. For example, relating God's

---

40. Oecolampadius, *In Iesaiam*, 104v (ad loc. Isa. 13:1).

41. Calvin, by comparison, tended to emphasize a more emotional understanding. So he stated in his comments on Isaiah 37:14 that Hezekiah's purpose in presenting the letter before the Lord was "that he might excite his own earnestness, and inflame his own ardor, in prayer." Compare Oecolampadius on why Hezekiah went to the temple: "God had promised to Solomon that He would hear the prayers of His people there." Oecolampadius, *In Iesaiam*, 200v (ad loc. Isa. 37:14).

42. Oecolampadius, *In Iesaiam*, 3r (preface).

concern for Jerusalem, Oecolampadius wrote, "as if He were saying: 'I consider well how the injury of the enemy has affected you my beloved, and tender daughter.'"[43] In another place, the Basler imagined Sennacherib saying, "If the other kingdoms could not resist my parents neither can you resist me."[44] Calvin used the same device in the same place. He imagined Sennacherib as boasting, "They conquered the gods of other nations, and I am far superior to my ancestors; therefore the God of Israel will not conquer me."[45] Luther, in his commentaries, reveled in this literary form. Why was it so popular? The created monologue produced an amplified commentary while simultaneously drawing the reader into a character. It proved a useful connection between exegesis and commentary.

Application

After all of Oecolampadius's careful exegesis was completed, there still remained the task of application. We will look at a couple of applied themes that were woven throughout the text. One was the cause-and-effect relation between revealing God's mercy and strengthening man's faith. Oecolampadius urged, "I should like, as often as in sacred letters the divine mercy is commended to us, it [God's mercy] should be diligently pondered, and minimally weakened."[46] Why? Because mercy only came from the mercy seat, Christ, to whom all glory was due. Therefore, the glory of God was more transparent through the window of His mercy. Seeing God should increase faith.

Christ Himself was the mercy of God, the love of God. He was the healing balm for the sinner's soul, the One promised as the sinner's substitute for just judgment: "The divine vengeance has ceased, and there is nothing by which we may reconcile divine vengeance to ourselves, unless God sees fit to give it through His mercy."[47] Jesus epitomized the mercy of God, which then fueled the flame of love

---

43. Oecolampadius, *In Iesaiam*, 202r (ad loc. Isa. 37:22).
44. Oecolampadius, *In Iesaiam*, 200r (ad loc. Isa. 37:11).
45. John Calvin, *Commentary on the Book of the Prophet Isaiah*, trans. William Pringle (Grand Rapids: Eerdmans, 1947), 3:117.
46. Oecolampadius, *In Iesaiam*, 6v (ad loc. Isa. 1:2).
47. Oecolampadius, *In Iesaiam*, 211r (ad loc. Isa. 40:2).

in a forgiven soul. As did Calvin, Oecolampadius believed that one purpose of the law was that unbelievers would apprehend their need for a Redeemer, for by it they could see how far short of perfection they fell and could then run to Christ.

Oecolampadius said that God Himself even ordained history in such a way that it would show His mercy and glory for the purpose of strengthening man's faith.[48] This gave commentators an example as to how to use history. The exegete's task was to build up faith also. Oecolampadius took every opportunity to do this in his commentaries, as can be seen in a discussion of the history of the bronze serpent: "As they, believing in the Word, fled for refuge to the bronze serpent, so we also should not doubt that we are saved in the cross of the Lord."[49] Here a historical demonstration of God's mercy drove Old Testament believers toward a saving trust, and so it should do for us.

Evangelism

Oecolampadius believed that if God desired to bring men to faith by revealing His mercy, then men need to imitate God by doing the same. Christians have to use models and arguments from the Bible to draw the believer, as well as the unbeliever, out of sin's deception that they might see God's mercy. The world and church traditions teach men that they can achieve fellowship with God by their own effort. This is a delusion that even Christians could fall into: "We sin no less than they and leaving the Word of God like them we follow human traditions."[50] God's Word, not traditions, explains the true grace of God: "Nevertheless we wait upon the words of God, from which it is not permitted to deviate even if an angel from heaven should order something."[51] So Oecolampadius was keen to use God's Word apologetically to encourage faith.

---

48. Oecolampadius, *In Iesaiam*, 104v (ad loc. Isa. 13:1).
49. Oecolampadius, *In Iesaiam*, 5v (ad loc. Isa.1:1). See Calvin on Isaiah 37:26, where he emphasized doctrine as a consolation; compare Oecolampadius, who pointed to God's love and scriptural promises.
50. Oecolampadius, *In Iesaiam*, 5v (ad loc. Isa. 1:1).
51. Oecolampadius, *In Iesaiam*, 195r (ad loc. Isa. 36:4).

Christocentricity

For Oecolampadius, Christ was the hermeneutical key to Scripture, its subject, and its purpose: "Because the Word of God is inspired by the Holy Spirit, I am unable not to affirm that in all places the Spirit of the Scriptures has regard for Christ Jesus in purpose, goal [*scopus*], and method."[52] The Bible's central plan of redemption is found in Christ Himself. He satisfied God's wrath, bearing our griefs and the discipline for our sins in order to gain God's peace and healing for us: "He Himself is the just servant of God, having power also to make others just, for He Himself is our righteousness."[53] Christ was the Word itself. That meant He created not only the gospel but even the law, which He established and mediated. Through Christ alone, all of the Old and New Testament could be understood.

All of God's promises were affirmed in Christ, who was the incarnate mercy of God. Christ was in Numbers 21 (the One lifted up, as explained in John 3:14), in Isaiah 37 (the trampled One, sprung anew), in Ezekiel 34 (the Davidic Shepherd), in Isaiah 53 (the Suffering Servant and shoot springing up), in Zechariah 13 and Romans 8:36 (the One over whom the spear is raised), in Hosea 6:2 (the resurrection on the third day), in Psalm 8 (the One under whom all is subjected), in Isaiah 6 (the final King).[54]

All typologies and prophecies point to Christ: "In vain, therefore, they waste all labor who in the prophets seek anything except Christ and the Christian life."[55] Understanding Scripture means primarily understanding Christ. The beatific vision inspires the heart to repentance and love. So one most fully employs exegesis by praising Christ.

We can look at the example of how Scripture encourages believers to praise Jesus in a situation of suffering. Oecolampadius applied Christ as the balm to a sinner's heart. All instances of suffering point

---

52. Oecolampadius, *In prophetam Ezechielem commentarius* (Basel: Apiarius, 1534), 73v (ad loc. Ezekiel 10).

53. Oecolampadius, *In Iesaiam*, 264r (ad loc. Isa. 53:11).

54. Hammer notes that Oecolampadius's Isaiah commentary was Christological, with chapters 49–66 being the book of the Messiah. "Der Reformator Oekolampad," 167.

55. Oecolampadius, *In Iesaiam*, 2r (preface).

to Jesus. Oecolampadius taught that Satan has made God his target and only secondarily wounds Christians who chose to stand with Him. They share in the suffering aimed at Christ. He counseled that man's greatest grief should not be over his own trials, but over the world's blasphemy of God: "This last thing, for the faithful, is Hell and the pain is compared to those in labor.... Holy men burn with zeal, and grieve that they are unable to vindicate the glory of God's Name."[56] Certainly Christians suffer when they reject the glories of this world. In return, God assures them that He has overcome the world. Oecolampadius confronted suffering with the sure foundation of faith that God sovereignly knows what happens to His people and uses it for their good. Trials do not come separate from a Fatherly hand. God has arranged every enemy field position, and even things as seemingly unmanageable as rumors.[57] Why? For the strengthening of His people. The believer's future stands firm because all the prophecies and typology demonstrate the truth of Christ: "Hope is confirmed by the power of God, because nothing is able to prevent the Word of God [Christ], by which salvation is promised to us, from coming to pass."[58] The Basel Reformer's exegesis was thoroughly Christocentric. The application also had to be Christocentric.

It is difficult to isolate the sophisticated hermeneutical principles of this scholar. He could take the word *covenant*, do a parallel word study with the "ark of the covenant," and then compare it with the typological fulfillment in Christ as our mercy seat, almost in one breath. For the Basel Reformer, the hermeneutical methodology and exegetical goal met in Christ and produced an application. To know Him was to be sanctified in love for Him. Rather than effecting Christian repentance through law or scolding, he displayed the beatific vision of Christ that both glorified God and compelled

---

56. Oecolampadius, *In Iesaiam*, 199r (ad loc. Isa. 37:2).

57. Oecolampadius, *In Iesaiam*, 202v (ad loc. Isa. 37:26). In terms of theodicy, man remains guilty. "From this it is also clear enough that Sennacherib served the divine will as an instrument and nonetheless was culpable by his sin." Oecolampadius, *In Iesaiam*, 212v–213r (ad loc. Isa. 40:12).

58. Oecolampadius. *In Iesaiam*, 213r (ad loc. Isa. 40:12).

the Christian: "But when the beauty of that splendor is loved, our own foulness is visited on us."[59]

Oecolampadius's hermeneutics and exegesis began with man's heart (you could not understand God's Word unless you were born again), then traveled through language, grammar, historical background, parallel Scripture, genre, typology, and theology before culminating in Christ, only to return to man's heart. The eyes of the soul would be opened in faith through the loving Word Himself. Christ, the Word, both spoke and opened the meaning of Scripture, therefore, Oecolampadius preached Christ. Oecolampadius proved to be among the elite exegetes of his day, and continues rivaling many moderns of today.

---

59. Oecolampadius, *In Iesaiam*, 59v (ad loc. Isa. 6:5).

CHAPTER FOUR

Reformation Renewal

How did Johannes Oecolampadius's work effect reformation and renewal among the people of God? What was the context that called forth specific theological and practical changes?

Oecolampadius found plenty of fodder for cultural applications of Scripture in his day. The dissolute condition of the sixteenth-century church provided pundits with a constant source of mockery. For example, Martin Luther frequently referred to papal Rome as the great whore of Babylon. Oecolampadius remarked about it more judiciously with a double entendre, saying: "Therefore, by 'Babylon' understand the kingdom of the world in which indeed there is much confusion, and whose captivity many experienced. What if you say that [it is] also Roman tyranny, on account of which many of the Christians were unable to carry out rightly legitimate things?"[1] His comments had to be circumspect. One untoward published statement could keep a book from being published, incarcerate the publisher, place the city under a papal ban, or cause the book and author to be burned.

The problem was that the Roman Catholic Church through the centuries had accrued certain respected habits, routines, and

---

1. Oecolampadius, *In Iesaiam*, 104v (ad loc. Isa. 13:1). For an extended analysis of Oecolampadius's doctrine as it might have appeared in a systematic theology, with additional quotations, see Poythress, "Johannes Oecolampadius' Exposition of Isaiah, Chapters 36–37," esp. chapter 4.

interpretations that contradicted the Bible. Unbiblical traditions were common because copies of the Scriptures were not available; priests did not know the original languages; and a general neglect of biblical studies had occurred. Entrenched falsehoods had become identified with power structures. Visibly practiced tradition had replaced the unknown Scriptures.

Doctrinal Renewal

Oecolampadius and other Reformers worked to renew the church and the people by teaching biblical doctrine. The Reformation grew from the Bible, and one of the foundational principles was that doctrine and the church had to be founded on Scripture, not on traditions, however venerable.

Sola Scriptura

During the Reformation, there were men in the Catholic Church who held church tradition to be of equal or higher authority than Scripture. Oecolampadius usually referred to these traditionalist papists more broadly as "antichrists" rather than identifying them with Rome. He noted, though, that all rebels against God partook of the spirit of the antichrist.[2] The traditions of men pulled people away from God into servitude to the traditions themselves. This was a result of the idolatrous spirit of the antichrist of which 1 John 2:18 warned and was tantamount to denying Christ Himself. Referring to tradition as a corrupted base of teaching, Oecolampadius scolded:

> They cry out: "The most holy high priest commands," "the most just king enjoins," "the church observes this custom," "the authority of councils has it so." Thus it has seemed right to the leading schoolmasters of the age. Nevertheless we wait upon the words of God, from which it is not permitted to deviate even if an angel from heaven should order something.[3]

Oecolampadius, like Luther, took his stand on the Bible alone. The Reformation trumpeted *sola Scriptura*, or "Scripture alone." The

---

2. Oecolampadius, *In Iesaiam*, 5v (ad loc. Isaiah 1:1).
3. Oecolampadius, *In Iesaiam*, 195v (ad loc. Isa. 36:4).

Reformers believed that Scripture alone should serve as the Christian's foundation for belief.

> Already by August of 1523, the Basel Reformer had convincingly asserted the principle of *sola scriptura* in his theses that he posted for public disputation. Thesis I reads, "since the words...are spirit and life and deserve to be called the bread of life, by which souls live, so all worldly philosophy, all secondary traditions of the Pharisees, and finally all human erudition are flesh.... Therefore in the schools and the temples of Christians the teaching is of Christ alone in all; so the authority of ethical philosophers and all other teachers, however many they be, is contemptible."[4]

He further defends the Bible's unique authority in his sermon on Psalm 57: "Scripture will not be holy because it is received by the Church, but the Church has received the sacred Scripture because it is holy and from God...for the Church received the biblical books prior to the great councils."[5]

Not only was Scripture authoritative, but it was also divinely inspired. God's Word came from His mouth, untainted by men. Oecolampadius wrote, "Before all things Christians should be persuaded that the sacred Scriptures are divinely inspired."[6] He added: "Were not the Apostles human beings like ourselves? They were indeed Apostles and human beings, but they did not teach nor write by the human spirit, but by divine overflow. They did not provide their own opinions, but that which they had seen with their eyes, or had received from the Lord."[7] Therefore, what we read in the Bible is God's direct communication, breathed out from Him, inspired. This means that the Speaker and what is spoken are inseparable.

---

4. Oecolampadius, *ad Rhomanos*. Cited by Demura in, "Calvin and Oecolampadius," 185. Translated by D. Poythress.

5. Johannes Oecolampadius, *In Psalmos LXXIII, LXXIIII, etc. conciones* (Basel: Robert Winter, 1544), 318, from "A Sermon to the People on the Invocation of the Saints, on All Saints' Day."

6. Johannes Oecolampadius, *In Epistolam Ioannis apostoli Catholicam primam, Ioannis Oecolampadii demegoriae, hoc est homilae una & XX* (Basel: Cratander, 1524), 64v (ad loc. 1 John 4:1).

7. Oecolampadius, *In Epistolam Ioannis*, 7v (ad loc 1 John 1:1).

To trust the Bible is to trust God Himself: "For when we believe the Word of Christ, we believe Christ."[8]

Perspicuity of Scripture

People had heard that only a priest could interpret Scripture, yet many priests could not read Scripture, nor had they ever seen a Bible. As a priest, Luther stood in awe when he first beheld a Bible chained to a library desk. So parishioners needed encouragement about the perspicuity of the Bible. Oecolampadius taught them not to be confident in their own innate ability to understand, but in the Lord, who promised to open His Word to them through His Holy Spirit: "But trust, and if you be of good heart, I will strengthen you with an example [of the Ethiopian eunuch], which if you approach it with pious and diligent study, you may go away more consoled than anything else would be able to do. So good and propitious is the Lord to all who seek Him in truth."[9] In fact, he remonstrated that the believer's obligation was always to feast on the fruit of the Word, and never abstain from it.

This means it is incumbent on any Christian to seek for and cherish the Word. Through this divine speech, our hearts are divinely moved and re-created: "The Word of God...thus works wonderful things in man. It is also a coal ravaging, burning up the whole old man."[10] Salvation itself is an effect of God's Word: "Believing in the Word of God makes us saved and this power of the Word is that this same Word is the power of God and see how necessary it is to hear the Word of God for it would be better...to bear all ceremonies than to have the Word of God cease."[11]

---

8. Oecolampadius, *ad Rhomanos*, 9r (ad loc. Rom. 1:17). [*ad Rhomanos* is sometimes referred to in research literature as *Annotationes* or *Adnotationes*.] See also Oecolampadius, *In Iesaiam*, 57r (ad loc. Isa. 6:1): "In the Scriptures, however, if you search them, you will see God."

9. Oecolampadius, *In Iesaiam*, 2v (preface).

10. Oecolampadius, *In Iesaiam*, 60r (ad loc. Isa. 6:6). See also, Oecolampadius, *In Epistolam Ioannis*, ad loc. 1 John 5:24: "It is necessary that our hearts hear. We hear the internal teacher, the Holy Spirit."

11. Oecolampadius, *ad Rhomanos*, 8v (ad loc. Rom. 1:16).

Theology Flowing from Exegesis

Biblical exegesis led to theological conclusions. Thus, biblical theology arose from the text. Scripture defined theology. That was why, when Oecolampadius restructured the university, the theological department was replaced by the biblical department. When Scripture was meticulously examined, it would teach the truths about the person of God, the work of Christ, and the condition of man. For example, Scripture defined sin and man's nature in Genesis 18, Jeremiah 1, Isaiah 6, Exodus 4, Job 14 and 42, Psalms 1, 8, 116, and 120, and 1 Timothy 1, leading to the conclusion that "we are liars, if we deny sin dwells in us," so we must have the remedy of Christ applied to us by God's love as seen in 1 Corinthians 8.[12] From Isaiah 40, Romans 3, and 1 Corinthians, the Reformer concluded that Christ was made for us sanctification, redemption, and righteousness from God, so that "by the works of the law no flesh shall be justified" (Gal. 2:16). Even biblical objects, while symbolizing the covenant, also led to a theological point; thus, the ark of God pointed to Christ as our mercy seat, as seen in Romans 3 and Hebrews 9.

Long-debated theological questions could be answered by God's Word. For example, the often-discussed "holy, holy, holy" of Isaiah 6 was defined by other Scripture passages, with the interpretative emphasis resting not on the threefold formula or on the usage of the words, but on the understanding of the holiness of God as presented in Scripture as a whole.[13] Looking at the controversial meaning of "angel," Oecolampadius disputed the practice of confusing the angels with the Lord by again quoting Scripture, which defined the nature of angels as separate from God. The question of whether Christ's death on the cross accomplished man's physical or spiritual healing was solved by the exegesis of Matthew 8 and 1 Peter 1, with the answer being both. To answer the question of who received God's Spirit after the prophesied blinding of the Jews, Oecolampadius employed another biblical reference, Matthew 11, which reported that it would be the poor and humble who believed.

---

12. Oecolampadius, *In Iesaiam*, 59v (ad loc. Isa. 36:1).
13. Oecolampadius. *In Iesaiam*, 58r (ad loc. Isa. 6:3).

So along with the other Reformers, Oecolampadius used Scripture as the pure Word of God to purify church doctrine and practice, and to critique unbiblical traditions.

Original Sin

Gross theological impurities infected the sixteenth-century church. How could this have happened, given the purity of Scripture? The church had mistakenly trusted in its own intellect. It had weakened the effect of original sin by proposing an unfallen reason. Oecolampadius espoused the view of original sin that included a corrupted intellect. Sin, he taught, clings to us during our entire earthly life.[14] It invades all our faculties, including our minds. So Oecolampadius, along with Augustine, taught total depravity: "In what way should not the lips be polluted, when our whole body is polluted, and as he witnesses below, our righteous acts are like a menstrual rag?"[15]

This sinful disposition from Adam invaded every human heart. We are sinners not merely because we sin, but because we were born with rebellious hearts: "For in Adam we all sinned not by imitation alone by which we sin freely but being made participant in His flesh in which sin separately dwells."[16] Our faithless hearts were a condition of our birth, "because sin dwelt in us, which we inherited."[17]

Salvation did not create an immediate purity of thought. Likewise, sanctification does not produce perfection: "Here appears the life of the righteous to be a perpetual wrestling, for they are empowered by the Holy Spirit to do good, but the flesh interferes and deforms the work."[18] Even the so-called saints could not claim sinlessness: "You have here clearly that the saints also have sinned.... And he does not say that they were imperfect, neither

---

14. See Oecolampadius, *ad Rhomanos*, 43v (ad loc. Rom. 4:14): "As long as we live, concupiscence remains in us." Also *ad Rhomanos*, 80r (ad loc. Rom. 9:20): "Therefore as long as we live, we dwell in crass bodies and so we are not able to see divine things."

15. Oecolampadius, *In Iesaiam*, 59r (ad loc. Isa. 6:5).

16. Johannes Oecolampadius, *Ioannis Oecolampadii doctoris undecunque doctissimi in librum Iob exegemata* (Basel: Henrie Petris, 1532), 80r (ad loc. Job 14:4).

17. Oecolampadius, *ad Rhomanos*, 49r (ad loc. Rom. 5:12).

18. Oecolampadius, *ad Rhomanos*, 61v (ad loc. Rom. 7:15).

that they have a propensity to evil, but they sinned. We know therefore that we are sinners...for always certain stains adhere to the
saints."[19] This last remark both upholds original sin and down-
grades the worship of saints. Even the apostles, after being saved,
fought with their own sin: "[Paul said], 'what I do,' that is in the
flesh I disapprove through the Law and hate in the spirit; and he
acknowledges here the apostle is still a sinner while justified and
has the desire to sin."[20]

In describing fallen man, Oecolampadius summarily defined
sin as the lack of faith. The human core of iniquity spews scorn
at God. But man's unbelief also expresses itself in a failure toward
others, a failure to imitate God's love, a failure to show mercy.[21] The
Basel Reformer grasped the essence of sin. He also knew that the
only remedy is faith in Christ. So he repeatedly displayed the beauty
of the Savior to the broken heart.

Free Will

The question remained as to whether faith was initiated by man, and
therefore a work contributing to salvation. A published debate took
place between Luther (*Bondage of the Will*) and Desiderius Erasmus
(*Freedom of the Will*). Luther maintained that the will of reprobate
man can only obey the sinful nature that enslaves it. Erasmus taught
that man is able to choose to love God out of an unregenerate heart.
The idea of man saving himself appealed to pride. From Eden to
Pelagius, to Arminius, and to sects, cults, and false religions, the
temptation continued for man to take the glory of Christ's work to
himself. Oecolampadius stood firmly with Luther: "Not that justification is attributed to our faith as if you would speak of it in an
exact manner as our work, for this would be an abusive faith if I
would trust in my faith, as if it were something in me that should
be remunerated. But in this way justification is attributed to faith, in

---

19. Oecolampadius, *ad Rhomanos*, 35r (ad loc. Rom. 3:23).
20. Oecolampadius, *ad Rhomanos*, 61v (ad loc. Rom. 7:15). Note that Oecolampadius's idea of *ego* here in Romans is taken over exactly by Calvin.
21. Oecolampadius, *ad Rhomanos*, 61v–62r (ad loc. Rom. 7:15).

that faith attributes everything to the mercy of God."[22] No element of Pelagianism was allowed to diminish the work of Christ. Faith is not a product of a free will, as Erasmus claimed, but a gift from God: "For this [is] the greatest gift of God…that He has given to us this faith by which we may believe in our redemption."[23] Since we are born in faithless sin, it must be God's initiation of faith in us that destroys sin's origin. Man left to himself is able only to die: "Free will is endangered also in this place: for if all people are not able to do anything other than dry up and fall down, what is the faculty of their free will?"[24]

Election

Since man cannot save himself, then it is God who saves, who *decides* to save: "Perfectly, however, He will immediately console the humble and those hoping in Him, such as whom He elects, from whom He does not draw away His mercy."[25] The whole idea of election contrasted starkly with the late medieval belief that being a baptized member of the church or buying an indulgence secured one's place in heaven. The Reformation returned to the biblical emphasis on God as initiator. This led to the understanding of predestination. The Reformer wrote: "Now he [Paul] consoles himself in two ways; first that predestination remains immutable. Then that the promises

---

22. Oecolampadius, *ad Rhomanos*, 10v (ad loc. Rom. 1:15). See also Johannes Oecolampadius, *In Hieremiam prophetam commentariorum libri tres* (Basel: Apiarius, 1533), 37v (ad loc Jer. 5:3): "We are therefore justified by faith before God as Paul clearly shows."

23. Johannes Oecolampadius, *Annotationes piae ac doctae in Euangelium Ioannis* (Basel: Cratander, 1533), 110r (ad loc. John 6:1).

24. Oecolampadius, *In Iesaiam*, 211v (ad loc. Isa. 40:8). Also, "Therefore perfidy or unbelief is the true root of all other sins…therefore faith alone suffices for destroying all sins." See also Oecolampadius, *In Iesaiam*, 263r (ad loc. Isa. 53:5): "Not only from original sin but from all sins He freed us, and so reconciled us to the Father." Also, Oecolampadius, *In Iesaiam*, 195v (ad loc. Isa. 36:8): "Our enemy knows that there is nothing found in our strength, and do we still continue to boast in our attempts or in the power of free will?" Also, Oecolampadius, *In Iesaiam*, 203r (ad loc. Isa. 37:29): "Therefore 'free will' has no dignity as long as we are looking to the divine things, by which everything subsists by sure laws."

25. Oecolampadius, *In Iesaiam*, 6v (ad loc. Isa. 1:1).

of the prophets are not empty, and this is what he says, 'the Word of God falls out,' which pertains to predestination."[26]

Oecolampadius binds together sovereignty and predestination, as can be seen throughout his commentaries.[27] This marriage of God's attribute and decree fits with the hardening of Pharaoh's heart and the idea of double predestination. For example, he comments on Isaiah's prophecy, "The people of the Jews, who were the temple of God and despised His Word, are to be blinded most justly."[28] Here we can see a fully mature doctrine of election and predestination, common among the early Church Fathers, but not the sixteenth-century clergy.

Solus Christus

In the early 1500s, most Christians believed they could placate God's righteous anger. This could be done through suffering, such as whipping themselves, climbing glass-strewn steps on their knees, or fasting. Or they could make a pilgrimage to Rome or pay money to the church and its charities. By these actions, they could procure mercy, and even salvation itself, for themselves and their relatives, living or dead. Daily sins could be forgiven through acts of penance, usually involving repeated prayers.

Oecolampadius was particularly irritated by conventional confessions after having been a penitential priest. But he saw this as only one strand of a confused web of unbiblical practices. First and foremost, men had to see their salvation as coming from the work of Christ alone (*solus Christus*). No sinful human could pay for a single sin, a cosmic rebellion against the almighty God: "Not by works of righteousness that we ourselves did, but according to His mercy He saves us.... Even if we all suffered all things, we could not

---

26. Oecolampadius, *ad Rhomanos*, 77r (ad loc. Rom. 9:6).
27. Oecolampadius, *ad Rhomanos*, 47v (ad loc. Rom. 5:6), refers to the time of the Incarnation as "predestined time." Contrary to Demura, "Calvin and Oecolampadius," 174, there is no conflict between Calvin's commentary on Romans 5:6 and Oecolampadius's, since Calvin is critiquing Augustine not on his doctrine but on the fact that he is off topic.
28. Oecolampadius, *In Iesaiam*, 58v (ad loc. Isa. 6:4).

make satisfaction for one little sin."[29] The most definitive example
was the thief on the cross: "It does not describe any good work of
his but that he cried, 'Remember me, Lord, when thou comest into
thy Kingdom.' And on account of this faith alone he heard, 'Today
shalt thou be with me in paradise.' The thief, therefore, is opposed
by abundant other [evil] works so this thief is justified without works
of the Law."[30] Man can do nothing to accomplish his salvation. He
can only respond in a faithful life of love. Good deeds are the fruit
rather than the basis for salvation (see below on good deeds).

Sola Gratia

Oecolampadius's normally irenic tone turned fiercely implacable on
the issue of dependence on God's grace alone (*sola gratia*) for salvation. In his commentary on Isaiah 40, he admonished, "Cursed is
he, according to Jeremiah, who makes flesh his arm…sin comes
before grace, and there is no room for congruent merit…. For we
are in sins before grace…. It is well-pleasing to God to pardon sins
in His Son, not by obligation, but from His good will…there is
nothing by which we may reconcile divine vengeance to ourselves,
unless God sees fit to give it through His mercy."[31] In a time when
people thought the righteousness of Christ was insufficient to satisfy
God's standard of perfection, here was a clear and culturally necessary explanation from Scripture of *sola gratia*. Man can be saved by
faith alone, through God's grace alone, found in Christ alone.

Sola Fide

Since man is born a sinner and can do nothing apart from sin, he
cannot save himself. However, by the late Middle Ages, the church
had gradually added ways in which man could supposedly aid in his
own salvation. These included the infamous buying of indulgences.

---

29. Oecolampadius, *In Iesaiam*, 210v (ad loc. Isa. 40:2).
30. Oecolampadius, *ad Rhomanos*, 37r (ad loc. Rom. 3:28).
31. Oecolampadius, *In Iesaiam*, 211r (ad loc. Isa. 40:2). For example, he
warned in his commentary on Isaiah 36, "all the antichristian rhetoricians defend
themselves and strive to whitewash a collapsing wall." Oecolampadius, *In Iesaiam*,
197r (ad loc. Isa. 36:15).

The Reformation returned to the Bible's teaching of *sola fide*, by faith alone. The Reformers insisted that man had nothing to contribute to his salvation, despite papal views on merits. Oecolampadius never hesitated to defend justification by faith alone.

If our good deeds cannot save us, what about the good deeds of dead saints? Did not some of these people have an overflow of goodness beyond what they needed? Could that extra goodness be bought and applied to others? These ideas were being propagated in the early sixteenth century. Oecolampadius attacked these fallacies: "Still do we sell merits and our works, as if we even overflowed to help others, as if it were in us to dispense them?"[32] No, we are only miserable sinners apart from Christ. We have already mentioned the Basel Reformer's teaching that saints were also sinners and could not save themselves, let alone anyone else. No human, apart from the God-Man Himself, could save men. None was righteous before the holy God; not one.

Imputation

Then do sinners, forgiven by God, appear before a holy God as sinners? The medieval priests told the people that after death they would work in a "waiting room" until they could appear holy before God. This was a post-mortem works-righteousness that had to be addressed. Christ took the penalty for the sins of all believers and gave His righteousness in exchange. Oecolampadius explained: "For the righteousness of God is for all who believe from faith to faith."[33] As soon as a believer is justified by faith, he receives the imputation of Christ's righteousness. "Now in this place the righteousness is that by which God counts us as just when we are in His grace."[34] This exchange does not wait until after death. "For this righteousness is in the present time. For in the future after this life, the righteousness of God is that each would receive according to his works." This latter refers to God's goodness in rewarding fruits

---

32. Oecolampadius, *In Iesaiam*, 195v (ad loc. Isa. 36:5).
33. Oecolampadius, *ad Rhomanos*, 10r (ad loc. Rom. 1:17).
34. Oecolampadius, *ad Rhomanos*, 34r–v (ad loc. Rom. 3:21).

of faith. Man has no righteousness of his own but fully receives
Christ's righteousness when he believes.[35]

Good Deeds

The late medieval believer found himself in a quandary. On the one
hand, he was told that his salvation was settled when he became a
baptized member of the church. On the other hand, he was threatened with purgatory, God's post-death penance room, if he did not
behave in this life. That left some, like Luther, scrambling at every
opportunity to gain God's approval. It left others living immorally,
knowing they were "saved" and not caring about future consequences. The Reformation clarified that good deeds are a result,
not a cause, of salvation: "This is the cause, namely, that it [the
gift of justification] is initiated by promises. The promises precede
justification.... Not that in any way we are prohibited from doing
the works of the Law, but we are free to do them, as faith and love
teach. He only says that these works are not to be reckoned for
justification."[36] The gift of faith, given by God, frees the soul to do
good deeds. The greatest deed is to love God and our fellow man.
But even this deed is not salvific: "Although love is great, it nevertheless does not justify; because no one loves as he ought to...for by
faith we are justified and made sons of God. So justification is not
to be attributed to love."[37] Neither a man's love nor any other fruit
of faith can save him. We cannot earn God's love or His blessings
by what we do.

    Yet salvation through faith alone does produce effects: "First,
faith justifies before God.... Second, it restores our consciences
after sinning. Third, it has made us into people who stand and persevere. Fourth, it confirms that we will be glorified and will rejoice."[38]
Earthly and heavenly rewards accompany salvation, but not by
compulsion, as if God owed them to us: "The benefits which God
does not take away from us are not on account of our merit, but

---

35. Oecolampadius, *ad Rhomanos*, 36r (ad loc. Rom. 3:26).
36. Oecolampadius *ad Rhomanos*, 34v (ad loc Rom. 3:22).
37. Oecolampadius *In Epistolam Ioannis,* ad loc. 1 John 3:10, trans. by the author.
38. Oecolampadius *ad Rhomanos*, 46r (ad loc. Rom. 5:1).

He gives on account of His own greatness and out of pure grace."[39] Such teaching may seem mundane to us, but it proved revolutionary to the church at that time.

Perseverance

Perseverance was not really an issue in the early Basel church, since salvation was secured by becoming a baptized member of the church. However, the Bible teaches that God keeps a man faithful and that man willingly participates in being faithful. Oecolampadius shows a balanced approach to perseverance. He teaches that God's power and the determinate character of His purpose guarantee eternal salvation, but we are to continue to exercise faith as we persevere: "Perfectly, however, He will immediately console the humble and those hoping in Him, such as whom He elects, from whom He does not draw away His mercy."[40] He adds, "We will not be left destitute of divine help, provided that our faith abides healthy."[41] The Basel Reformer maintained the mystery of sovereignty and free agency.

Covenant

The doctrine of covenant in the Bible had long been neglected. The word *covenant* had come to mean primarily a marriage bond. It remained for the Reformers to recover the doctrinal meaning.

In his understanding of the concept of covenant, Oecolampadius preceded John Calvin. He bound together Old Testament believers and New Testament believers through the cross. In speaking of the temple, he identified "the elect of God—at that time the synagogue, now the Church."[42] All believers throughout all time were joined by faith in Christ. There was one covenant of salvation between God and believers, the promise made in the cross. Peter Gorday pointed out that this approach was similar to the Church Fathers, who emphasized a "Christological salvation-history and

---

39. Oecolampadius, *Annotationes in Euangelium Ioannis.* [*Annotations on the Gospel of John*]. (Basel: Tigurinus, 1533/1535), 111r (ad loc. John 6:5).

40. Oecolampadius, *In Iesaiam*, 6r (ad loc. Isa. 1:1).

41. Oecolampadius, *In Iesaiam*, 194r (ad loc. Isa. 36:1).

42. Oecolampadius, *In Iesaiam*, 56v (ad loc. Isa. 6:1).

thus made possible a unification of biblical thought that was claimed to be 'Historical' without falling into philosophical historicism."[43]

God's covenantal promises, whether in the Old or New Testament, provided strength for believers in every age, in every generation. The promises of judgment and of redemption had always been available. Because of continuity in the covenants, God's judgments persisted, so that perils of condemnation pronounced in Isaiah's time could be applied currently. Both law and gospel were present through the covenant Executor in the Old and New Testaments. Since God is immutable, so are all His promises, whether they be of blessing, curse, or salvation. Therefore, His promise to be God to the faithful remains eternally. The Basel Reformer demonstrated that God's perpetual covenantal promise to be God to His children was exhibited even in His Name, "YHWH, Father, Lord," which implicitly demanded a covenant relationship.[44] Apparently, according to Oecolampadius, the covenant itself could be viewed as one intensified promise. The epitome of the promise was God's giving of Himself on the cross.

Assurance

In contrast with medieval Roman Catholic tradition, which said that no one could be sure of his final salvation except by special personal revelation or by buying an indulgence, Oecolampadius, along with other Reformers, stressed the confidence that we can have through faith that looks to Christ and to God's promises: "We should imitate the faith of the fathers, and as they, believing in the Word, fled for refuge to the bronze serpent, so we also should not doubt that we are saved in the cross of the Lord."[45] He added, "Everything in this book is to confirm us in faith."[46] Finally, he said, "However, hope is confirmed by the power of God because nothing is able to prevent the Word of God, by which salvation is promised to us, from com-

---

43. Peter Gorday, *Principles of Patristic Exegesis: Romans 9–11 in Origen, John Chrysostom, and Augustine* (New York: Edwin Mellen, 1983), 32.

44. Oecolampadius, *In Iesaiam*, 200v (ad loc. Isa. 37:16).

45. Oecolampadius, *In Iesaiam*, 5v (ad loc. Isa. 1:1).

46. Oecolampadius, *In Iesaiam*, 213v (ad loc. Isa. 40:12).

ing to pass."[47] Christians could be assured of their salvation by God's certain promise in the Word. The hope rested on God, not men.

Law

What, then, was the purpose of the law? Several options were discussed during the Reformation. 1) The law was completely abrogated, being fulfilled in Christ. 2) The law continued to be authoritative except in its sacrificial dimensions. 3) The law was fulfilled in Christ but was used to show God's standard and drive a soul to Christ.

Oecolampadius first addressed the nature of the law: "From these things that are said there arises the question of the holiness of the Law. For he [Paul] had said the law works wrath; and those who are under grace are not under law. Besides he had linked together the old man and the Law as an incitement to sin.... It is as if he should say, 'I would not say that the Law as given by Moses is impious when sin is the transgression, but rather to deplore our infirmity and inability with these words.' For after the sin of our first parents our nature is so vitiated that the Law given by God however much it may be truly holy, not only does not assist us, but makes us worse."[48] In other words, the law, which showed how a good person behaved, ended up being a source of judgment because all men were sinners: "The Law was holy, just, and good. However, it was from our infirmity, which became worse by a good medicine.... Hence Moses will not be contrary to Christ, but will serve him."[49]

The law helps in two ways. First, we realize that we cannot be saved by obeying the law, for all have fallen short of perfection. The law had to be given in order for us to see God's standards, which could not be compromised by our rationalization. We had to see that only Christ, as God's righteous Son, could fulfill the

---

47. Oecolampadius, *In Iesaiam*, 212v–213r (ad loc. Isa. 40:12).
48. Oecolampadius *ad Rhomanos*, 59r (ad loc. Rom. 7:7).
49. Akira Demura, "Two Commentaries on The Epistle to the Romans: Calvin and Oecolampadius." In *Calvinus sincerioris religionis vindex*. [Calvin as protector of the purer religion.] Wilhem H. Neuser and Brian G. Armstrong, eds. (Kirksville, Missouri: Sixteenth Century Journal Pub., 1997), 175. He quotes Johannes Oecolampadius, *Enarratio in Euangelium Matthaei* (Basel: Cratander, 1536), 3r.

law: "Everywhere Christ shows the Law as necessary, although we will not be saved by the Law. It does not follow, the Law is necessary, therefore it saves."[50] No one is saved by keeping the law, but by it everyone can see what true righteousness looks like and then recognize it in Christ.

Second, the law drives us to Christ. Because the law shows me to be an unsaved sinner, I must seek the remedy found in Christ alone: "This one thing the Law presents to me so that it may come to my eyes to know sin."[51] As a sinner, I must know that I am condemned and in need of a Savior: "The law makes us despair of our own capabilities."[52] The purpose of the law is to unveil righteousness in the Righteous One, to show man's inability to save himself by being good, and to show the necessity of receiving Christ as our saving Representative. In short, Moses helps us to Christ.[53] The law is essentially inward, not outward behavior:[54] It is through Christ alone that the law is perfectly performed and through Him alone that a sinner is made spiritually perfect.

Church Renewal

Doctrine and practice are always inextricably joined. Through the Middle Ages, the pollution of doctrine, along with general biblical ignorance, led to problems in practice. The outworking of the institutional church, as well as daily thoughts and habits of Christians, became aberrant. The whole structure of the physical building,

---

50. Oecolampadius, *Enarratio in Euangelium Matthaei*, 65v (ad loc. Matt. 5:17).

51. Oecolampadius, *ad Rhomanos*, 59r (ad loc. Rom. 7:7).

52. Oecolampadius, *ad Rhomanos*, 83v (ad loc. Rom. 10:4).

53. Oecolampadius, *Enarratio in Euangelium Matthaei*, 3r.

54. See Johannes Oecolampadius, *Enarratio in Euangelium Matthaei,* 65r (ad loc. Matt. 5:17). Cited by Demura, "Two Commentaries," 176. See also *ad Rhomanos*, 61r (ad loc.Rom. 7:14): "However, note that it is not the same to say the law is spirit and to say that it is spiritual." Note that he makes a fine distinction between "spiritus" [spirit] and "spiritualis" [spiritual]. Commenting on Isaiah 24:5, Oecolampadius has a similar expression that reads: "But Law is from love, the law is spirit." ["Charitatis autem lex, lex est spiritus."] Oecolampadius, *In Iesaiam*, 156r. Nonetheless, the law has become incapable of salvation. In the Romans commentary, Oecolampadius pointedly does not say that the law is spirit, only that it is spiritual. On the other hand, when defined by love, the law is spirit.

actions inside and outside of that building, who was in the building, who was in charge there and what they had authority to do, and how Christians were to be discipled had to be reformed. Oecolampadius therefore undertook practical reform of the church and of Christian living, in addition to his work to establish doctrinal soundness.

Icons

One key Reformation issue concerned the idolatrous worship of pictures, statues, and pieces of dead saints' bodies. These practices crept into the church during the Middle Ages. People had become superstitiously attached to the creature rather than honoring the Creator.

For example, some thought praying in front of a particular statue or relic strengthened their petition. Erasmus ironically noted that statues that reportedly had worked miracles, according to citizens, now could not save themselves from being dismantled.[55] Satan had used pictures and carvings to entrap hearts, turning people away from God: "For the thing is extremely difficult, to liberate from such captivity when the world and demons resist us in proceeding toward true piety; he [Isaiah] tells many things concerning the power of God and His goodness: but he thus overthrows the power of idols and demons and other powers of this world, in order that without hindrance the way to God may be evident to believers.... But these [idols] are never rejected, unless the power of God is known which now he places before the eyes."[56] God did work through the Reformation to free people to worship God in Spirit and in truth.

When people realized the heinousness of their sin, they sometimes smashed or burned statues and painted over pictures. Hence, as we witnessed in Basel, the iconoclastic rebellion occurred.

However, Oecolampadius lifted Christians' eyes beyond the idols themselves to warn them of the inward battle against sin and of the outward battle against principalities. The solution to idolatry lay in knowing God and wholeheartedly turning toward Him, not in

---

55. Froude, *Life and Letters*, 359–360.
56. Oecolampadius, *In Iesaiam*, 212v (ad loc. Isa. 40:12).

crushing statues. Nevertheless, city governments often ordered the removal of statues, icons, and painted wall images.

Relics

People often collected badges from reliquaries they visited, similar to the silver souvenirs from the temple of Diana in Paul's day. These were variously supposed to carry a certain power of blessing from the dead saint, or at least symbolically provided merit before God. So Christians were encouraged to make pilgrimages to view relics. At the same time, churches and towns grew rich by these visits and tried to purchase numerous and significant relics. The black market from the Holy Land to the West flourished, with skeptics commenting that enough supposed splinters from the cross existed to build several crosses. Christians had been misled to attribute to creaturely things (such as bones, hair, or teeth of the dead) the grace that comes from God's Spirit: "Today we have heard of similar things happening in regard to the sacraments, images, and other things which thus far in the eyes of the common people appear impressive; but in reality, on account of the abuses, they are held to be harmful."[57] These items were not sinful in themselves, but man's abusive attachment to them was.

Worship of Saints

The issue went deeper than using a creaturely item as a type of good-luck rabbit's foot. It involved the actual worship of departed saints, dead Christians. Some believers had grown up praising a saint buried in the local church, annually celebrating a patron saint of the city, or hearing their families call on a saint for help.

To combat this practice, Oecolampadius first clarified who qualified as a saint: "And so all Christians are saints."[58] There was no separation in status between Christians, as the papist church claimed. All were sinners saved by grace and made holy through Christ.

---

57. Oecolampadius, *In Iesaiam*, 196r (ad loc. Isa. 36:7).
58. Oecolampadius, *In Iesaiam*, 105r (ad loc. Isa. 13:3).

Then he proceeded to critique the adoration of dead believers. This practice contradicted God's command in Deuteronomy 18:11 and Isaiah 8:19, and bordered on necromancy. More important, it diminished the glory due to God: "It is superstition, therefore, that we believe saints wish us to be occupied with worship dedicated to them. They throw down their crowns in order to accomplish (also from us) that all honor be given to God."[59] Oecolampadius insisted that a Christian could not worship anyone except God alone, as was demanded in the first and second commandments.

If Christians could not worship remnants of dead believers or departed believers in heaven, could they at least ask the saints to intercede for them? This had become a common practice, with various dead saints specializing in different areas. One might have particular influence over the sea and sailors. The guilds adopted patron saints acquainted with their skills. Cities invoked the special protection of particular saints. To all this Oecolampadius replied: "Hope is not to be put in externals, that is, in men or any other creature.... Therefore, they act foolishly who, abandoning Christ, trust in the prayers of the saints.... For through Christ we offer our prayers to the Father who is our only Mediator, Advocate, and High Priest in the presence of God."[60] Elsewhere he wrote, "Christ is the altar on which we offer our sacrifices of entreaty, in order that He may commend us to God the Father."[61] Oecolampadius championed the unique priestly office of Christ in intercession. He continued by pointing out that God specifically commanded believers to pray in the name of Christ only.[62] Thereby, he left no room for corrupt, sinful disobedience that invoked the dead. Christ alone received the honor of Mediator, the only High Priest.

Worship of Angels

The idolatrous worship of angels also needed to be addressed. Some citizens would call on a particular angel for help rather than on God.

---

59. Oecolampadius, *In Iesaiam*, 58r (ad loc. Isa. 6:2).
60. Oecolampadius, *In Iesaiam*, 198v (ad loc. Isa. 36:2).
61. Oecolampadius, *In Iesaiam*, 60v (ad loc. Isa. 6:8).
62. Oecolampadius, *In Iesaiam*, 195v (ad loc. Isa. 36:4, 6).

This again substituted the creature for the Creator. It stole from God His authority, as if the angels could decide or act independent of God's command. Calling on an angel gives it honor and worship that belongs to God alone. Oecolampadius condemned the practice of worshiping angels since Scripture says they are "assistants and ministrant spirits...not equal to God or above God, but greater than us and others...so also the angel who appeared to John did not permit himself to be worshiped."[63] "Only God. Only God. Only God" became the repetitious exhorting cry of the Reformation.

Not only laymen but clergy were distracted by angels. Oecolampadius was troubled by the allurement angelic studies had for scholars such as Origen and Jerome, maintaining that curiosity beyond Scripture demonstrated impiety: "It is not necessary to treat exhaustively concerning these angels, but rather to take care that we lead an angelic life, through which we may be joined to any troops of angels."[64] Here he clearly eschewed medieval philosophical scholasticism in favor of the biblical text alone. He concluded that angels deserved respect, not worship. Men had to worship God, hallowing His name on earth as the angels did in heaven.

The Lord's Supper

Badges, paintings, icons, dead saints, and angels could not be worshiped. But what about external representations associated with the presence of Christ Himself? Was not Christ in the Lord's Supper? At that time, the Eucharist had come to be regarded as a magical practice, wherein men turned bread into flesh and again sacrificed on an altar the Son of God, Christ, who gave Himself up once. As mentioned earlier, Oecolampadius, Luther and other Reformers researched, published books about, and debated the issue in order to bring thinking

---

63. Oecolampadius, *In Iesaiam*, 57v (ad loc. Isa. 6:2).

64. Oecolampadius, *In Iesaiam*, 58r (ad loc. Isa. 6:3). He referred to Scripture passages such as Hebrews 1, Daniel 7, Revelation 4, Malachi 2, and Romans 10 in order to interpret angelic visions in the Bible. By looking at the Hebrew Bible passages, he noted a broader use of "seraph," which translated meant "burning one." He then identified Isaiah and Paul as seraphs. "Also the other evangelists and apostles are seraphim. For they are such a furnace of love, desiring to make the whole world saved." Oecolampadius, *In Iesaiam*, 60r (ad loc. Isa. 6:6).

back into line with the Bible. Christ was not an "imbreaded god."[65]
Also as mentioned earlier, Oecolampadius countered this fallacious
interpretation of the Lord's Supper through his extensive tome *De
Genuina Verborum Domini*, in which he proved transubstantiation to
be an innovation not found in the Church Fathers.

He urged parishioners to recognize that Christ had been sacrificed once for all, as stated in Hebrews. Therefore, the bread and
wine could not belong to an ubiquitous body repeatedly being sacrificed. However, neither were the elements empty symbolism: "For
they declare their unbelief...if they say they have eaten the sign
only and not also the thing signified.... I freely confess the Body
of Christ to be present in the bread in that mode in which it is present in the Word itself."[66] Christians had to rethink this sacrament,
understanding its biblical meaning as a confirmation of faith for
those who commune with Christ. A child of God, by faith, par-
ticipatorily received the pledges of God for forgiveness of sins and
eternal life in union with Christ. He was taken up into heaven to
meet Christ in the Eucharist.[67] It also served as a sign to others that
the church is "the unleavened bread of Christ."[68]

Baptism

Other sacraments, not ordained by Christ, had become prevalent
in the church and had to be dropped. The command by God to be
baptized was confirmed, yet not without controversy. As mentioned
before, the Anabaptists objected to infant baptism. Within the main-
stream church, misunderstanding had led to an interpretation of

---

65. Locher, *Zwingli und die schweizerische Reformation*, 303.

66. Staehelin, *Briefe und Akten*, 2:38–40, #470.

67. Staehelin, *Lebenswerk*, 144. Staehelin quotes from Oecolampadius, *Para-
doxan* (1521), a publication on confessions. Compare John Calvin, *Institutes of the
Christian Religion*, trans. Henry Beveridge (Grand Rapids: Eerdmans, 1970), 4.17.31.

68. Oecolampadius, *ad Rhomanos*, 41v (ad loc. Rom. 4:11). "They [partici-
pants] are confirmed more by this mystery which mystery has the promise added
to the sign when by faith they regard not the water, not the bread, not the wine as
themselves signs but Christ Himself, whose flesh given and blood poured out for
remission of sins, according to the promise.... In addition also the unity of religion
is served by this symbol in that by it we distinguish Christians from non-Christians
and members of Christ; so that we are all the unleavened bread of Christ."

salvation by water. A believer was told that he was saved if he was a baptized member of the church. Again, a visible creation was substituted for the Creator. Water took on salvific power. The Reformers countered that the sign meant nothing without the Word and without faith: "External water does not make a Christian, unless one is baptized internally by the Holy Spirit and amends the way of living thereafter according to the prescription of the Word of God."[69] Through an external sign, baptism, similar to Communion, demonstrated union with the Lord and the fellowship of believers.[70]

Definition of the Church

The late medieval church had not defined itself in biblical terms. Luther once confronted a drunken citizen who had embraced antinomianism. The man protested that he had the church's assurance that he was going to heaven: he had been baptized and had bought an indulgence. This citizen had placed his trust in a false implication arising from false doctrine. For such people, Oecolampadius had to define the church as God defined it. Not every baptized church member belongs to the true, invisible church. The church, simply stated, is the elect.[71] The invisible church consists of those throughout all time who are made regenerate.[72] Oecolampadius taught, "It is not those who honor God only with the mouth and in pretense, but those whom God has predestined from eternity: so you may see that we are saved by grace and election, not by the merits of our works."[73] God gathers the true church through His Word, not man's will. Rather than an institution, a power structure,

---

69. Oecolampadius, *In Psalmos LXXIII*, 52 (ad loc. Ps. 74:2).

70. See Staehelin, *Briefe und Akten*, 2:41, #472.

71. See Oecolampadius, *In Iesaiam*, 202v (ad loc. Isa. 37:26): "Thus also the Church has been chosen by God, as in Romans 8." In Johannes Oecolampadius's *Iacobi Latomi theologiae professrois de confessione secreta. Ionnis Oecolampadii elleboron, pro eodem Iacobo Latomo* (Basel: Cratander, 1525) [Also referred to as "Elboron"], Oecolampadius stated that God's election designated the community of the elect.

72. Oecolampadius, *In Iesaiam*, 59v (ad loc. Isa. 6:5): "This temple doubtless signifies the elect of God—at that time the synagogue, now the Church."

73. Oecolampadius, *ad Rhomanos*, 72r (ad loc. Rom. 8:28). See also, "And many with the mouth confess that they believe Scriptures, but with the heart they deny it." Oecolampadius, *In Iesaiam*, 262v (ad loc. Isa. 53:1).

or a social establishment, the church had to be redefined as what it is—the spiritual body of Christ. The Son redeemed and glorified the church, and the Spirit inhabits it. Man does not choose to join the church as if it were another guild. "The true Church of God of which we are made citizens through true faith in Christ" is the creation of God.[74] Only those who are justified by faith; demonstrate sanctification; acknowledge Christ as God and man; and follow Him with a love that cleaves to Him only as head of the true church are saved. Only these are members of Christ's church.

Since faith does not make a person sinless, the visible church will always have sinners. Christ's blood is the basis for the church's holiness and unity, not an outward organization. True believers within the invisible church are being sanctified. Their behavior increasingly reflects God's person and Word. Holiness is both imputed and actual: "Christ for us was made righteousness from God and sanctification and redemption [1 Cor. 1:30]."[75] Moreover, "through Him every day we conquer Babylon in ourselves."[76] The church, and individuals in it, eventually image her Lord. Then the temple of God, formed by believers who decorate her with works of mercy, reflects His glory.

The drunken man above either had to repent or acknowledge he was not a member of the church. If he refused to repent, then excommunication had to be enjoined. According to Oecolampadius, excommunication from Christ's body comes when someone falls away from love. Faith and love are both the basis and binding of the church. An unrepentant sinner who has been confronted three times according to Matthew 18 has to be separated from the Lord's Table. The goal is not to create a pure church but to support holiness. The visible church will never be entirely pure and therefore never identical with the invisible church. Oecolampadius rejected the isolationism of the Anabaptists, caused by their supposition of this

---

74. Oecolampadius, *In Iesaiam*, 194r (ad loc. Isa. 36:1). See also 6r (ad loc. Isa. 1:1).

75. Oecolampadius, *In Iesaiam*, 210v (ad loc. Isa. 40:2).

76. Oecolampadius, *In Iesaiam*, 104v (ad loc. Isa.13:1).

premise. Conversely, neither does it mean that an apparently good person with good works necessarily belongs to the invisible church.

If the elect comprise the invisible church and if they are still in various stages of holiness, how is the true church to be recognized? What distinguishes the visible church? First and foremost, one seeks "the true Church of God which trusts solely in the Word of God."[77] Three necessary elements to build the church will be present: 1) prophets will call people to repentance through God's Word; 2) men will stop sinning through renouncing the world and crucifying the old Adamic nature, rising as new men; and 3) the church will seek, hope, and trust God, all of which comes from the Word of God and faith.[78] The true marks of a gathered church include baptism and the Lord's Supper, where the true Word of God is given. Christians confess faith in Christ and hold to the marks of the true church, especially in the Lord's Supper and baptism. Oecolampadius explained the larger debated topics—namely, a purified Lord's Supper and a simplified infant baptism, both conducted in the common language—in printed tracts circulated throughout the 1500s.

Church and State

The implication of church discipline was extensive. It was all well and good to say that someone had to confront a public sinner who professed to be a Christian. But who should do this? And who should inflict consequences if the person remained unrepentant? Church discipline was a means by which to encourage and protect the holiness of the church, and therefore the name of Christ. But who was to have charge of such discipline?

In Europe in the Late Middle Ages, church and state were seen as somewhat synonymous. The civil ruler would decide matters of the church that he would enforce: which books could be printed or possessed, which churches or cities were acting outside the bounds of orthodoxy, who should be burned or promoted, which language

---

77. Oecolampadius, *In Iesaiam*, 194r (ad loc. Isa. 36:1).

78. Johannes Oecolampadius, from his lecture on Haggai. *A commentary of Jo. Oecolampadius on the last three Prophets: Haggai, Zechariah and Malachi* (Basel: Cratander), 1527.

should be used in worship, where people could gather to worship, what type of education qualified a man for ordination, who could sing, pray, preach, or baptize, which Bible could be used in which language, who had sinned and how the consequences should be applied, which prayers were to be prayed, and the theological meaning behind every movement of the church. The onerous magnitude of the task undertaken by King Edward VI in England to bring about the reformation of the church becomes obvious with such expectations. Some envisioned a government where the state ruler would always call himself a believer and therefore would work for the church. Any presupposition that the civil ruler would necessarily be a Christian was quickly dismissed in the events of the following centuries. Political intrigues and fights to maintain or gain power proliferated, creating many Christian martyrs. However, during the Reformation relations between church and state were rethought. Some presupposed a Christian government; others did not. Each stance required a different approach to who administered church discipline.

In his thinking about the church, Oecolampadius introduced a radically new idea for the time, namely, a separation between the spheres of church and state. Each would have its own domain. This did not prevent Christians from being involved in politics, as the Anabaptists insisted. Christians could and should be involved in civil government; in fact, Oecolampadius believed that no one was better suited to be a judge than a Christian. The ideal city would have Christian leaders and Christian laws that would be followed willingly by citizens as in 1 Timothy 4:8. Society was spiritual, not just secular, in nature, so government should guide people in trusting God. The government's job was to bear the sword for the enforcement of public peace, primarily for the sake of the church.

The church also had its sphere of authority.[79] It had its own spiritual weapons: forgiveness and excommunication, which bring about

---

79. Oecolampadius: "You [magistrates] give good and peace-loving citizens; the church produces pious and blameless Christians." The quote is from "Oecolampadius advocates in a speech before the Basel Council the new [church] order and the carrying through of church discipline." (2:448). Staehelin also indicates that the

peace with God. The civil government should have no ultimate authority here. It could enforce consequences on those whose sin broke civil law, but not on those breaking only church law. That meant the state could not punish heretics or Anabaptists for their beliefs. Separation of church and state meant that Christian faith was neither hindered nor forced; God's Word should be taught and lived freely.

The city of Basel, like other cities of that time, was a self-sufficient political entity with its own taxes, army, and laws. When Anabaptists refused to take oaths, this included the yearly oath of allegiance taken by all Basel citizens promising to defend the city and its laws. This refusal was deemed a civil offense. Citizens of Basel were endangered by those who chose to live in their midst yet not defend their city. In fact, Anabaptists took no oaths of any kind, but rather made "promises." These promises, usually to leave town, could be broken, and often were. Yet sworn agreements were necessary to carry on society among sinners. According to Pries, Oecolampadius's opinion was that it would be a "remarkable society...indeed be a blessed life" if everyone spoke the truth. But the reality of sin made legal oaths a necessity.[80]

Elders

The proposed plan to choose those responsible for deciding church discipline seemed a compromise step by the Reformer. Ever since Oecolampadius had been the confessor priest of Basel, he had desired to see true repentance and holiness in the church. He alone among the early Reformers emphasized the necessity of church discipline and its execution by the church. His proposal specified twelve censors who could exercise the required discipline with *gravitas* and

---

speech was given either on June 8, 1530, or somewhere between May 2 and June 8. Staehelin's first endnote, which note actually is on p. 2:458, gives his written source: Stadtarchiv Strassburg, Thomasarchiv, No. 177, fol. 200ff. Cited in Staehelin, *Briefe und Akten*, 2:456, #750.

80. Pries, "Anabaptist Oath Refusal," 77, citing as a source Oecolampadius, "Unterrichtung von dem Widertauff von der Oberkeit und von dem Eyd auff Carlins N. widertauffers artickel. Antwort auff Balthasar Hubmeiers büchlein wider der Predicanten gespräch zu Basel von dem kinder tauff" (Basel: Cratander, 1527), p. Eiiii(V).

without clerical tyranny. As a checks-and-balances measure, he proposed that the body of censors consist of four town pastors, joined by four representatives of the church and four city councilors. The representatives from the church were to be elders: "This power cannot be handed to the congregation, which includes women and children. The true representatives of the Church ought to be, as in the early Church, elders, whose judgment, as of the more prudent, expresses the mind of the Church."[81] As Scripture taught, these were to be men who were not new believers, but those who had been tested in their piety and had proved themselves wise and godly.

Prayer

During the Reformation, prayer itself needed clarification. Some parishioners took confidence in the empty repetition of rote words as a way of influencing God. Employing a statement by Rabshakeh in Isaiah 36, concerning a person's trusting in his own words, Oecolampadius revealed the presumptuousness of attempting to obligate God by our prayers: "In the same manner, it is not surprising that many are not heard, however much they persist in prayers, for they attribute more to themselves than to divine mercy. And it happens to them, just as to the Jews who lost the victory along with the ark of God which had been led forth into battle. Therefore, nothing of our works suffices to free us."[82] He allowed no room for an arrogant bribery of the Divine through Pharisaical petitions. However, he admitted there was profit in enlisting the prayers of others, since God had promised to hear the joint prayers of many believers.[83] He wrote, "But we are heard through Christ alone who is a beloved Son of the Father in whom God is well pleased."[84]

---

81. Oecolampadius, from a Spring 1530 oration to the synod of Basel clergy, "*De reducenda excommunicatione.*" Cited in Rupp, *Patterns*, 39.

82. Oecolampadius, *In Iesaiam*, 195v (ad loc. Isa. 36:4). Also Oecolampadius, *In Iesaiam*, 195v (ad loc. Isa. 36:2): "And yet we must not pray in such a way as if we were trusting in our own prayers and making God indebted."

83. Oecolampadius, *In Iesaiam*, 198v (ad loc. Isa. 37:2). Oecolampadius commended Hezekiah for seeking Isaiah's intercession, *In Iesaiam*, 199r (ad loc. Isa. 37:4).

84. Oecolampadius, *In Iesaiam*, 195v (ad loc. Isa. 36:5).

Forgiveness

An array of self-inflicted punishments, assigned by a priest, had usurped Christ's finished atonement. In contrast to the Roman tradition of penance, which burdened the consciences of the people, Oecolampadius proclaimed free forgiveness through Christ, offered in biblical promises: "Now then, you should no less diligently hearken to the words of the most glorious and certain testament, resting firmly on the promises of Christ; and you should be convinced that you have received in Christ eternal life and forgiveness of sins, under the inexpressible divine pledges."[85] Parishioners were confused by this, wondering how absolution was obtained. He answered biblically that only God could forgive sins, not a priest. This was particularly clear to him after having served as a parish penitential priest. He explained, "And the preaching of the Gospel not only simply cleanses me, but absolves.... For the Word of God, through faith, cleanses from all sins."[86] God in His Word has promised forgiveness to those who believe in Christ.

Priests/Ministers

Oecolampadius also devoted energy to reforming the priesthood. *Priest* was a theologically loaded term for the corrupted ministerial office. The unbiblical tradition had arisen that the official presiding in the Mass (the Lord's Supper) actually re-offered Christ's body as a sacrifice. Therefore, he was akin to an Old Testament priest. With the Reformation came a return to what Scripture actually taught about Christ's finished, one-time sacrifice. That left the clergy to be redefined as shepherds of the faith, proclaiming the gospel to the saved and unsaved. In another judicious act of peacemaking,

---

85. Jack W. Cottrell, "Covenant and Baptism in the Theology of Huldreich Zwingli" (PhD diss., Princeton Theological Seminary, 1971), 349–350, quoting Oecolampadius from a sermon and letter originally printed around June 1, 1522, as *Quod Expediat Epistolae et Evangelii lectionem in Missa, vernaculo sermone plebi promulgari, Oecolampadii ad Hedionem Epistola.* [A letter of Oecolampadius to Hedio, that it is fitting for a reading of the Epistle and the Gospel to be read to the people during Mass in the common language.]

86. Oecolampadius, *In Iesaiam*, 60v (ad loc. Isa. 6:7).

Oecolampadius retained the usual term *priest*, but undertook to transform the office inwardly.

Corrupt Priests

The immorality of the priests was so rampant that they were objects of disdain among the people. Anyone with even the smallest notion of scriptural morals viewed the hypocrisy of the clergy with horror. Some priests took mistresses, since they could not marry. Others accumulated large sums of money by exploiting the poor. Clerical offices could be bought by the wealthy and bestowed on children, who would then be secure with a steady income from parishioners. These children often never preached nor studied Scripture. The majority of trained priests studied the Latin liturgy rather than Scripture itself, and some disbelieved. Oecolampadius usually referred to unconverted priests as "Pharisees," chiding them that they could not believe because knowledge puffed them up and because they sought the accolades of men rather than God's glory.[87] He denounced abuses, warning, "The antichrist seeks various ways in order to betray the truth; for he ensnares some with sacerdotal offices, others with privileges, and others with gold coin, so that those whom he cannot conquer by threats, he may conquer by gifts."[88] The Reformer spoke earnestly from his own experience about the transience of this world to the compromised priests of his day.

Training of Priests

Given the poor training and general ignorance of the clergy, how were priests to be trained? Oecolampadius had to think through the whole educational model as he restructured the university. To begin with, he said, a priest should be a true Christian who obeys God's Word: "He should receive the teaching of Christ from the altar of sacred Scripture, indeed, from Christ Himself, not human dreams and frivolous traditions from the fathers."[89] Traditionally, priests

---

87. Oecolampadius, *In Iesaiam*, 2r (preface).
88. Oecolampadius, *In Iesaiam*, 196v (ad loc. Isa. 36:8).
89. Oecolampadius, *In Iesaiam*, 60v (ad loc. Isa. 6:6).

supposedly received salvation or ordination as a function of another priest's pronouncement. The Reformer countered: "This is not a perceptible unction to you, or a rite consisting in ceremonies, nor were bishops' hands furnishing [it]. But the sincere heart will be fit for the Holy Spirit and the heavenly unction."[90] Even their salvation by faith did not come through man, for "faith is had by those who see with the eye of the heart, who had God Himself as teacher."[91] So a priest had to be saved, sanctified, and anointed by God for his office.

In addition, as mentioned previously, the new university education emphasized fluency in the original languages and theology flowing out of the Bible itself. It also encouraged familiarity with the Patristics and excellence in exegesis.

Oecolampadius's redefinition of the ordination to priesthood as "the sincere heart" with "heavenly unction" injected more spiritual responsibility and life, resulting in the priesthood of all believers. Each person received an unction from the Holy Spirit. In this power, Christians were to exhort one another, edify one another, and offer sacrifices of prayer and praise directly through Christ. Since it was God Himself who called and enabled them, "now He exhorts the whole Church to announce the blessings of God."[92] Therefore, although the priest had specific clerical responsibilities, all Christians were called to a living involvement in the gospel.

Duties of Priests

Everyone could criticize the bad behavior of sixteenth-century priests, but what was a Reformed pastor to do positively? What did a good pastor actually look like? Oecolampadius instructed that the true pastor should "announce the joy of liberty," "discharge an apostolic office," "preach not a hard law but the Gospel and consolations," "build up, not destroy," and not "impose insupportable works."[93] Ministers primarily were to shepherd people: "Take care, that you take away sorrow from the hearts of men, gently teaching them, not

---

90. Oecolampadius, *In Iesaiam*, 57r (ad loc. Isa. 6:1).
91. Oecolampadius, *In Iesaiam*, 4r (ad loc. Isa. 1:1).
92. Oecolampadius, *In Iesaiam*, 212r (ad loc. Isa. 40:8).
93. Oecolampadius, *In Iesaiam*, 210v (ad loc. Isa. 40:1).

imperiously, not coldly, but fervently, in order that the words should penetrate the innermost part of the heart."[94] Using the example of John the Baptist, he exhorted ministers to expose sin through the law and then sanctify souls through the gospel: "The herald ought to announce by two things, the law and the Gospel: by the law he brings down, by the Gospel he raises up. For He commands to cry, that all flesh is grass, that is, that we know ourselves to be sinners, our strength vain. [As in] 1 Corinthians 1, that no flesh should glory, [or in] Romans 3, by the works of the law no flesh shall be justified. Whence it is to be mortified and crucified with its passions."[95] Like John the Baptist, preachers needed "to cleanse, to empty out, to remove from the midst the impediments of life, such as inebriation, drunkenness, cares of the age, and the things that do not admit one to the beginning of the Christian life, and exclude the Word of the Lord."[96]

Priests who denied the gospel did not always do so out of hedonistic wantonness, but sometimes out of fear. For these men, Oecolampadius proffered the following advice: Do not be surprised that preaching Scripture brings turmoil. God's Word has always precipitated opposition and agitation. Why? Because "the preaching of the Word of God damns all men; all are frightened and begin to struggle," even kings.[97] He referred weak priests to the example of Hezekiah, so they "will not be frightened by threats of this sort, since they know that there is no other zeal more pleasing to God than to live according to His Word.... Also there is no peril in exhorting the people to worship before the one and only altar, that is according to the commandment of God, and as it is prescribed in the canonical Scriptures."[98] He then encouraged these fearful clerics to take strength through God's Word and His promises: "Act, strong men! For the Lord has a reward in hand, which He will give to everyone trusting in Him and acknowledging Him."[99] In this way, he steadied

---

94. Oecolampadius, *In Iesaiam*, 210v (ad loc. Isa. 40:2).
95. Oecolampadius, *In Iesaiam*, 211v (ad loc. Isa. 40:6).
96. Oecolampadius, *In Iesaiam*, 211r (ad loc. Isa. 40:4).
97. Oecolampadius, *In Iesaiam*, 58v (ad loc. Isa. 6:4).
98. Oecolampadius, *In Iesaiam*, 196r (ad loc. Isa. 36:7).
99. Oecolampadius, *In Iesaiam*, 212r (ad loc. Isa. 40:10).

weak knees. Having himself been through the divestment of office and the hollow mockery of the world, he spoke powerfully without fear, and so could lead others.

Calling of Priests

If the preacher's duty was to encourage others in holiness, what sort of man should he be? Oecolampadius gave the following charge to God's called men.

> Observe here whoever acts as a preacher, your office. For the task is, that with Isaiah you may first be a disciple rather than a teacher, and may be among those who have seen God, whom Scripture calls 'theodidaktous' [taught by God]. May you also be called by God, as was Aaron, and not like Nadab and Abihu, and Korah, and others. May the desire of Uzziah first die to you, who intruded into sacred things from his own audacity. [Such desire] dies however, if you do not receive glory from people. For from arrogance is born in the mind the contagious disease of leprosy, which is a symbol of heresy. That you may see, with Moses, that great vision in the burning bush, take off your shoes, throwing off the garment made of skins and earthly filthiness and dirtiness of passions, for you will not be fitting to them, in order that you may be sent or may teach. That you also may be a surety of election, the task is, that in you may be prostrated Saul, and may rise up Paul; that you may no longer seek the things which are of the flesh, the things which belong to pharisaical righteousness, the things which are yours, but those of Jesus Christ, and those of others [who are] in Jesus. Withdraw also with Ezekiel to the river Chebar, lest you seek to be praised by people and to be called 'rabbi.'
>
> And when you know God and see how great is His majesty, beyond profound and inscrutable judgment, and how great is His goodness, then, if the vision be to that [such a calling], teach, lest you be among those who run but are not sent, and instead of the Word of God you offer the trash of your dreams. In the Scriptures, however, if you search them,

you will see God. And when Uzziah has died you may at once declare God fullest and best.[100]

Sermons of Priests

Oecolampadius encouraged Scripture-based, gospel-centered preaching, both by his own example and by his exhortation to others. The Reformation brought the Bible back into the center focus for directing and effecting the worship of God. No longer was ceremony the conveyor of grace, but the Spirit-filled power of the Word. Priests had to reshape their approach to liturgy and exhortation. Exegesis and sermonizing had to be resurrected.

1. The Word as a Means of Grace and Sanctification. Oecolampadius operated on the belief that the application of Scripture sanctifies the sinner. Therefore, sermons have to be based on Scripture, soundly exegeted. Through God's Word, the believer knows God and lives in sanctified obedience: "To follow God with heart and soul, wherever He may lead, this is to see God."[101] Knowing God demands a confession of sin, which comes from Scripture's conviction. This has to be accompanied by true repentance and commitment, for "many with the mouth confess that they believe the Scriptures, but with the heart they deny it."[102] Walking with God leads to prayer, the goal of which "ought to be that God be glorified and that it be known that He Himself alone is God."[103] Prayer that glorifies God, in turn, relies on knowledge of God, which flows from His empowering Word, as does faith: "Moreover, our faith is strengthened through the promises whether in the old or the new law."[104] In the entirety of the Bible, God covenanted to be God to His people and strengthen men. Pious faith also grows through examining biblical examples, "by which in all adversities we can be consoled [in the fact that] we will not be left destitute of divine help,

---

100. Oecolampadius, *In Iesaiam*, 56v–57r (ad loc. Isa. 6:1).
101. Oecolampadius, *In Iesaiam*, 56r (ad loc. Isa. 6:1).
102. Oecolampadius, *In Iesaiam*, 262v (ad loc. Isa. 53:1).
103. Oecolampadius, *In Iesaiam*, 201r (ad loc. Isa. 37:17).
104. Oecolampadius, *In Iesaiam*, 201r (ad loc. Isa. 37:16).

provided our faith abides healthy."[105] The whole of the Christian life in its many intertwined facets stands on Scripture, the God-breathed Word. Oecolampadius wrote: "For from Adam and from the flesh come sin, slavery and death; from the Spirit of God, sanctification liberty, life and security. He protects security by predestination; by all which things we will see that the glory of God is preached, which we pray would also be for sanctifying us."[106]

But most significantly, faith is encouraged through the Bible, even by God revealing Himself in His names, such as "Lord Sabbaoth." He wrote, "Sabbaoth...signifies just as much the physical armies as the spiritual ones which fight against us, and which He is able to destroy in one moment; or that all armies are His servants, the heavenly as much as the earthly, and He can send them for the aid of His own people."[107] God's names, like all of His communication, are a mercy intended to transform us. For all Scripture was written as a mercy from God and is to be studied, "Not so much in order that we may learn, but also in order that then we may receive something of advantage [spiritual profit], not merely of knowledge which may belong to vanity, but also belonging to life."[108] God's Word is not meant to be carved merely on stone tablets, but on hearts where He would live.

2. "Fencing" the Scriptures. Prior to the Reformation and the printing press, people usually had no access to the Bible, either through reading or hearing. Even priests were ignorant of its content. But by Oecolampadius's time, the Bible could be read by all who were literate. However, he did not believe everyone should necessarily read the Bible. Despite the priesthood of all believers, for whom the perspicuity of the Scriptures was blessed by God, others could be cursed by it. As mentioned previously, the Basel Reformer uniquely developed the doctrine of Scripture in a special direction. He "fenced" the Scriptures. That is, he made clear that exposure to the

---

105. Oecolampadius, *In Iesaiam*, 194r (ad loc. Isa. 36:1).
106. Oecolampadius, *ad Rhomanos*, preface.
107. Oecolampadius, *In Iesaiam*, 200v (ad loc. Isa. 37:16).
108. Oecolampadius, *In Iesaiam*, 5r (ad loc. Isa. 1:1).

Word brought greater condemnation to the unbeliever. Oecolampadius explained that for the unregenerate, "the understanding of his discerning will be hidden," and he will be blinded by "a spirit of sleep mixed by the Lord.... So the sense of Scripture is opened to none except those who seek Christ, and to whom Christ reveals Himself."[109] Some verses in Scripture warn against giving what is holy to the unholy. Concerning Matthew 7:6, he observed, "Doubtless it is unworthy and pernicious, where it is a matter of highest things, to discuss concerning vain things and to touch the ark with profane hands."[110] Jesus was restrained in His home town. Why? "He took thought for the fitness of the hearers."[111] So the individual had to exercise discernment before delving into the Word apart from God. Unregenerate scholars could not expect to understand it, nor should they attempt it. The proclaimer of Scripture must realize that God's Word will be life to some and death to others.

This idea of fencing the Scriptures penetrated the Basler's own exposition as well. Commenting on why Hezekiah's ambassadors remained silent in Isaiah 36, he observed that it would have been too great of a mercy for the ears of blasphemers to have heard God's precious Word. In fact, it was good that God's Word should be removed from them, so that they would not incur greater guilt. The reprobate could only damn himself further by hearing Scripture and not responding in faith. Therein lay the paradox. Faith for the unbeliever came by hearing, and hearing by the Word of God (Rom. 10:17). Yet without faith, hearing brought greater condemnation. The unbeliever had to be entreated through the gospel, yet discerningly.

Oecolampadius also warned Christians about the seriousness of hearing God's Word. Now that they could access the very speech of God, they had to take care. They had to feed on Scripture, yet not "dully or basely. Nothing could be said that ought and should make [us] so attentive, as that we hear what God says. As often as God speaks, no one who does not hear is excused."[112] The

---

109. Oecolampadius, *In Iesaiam*, 2r (preface).
110. Oecolampadius, *In Iesaiam*, 2r (preface).
111. Oecolampadius, *In Iesaiam*, 2v (preface).
112. Oecolampadius, *In Iesaiam*, 6v (ad loc. Isa. 1:2).

Christian is obliged to hear his Master whenever He speaks. As the Basel Reformer observed, if almighty God has stooped to accommodate Himself to us "and does not reject to speak Himself to us ingrates and sinners," should we not listen?[113] It is a mercy to be allowed to hear the living God's speech. But ears that are muffled by sin can hear only if opened by a heart of reverence. For those who attend His Word, it produces fruit, reflects God, and reveals inner hearts. The Bible communicates the unchangeable Word of God, which came with eternal certainty. Through it, the non-Christian is exhorted to believe God, while the Christian is exhorted not to be presumptuous. This obligation to hear God's Word is reinforced by the seriousness of the calling to the priesthood for all believers. Each Christian, whether clergyman or layman, has to attend God's Word.

3. Christ as the Goal of Preaching. The preaching office emerged through the humanistic movement, fresh and untamed. The content, form, and boundaries had yet to be defined. Preaching Scripture began penetrating beyond moralistic cultural aberrations to the individual sinner's heart. The source of obedience is faith in Christ, so Oecolampadius's own preaching centered on Christ. The Messiah, he said, is not a mere moral model, an assistant in self-help, or a ticket to heaven. He is almighty God, full of compassion toward those who turn to Him.

With this emphasis, the Reformer's messages were akin to Chrysostom's in that they appealed to the heart of a reborn soul. They appealed to his fundamental love for God. In Basel, the Reformer's preaching penetrated the believer's heart, not by goading, but through the beatific vision, through seeing Christ. All of life, with its temptations and difficulties, falls into proper perspective before Christ. Perception of Him and His presence sanctify and inspire. Since the reborn soul resonates with love at the sight of the Beloved, Oecolampadius displayed God and made the believer long for his Lover. "Indeed," he wrote, "the splendor of supreme

---

113. Oecolampadius, *In Iesaiam*, 6v (ad loc. Isa. 1:2).

glory and wisdom kindles souls with love for him."[114] Simply put, to preach the Word meant to preach Christ: "Because the Word of God is inspired by the Holy Spirit, I am unable not to affirm that in all places the Spirit of the Scriptures has regard for Christ Jesus in purpose, goal [*scopus*], and method."[115]

No harangues of "should do this," "need to do that," or "if you did this, then you would," were necessary according to Oecolampadius's approach: "But when the beauty of that splendor is loved, our own foulness is visited on us."[116] Such passion for God, he believed, propels men to destroy Babylon daily in their souls and in the world. Every virtue, including humility, springs from knowing God: "The true knowledge of God has this specially, that it may more greatly humble.... Do you understand from these things that the knowledge of God humbles, while worldly and pharisaical puffs up?"[117] Similar to the prophet Isaiah, a believer's reaction on beholding God encompasses both awe and shame. Oecolampadius's Christocentric preaching drew the spirits of God's children to their heavenly Father.

Man has blind eyes and deaf ears which no human preacher can open. God alone must heal the sinner: "The sense of Scripture does not come to any, except to those who also seek Christ and to whom Christ reveals Himself."[118] The preacher should understand that only God's Word and Spirit bring life, "lest namely the minister should glory in his ministry beyond what is fitting and that which belongs to God he should arrogate to himself."[119] The announcement of redemption must enter the believer's soul by God's loving action.

---

114. Oecolampadius, *In Iesaiam*, 58r (ad loc. Isa. 6:5). Oecolampadius, *ad Rhomanos*, preface: "For the goal of all Scripture is, to vindicate the glory of God, and that Christ may reign in all things, especially however in the hearts of men." Oecolampadius, *In Iesaiam*, 2r (preface): "For all Scripture sees Christ as its goal." Oecolampadius, *In Psalmos LXXIII*, 235 (ad loc. Ps. 137:3): "All our [Scriptures] are directed to this goal [scopus] that Christ Jesus be glorified, praised, and revered by all." Johannes Oecolampadius, *Commentarii omnes in libros Prophetarum* (Basel: Crispinus, 1558), Jona "Praefatio," 127: "Christ is the goal of all the prophets."

115. Oecolampadius, *In Ezechielem*, 73v (ad loc. Ezekiel 10).

116. Oecolampadius, *In Iesaiam*, 59r (ad loc. Isa.6:5).

117. Oecolampadius, *In Iesaiam*, 59v (ad loc. Isa. 6:5).

118. Oecolampadius, *In Iesaiam*, 2r (preface).

119. Oecolampadius, *In Iesaiam*, 60v (ad loc. Isa. 6:7).

Christ is the Shepherd who loved His flock unto His own death. He knew what it meant to be weak, and He carries, feeds, and protects His own, "leaving no stone unmoved" for their sake.[120] Seeing the splendor of this goodness sets a Christian's heart aflame with love.

4. The Glory of God in Preaching. Both the idea of God's mercy and the idea of man's faith can be strengthened by the preacher through looking at God's glory. The mere fact that man can hear God in His Word serves both of these purposes. God "accommodates Himself, as great and immense as He is, to our infirmity and does not reject to speak Himself to us, ingrates and sinners.... And He shows His beneficence: what is all flesh, that it should hear the voice of the living God, who speaks from the midst of fire, as we have heard, and is able to live?"[121] Oecolampadius emphasized this theme of glory throughout the Bible, because it elevated God while bending man in worship. For example, he rejoiced: "By the example of angels, pious priests are themselves exhorted to praise and bless God, that all things be to the glory of God. Truly this is greater glory, that the name of God began to become known in all the earth. For this reason the angels shout and rejoice, the archangels dance, and all the troops of angels. All earth is full of the mercy of God and His glory.... The glory breaks out [from the temple that is Christ] and communicates itself to the whole world."[122]

God's glory is so important that He ordained that everything done apart from Him should fall into the bottomless pit of vanity. The Basel Reformer highlighted this mysterious irony: the Immutable made earthly things mutable for His own glory. Even man's wisdom will be vanquished by the revelation of God, who is the true wisdom. In the consummate reversal, all things opposed to God's glory will serve His glory. These are glories to be proclaimed by the preacher.

120. Oecolampadius, *In Iesaiam*, 7r (ad loc. Isa. 1:2).
121. Oecolampadius, *In Iesaiam*, 6v–7r (ad loc. Isa. 1:2).
122. Oecolampadius, *In Iesaiam*, 58v (ad loc. Isa. 6:4).

5. Hope. Oecolampadius often directed Christians to hope in Scripture's final fulfillment, the consummation. At that time, Christ will finish the application of redemption. Justice, as accomplished in the substitutionary death of the just Christ for the unjust sinner, will be dispensed. God's justice will prevail over all creation. Just as Scripture demonstrates the Almighty's punishment of His enemies in the past, so it promises His complete victory in the future. Sin defeated at the cross will be completely crushed: "And through Him every day we conquer in ourselves Babylon. However, a full and true overthrow of the world will take place at the end of the ages of this world."[123] Liberation, in its truest sense, approaches when Christ approaches. Sin from within and all the results of sin from without will disappear when Christ appears. In all of life, this comforts the Christian. This was especially true during the Reformation, when plague, Turk, pope, and emperor threatened life.

6. Warnings. Dangers that arise from inside and outside the church have to be addressed by pastors. Oecolampadius knew that God's children should recognize impostors. He instructed believers to discern the antichrist by the way he uses deceit, self-confidently opposes God, prefers his own self-made rules, flaunts himself, employs the things of God for his own profit, mingles truth with falsehood, slanders godly leaders (especially "those who are purely teaching the Word of God, so that he may more freely tear in pieces the sheep left behind by them"), frightens believers where no danger exists, turns God's justice into injustice, pretends to be a friend, quotes Scripture, uses empty words to prevail, and extinguishes hope.[124] The hidden agenda of all evil, he explained, is "to lead us away from faith in God."[125] And why shouldn't Christians expect such warfare? Christ Himself had to withstand attacks tempting Him to not trust God, to misinterpret Scripture, to fear, and to be ensnared by worldly gifts.

---

123. Oecolampadius, *In Iesaiam*, 104v (ad loc. Isa. 13:1).
124. Oecolampadius, *In Iesaiam*, 195r (ad loc. Isa. 36:4).
125. Oecolampadius, *In Iesaiam*, 195r (ad loc. Isa. 36:4).

But the most grievous temptation that assails the heart is satanically whispered: "God does not love you." Oecolampadius wrote: "Behold, among these sure trials how often the Devil suggests that your faith is in vain and that you are among the number of the damned.... For just as when [we are] assured of God's grace, we are gladdened in conscience; so when we believe God is angry with us are we most greatly terrified; indeed, this is Hell itself."[126] Oecolampadius counseled those who needed their faith encouraged to look to Christ, who overcame evil: "And the demon can boast about his power because there is nothing like it on earth, but it is unfit for war against the City of God and the truly faithful.... And notice that the enemy says he can do nothing without the approval of God."[127] Christ unmasked Satan, defeated him, and sovereignly rules over all creation. Therefore, the believer can resist evil, knowing that his Lord Jesus is the faithful Victor.

7. The Gospel in Preaching. Scripture had to be applied by both cleric and layman not only to the faithful but also to the unfaithful. It was the apologetic plow that overturned the soil of hearts. Oecolampadius taught that Christians receive a commission to carry the gospel: "You have here what you ought to announce, namely the mercy and power and advent of Christ.... We who are the true announcers say, 'Behold your God.'... And our God is Christ."[128] No other message can suffice: "No one comforts, except the one who preaches faith."[129] The preaching of the gospel gives man the keys of the kingdom by which men are not only cleansed but absolved from their sins.[130]

What exactly was the gospel proclamation during the Reformation? How did someone evangelize early sixteenth-century souls? A key example is found in Oecolampadius's exposition of Isaiah 53:

---

126. Oecolampadius, *In Iesaiam*, 196r (ad loc. Isa. 36:10).
127. Oecolampadius, *In Iesaiam*, 196v (ad loc. Isa. 36:10).
128. Oecolampadius, *In Iesaiam*, 212r (ad loc. Isa. 40:9).
129. Oecolampadius, *In Iesaiam*, 210v (ad loc. Isa. 40:1).
130. Oecolampadius, *In Iesaiam*, 60v–61r (ad loc. Isa. 6:7).

How clearly it appears that none is without sin, and we all have
need of Christ the Redeemer; we have gone astray from Christ
the Shepherd, who brought us on [His] shoulders to the fold.…
We fall to our own way, when we do what is in us, left to ourselves, which when we do it, we sin. Our way is opposed to the
way that God shows. He says "we have turned" according to
the Hebrew, by which is indicated the internal passion of sinning.… He put on Him our sins.… Truly the blood of Christ
is precious which is reckoned for our sins…for you were like
straying sheep, but you were turned toward the Shepherd and
Healer of our souls.… Our sins which we ought to bear, He
bore. Not only from original sin but from all sins he freed us
and so reconciled us to the Father, reconciling things in heaven
and on earth.… He died not for His sins, but for the sins of
the people.… And in pledge, (that is in wound) our badness
is healed for us, that is in the resurrection of Christ, because
Christ died for our sins and rose for our justification.… For
He Himself is our righteousness, and bore iniquities, making
satisfaction for them…and He will be successful in what He
wants.… But He wants to kindle a fire, which He has come
to send into the world, that is, in order that the whole world
might believe.[131]

From this we see that the lay Christian also is obligated and
empowered by the overflowing love from Christ, known by faith
through the gospel.

In another section of his commentaries, Oecolampadius
declared the gospel message: "That is, He is said to have made
satisfaction and more than satisfaction for sins, since Christ made
satisfaction in our nature, because He with His innocent blood took
away the sin of the world. Even if we all suffered all things, we
could not make satisfaction for one little sin, Christ however made
satisfaction and more than satisfaction, as below [in chapter] 53."[132]
He added: "He triumphed over opposing powers, the Pharisees,
and the wise of this world, who are confounded by the word of the
cross, and made foolish and wrecked.… But our souls, captured and

---

131. Oecolampadius, *In Iesaiam*, 263v–264r (ad loc. Isa. 53:6).
132. Oecolampadius, *In Iesaiam*, 210v (ad loc. Isa. 40:2).

seduced by demons, were brought back by Christ, and He as a Victor brought away plunder from them."[133]

From these two examples, we can see the general content and tone of scriptural proclamation, at least according to one Reformer. It also contradicts the idea of any Mediator apart from Christ, of any sacrifice at the Mass beyond Christ's earthly work, and of any human ability to forgive sins which belongs to God alone. God lays His Word in a man's mouth so that through the Holy Spirit a hearer obtains salvation; thus, the speaker is given the keys of heaven, whether he be layman or clergyman. But Oecolampadius, as we have seen, was unique in his ability as a scholar and in his depth as a biblical expositor. His expansive comprehension of both God and His Word brought a powerful testimony to Basel.

8. Evangelizing Jews. Of particular evangelistic interest to Oecolampadius were the Jews, the descendants of Abraham by the flesh. This was at a time when the Jews were stigmatized, marginalized, and attacked. In his writings, he was careful to make his wording more accessible to Jewish readers. The Basel Reformer actually retranslated some biblical Hebrew names in his commentaries just to better communicate with contemporary Jews. Whenever there was a passage over which rabbis had stumbled, he would clarify the meaning. For instance, he rebutted the common Jewish interpretation that Isaiah 53 referred to the Jewish nation or Moses: "They are reproved in Scripture that they are in exile on account of their sins. And how truly shall they carry our iniquity, when they are not able to carry their own?... It is trivial to refute that some expound this saying concerning Moses. For he [Moses] did not make satisfaction for the Gentiles, or for the Jews, or even for himself."[134] Again, in Isaiah 6, Oecolampadius countered the Jewish interpretation of the threefold "holy," concluding that God Himself was holy in a threefold sense because of His trinitarian nature, apart from creation.[135]

---

133. Oecolampadius, *In Iesaiam*, 264r (ad loc. Isa. 53:12).
134. Oecolampadius, *In Iesaiam*, 264r (ad loc. Isa. 53:12).
135. Oecolampadius, *In Iesaiam*, 58r (ad loc. Isa. 6:3).

At the same time, he endorsed many rabbinical interpretations. For example, he indicated that the correct name for seraphim according to Jewish etymology was "burning ones." At one point, he referenced a Jewish tradition that claimed a timing coincidence of Sennacherib's defeat with the drowning of the Egyptians in the Red Sea. Later, he again mentioned a tradition that claimed that Sennacherib's death resulted from his plan to imitate Abraham's sacrifice in order to appease Israel's God. There was little or no evidence to support these observations. Perhaps these uses of Israelite traditions aided his solidarity with Jewish adherents and strengthened faith. The theme of Isaiah, the blinding of the Jews and the calling of the Gentiles, provided opportunity for him to call Jews back to God. His obvious heart's desire was to see Abraham's children embrace their Messiah. God blessed Oecolampadius during his ministry with the privilege of baptizing at least one Jewish believer.

Conclusion

Oecolampadius took the carefully exegeted Scriptures and zealously applied them to his culture, the church, himself, and lost souls. He believed all creation is intended to praise Christ. Each Christian through faith in Christ is to humble himself for the service of God and others, even as Christ did: "That which is most admirable, is that He who is most worthy and wise of all, should sink Himself to such astonishing servitude, so that in His appearance there appears no virtue.... Whence also He wants [us] to learn from Him humility and obedience, in order that no one might think himself too worthy to minister to others."[136] Men can learn the true way of life only by knowing God and His Word. This is a gift of God, not something manufactured by man: "Faith is had by those who see with the eye of the heart, who had God Himself as teacher."[137] Oecolampadius had been taught by the Master.

It remains a mystery of history how the life and writings of such a stellar saint slipped into the unknown. Clearly he was one of

---

136. Oecolampadius, *In Iesaiam*, 262r (ad loc. Isa. 52:15).
137. Oecolampadius, *In Iesaiam*, 4r (ad loc. Isa. 1:1).

the most outstanding Reformers of his time. His piety of life, wisdom in church and state affairs, boldness in preaching, concern for loving others, and decisiveness in humble leadership make his person a model for all time. The thoroughness, exactitude, philological and theological correctness of his scholarship, and the breadth and depth of his understanding, remain unsurpassed to this day. This is seen in the volumes of quality material he produced in a very short lifetime. The fresh biblical ideas of separation of church and state, church lay elders, excommunication, rewritten liturgy, Reformed catechism, university curriculum, and biblical exegesis, not to mention all the theological implications of a mature Reformed theology, flowed from him without pause.

Contemporaries would no doubt point to his ceaseless care for souls, visitations to the sick and grieving, circuits among outlying farms, pleadings for the lives and souls of wayward believers, and tenderness toward his wife and three little children. How many students, villagers, correspondents, and leaders were changed because of him? And yet, his sight was always set on the glory of the God whom he passionately loved and zealously followed, even when it was contrary to his retiring personality. As Karl Hammer points out, here was the ultimate combination of scholarship and practical Christian faith.[138]

Oecolampadius fulfilled his natal name "houselamp," proving to be a beacon in God's house. At the time of his death, he was writing an exposition on Colossians. His next verse could have been used to summarize the theme of his life: "If ye then be risen with Christ, seek those things which are above, where Christ sitteth on the right hand of God" (Col. 3:1). Several have pointed to church discipline as the Reformer's main contribution. Others are excited to see his connection with Calvin. My personal interest has been his

---

138. Hammer, "Der Reformator Oekolampad," 157–170, esp. 166. In fact, Hammer sees this as the main lasting result of Oecolampadius's life. He proposes that the Reformer blended the Reformation and humanism, orthodoxy and pietism, scholarship and praxis, doctrine and philology, being a professor and being a pastor. See also Karl Hammer, "Oecolampads Reformprogramm," *Theologische Zeitschrift* 37, no. 3 (May–June 1981): 149–163.

edifying exposition of Scripture. But Oecolampadius's own concern was always that God would receive glory from faithful men. God fulfilled that desire in his Reformation role, which continues today.

And I will give thee the treasures of darkness, and hidden riches of secret places, that thou mayest know that I, the LORD, which call thee by thy name, am the God of Israel. —Isaiah 45:3

CHAPTER FIVE

Worthy Words

PUBLICATIONS, TRANSLATIONS, WRITINGS

JOHANNES OECOLAMPADIUS was prolific in his writings. As a teenager, his bent for language evidenced itself first in a Latin poem written in elegiac couplets. But his first renown came as a collaborator with Desiderius Erasmus on the Greek New Testament of 1516, for which he penned a postscript and a hundred annotations on the Hebrew, and edited out theologically heretical statements. Their cooperation continued with a nine-volume edition of Jerome's works (1520) and later translations of John Chrysostom. During 1515–1516, Oecolampadius discovered an eleventh-century commentary by Theophylact that he translated and published. Four booklets on penance and confession, plus a Greek grammar (*Dragmata Graecae literaturae*) followed by mid-1518. The latter remained in use for at least one hundred years in various schools, including Paris.

While at the monastery from 1520–1521, he translated tracts by John of Damascus, the Gregories, and Basil the Great. A private document written for friends about Martin Luther's ideas called "Judicium" circulated at a time when it was most dangerous to be associated with Luther. Other works on pastoral concerns came out of this time, such as a litany for the sick and dying, "Confession and how it ought not to be burdensome to Christians" (1519), and *Paradoxon* (1521), on confession. In this latter work, an evangelical interpretation of Communion emerged: "Christ comes down from heaven in order to give Himself to us 'under the form of bread and wine' and so to incorporate Himself into His mystical body, the Church. In noteworthy manner, there already belongs to it also that we in Communion rise up to Christ in heaven."[1] Some will recognize similarities to the formulation that came later through John Calvin.

The stirring university lectures of 1523 on Isaiah and 1 John found their way into print as commentaries in 1524–1525. That same year, he confronted Erasmus in print with 154 passages from Augustine, Prosper, and Ambrose on free will. The next year, he produced a tract on the relief of the poor and another tract for the Frenchman Jacobus (Masson) Latomus. The massive and controversial *De Genuina Verborum Domini 'Hoc est corpus meum' juxta vetustissimos authores expositione liber* on Church Fathers' interpretations of the Eucharist appeared in 1525. Following this definitive tome, several short works on both baptism and Communion came into print in 1526–1527.

A rift, initiated by Luther, occurred in 1526. Oecolampadius had crafted two responses to a man who was afraid he might lose the mystery of faith if he conceded that the meaning of the words for Communion contained a trope. Luther viciously attacked the Basel Reformer in *Syngramma*. While Oecolampadius replied quietly in German with a summation of his own doctrine and a proposition for common ground, Luther enlarged and sharpened his *Syngramma*. Despite the antagonism, Luther admitted to reading during this time Oecolampadius's commentary on Isaiah, which was published before his own. There is at least one parallel in the commentaries. Oecolampadius wrote on Isaiah 37, "He who was seeking to slay the sons of God may be slain by his own sons." Luther observed, "[He] was finally massacred by his own sons, the one who wanted to kill the children of God." Considering the overlap in comments, at least a possibility of influence by Basel on Wittenberg may be conjectured.

Somehow, amidst his burgeoning responsibilities of 1528, Oecolampadius produced a translation of Cyril of Alexandria in three volumes. Then, using Erasmus's device of dialog with an imaginary

---

1. Locher, *Zwingli und die schweizerische Reformation*, 301.

character, he cited Church Fathers from Irenaeus and Athanasius to Theophylact and Hesychius concerning the Lord's Supper in "Quid de eucharistia veteres tum Graeci, tum Latini senserint, dialogus." This demonstrated his dual interest in truths from the Fathers and application to contemporary beliefs, which permeated his writing projects. Some even associated his name with the 1531 translation of a ninth-century monk's essay on the Lord's Supper ("Bertram" by Ratramnus). But the evidence remains tenuous, although an English contemporary, Nicholas Ridley, clearly assumed a connection.[2]

Biblical exegesis, however, filled more pages of Oecolampadius's corpus than translations and apologetics. Eventually, commentaries on Genesis, Job, Psalms, Isaiah, Jeremiah, Ezekiel, Daniel, Hosea, Joel, Amos, Obadiah, Jonah, Micah (chapters 1–2), Haggai, Zechariah, Malachi, Matthew, Romans, Colossians, Hebrews, and 1 John came into print. Both Jeremiah and Ezekiel were edited by Wolfgang Capito posthumously, with a biography of Oecolampadius attached to the Ezekiel foreword.

Dr. Ernst Staehelin, who devoted much of his scholarly life to locating and cataloging the writings of Oecolampadius, transcribed five hundred pertinent letters from 1527 to 1531 alone; some letters are to Oecolampadius, some from him, and some about him. The five hundred letters transcribed by Staehelin included only extant writings. Somehow, Basel's Reformer found time to communicate in script with famous personages such as Ulrich Zwingli, Heinrich Bullinger, Martin Bucer, Capito, Luther, Philip Melanchthon, Michael Servetus, Philip of Hesse, John X, William Farel, Johann Zwick, Leo Jud, Joachim Vadian, and the Waldensians. Correspondents also included the less-famous such as Simon Grynaeus, Willibald Pirkheimer, Otto Binder, Casper Megander, John Baptist Fischer, Thomas Gassner, Conrad Sam, Ambrosius Blaurer, Maris Stellae Wettingen, Johann Froben's family, Augustin Kramer, Jacob Augsburger, Johann Grel, Berchtold Haller, Franz Kolb, Erasmus Ritter, Niklaus Prugner, Melchior Ambach, Johann Mantel, Simprecht Schenk, Rudlof Ambühl, Wilhelm von Lupfen, Matthaeus

---

2. Jaroslav Pelikan, *Reformation of Church and Dogma (1300–1700)*, 199.

Alber, Johan Schradin, Martin Hans [Hubert], Martin Frecht, Nicolas Kniebs, George von Wurtemberg, Boniface Wolfhardt, and Boniface Amerbach. He also penned numerous memos to the City Council and councils in other cities, plus quarterly reports concerning his professorship. All this was accomplished by quill and ink. Clearly, God gave him a facility in the written word along with scholarly eloquence.

The following chronological compilation of Oecolampadius's writings comes mainly from Salomon Hess in the eighteenth century[3] and Staehelin in the twentieth century.[4] Not all entries have definitive publication dates. German spellings differ. An English translation of the entire publication listing is provided in quotes first, followed in brackets by the original title and listing. Some other explanatory notes may follow the brackets.

---

3. Salomon Hess, *Lebensgeschichte D. Johann Oekolampads, Reformators der Kirche in Basel*; nebst einem Anhang ungedruckter Briefe von Oekolampad an Zwingli (Zurich: Ziegler und Söhne, 1793).

4. Ernst Staehelin, *Oekolampad-Bibliographie*. 2. Aufl. (Nieuwkoop: De Graaf, 1963).

PUBLISHED WORKS DURING
OECOLAMPADIUS'S LIFETIME

1500   "Youth." ["Adolescentia."]

1512   "Declamations of Johannes Oecolampadius on [Christ's] Passion and Last Words." ["Declamationes Io. Oecolampadii De
passione & ultimo sermone."]; "Declamations on the Passion
and the Seven Words of Christ. 4 Argentor." ["Declamationes
de Passione et VII dictis Christi. 4 Argentor."]

1514   "A Poem on the History of Violence [Done to] the Cross."
["Carmen de historia violate crucis."]

1516   "*The entire New Testament*, carefully revised and edited by Erasmus of Rotterdam, with attention not only to the Greek..."
Basel: Froben, 1522. ["*Novum Testamentum* omne, diligenter ab
Erasmo Roterodamo recognitum & emendatum, non solum ad
graecam..." Basel: Frobenius, 1522.] Also 1523.

1517   "In this minor volume is contained a certain speech to the clergy by
Johannes Oecolampadius the theologian." ["Quae hoc, opusculo
continentur oratio Ioannis Oecolampadii Theologi ad Clerum."]

1518   "'On the Paschal laughter,' an apologetic epistle by Oecolampadius to W. Capito the theologian." Basel, 1518. The same book,
Ibid., 1540. ["'De Risu Paschali,' Oecolampadii, ad V. Capitonem theologum Epistola apologetica." Bas. 1518. Idem liber, 8.
ibid. 1540.]

Gleanings from Greek Literature, compiled by J. Oecolampadius
[*Dragmata Graecae Literaturae*, a Io. Oecolampadio congesta.
Also published in Basel 1520, 1523, in Paris de Gourmont,
1928; and another edition in 1535.]

"The Canons of Peter, Archbishop of Alexandria and Martyr,
on Penitence. The Canons of Gregory, the Bishop of Neocaesarea. The Encyclical letter of the Patriarch Gennadius of
Constantinople on Simony. The letter of Nicephorus Char-
tophylox the Archbishop of Constantinople on the Power of
Binding and Loosing. J. Oecolampadius translator." ["De poe-
nitentia Petri archiepiscopi. Alexandrini & martyris Canones.
Gregorii Neocaesariensis episcopi, Canones. De Simonia

Gennadii patriarchae Constantinopolitani Encyclia epistola. De Ligandi et Solvendi Potestate, Nicephori Chartophylacis Constantinopoli, archiepi. epistola. Io. Oecolampadio Interprete."]

1519 "Notes on the *New Testament* of Des. Erasmus of Rotterdam, newly revised, recently augmented by substantial addition." ["Des. Erasmi Roterodami in *Novum Testamentum* ab eodem denuo recognitum, Annotationes, ingenti nuper accessione per autorem locupletatae."]

"A sermon of Gregory Nazianzus, Bishop and theologian, on loving the poor. An admonition to a virgin, by the same. Praises of the Maccabees, by the same. Translated by J. Oecolampadius, preacher at Augsburg." ["De Amandis pauperibus, Gregorij Nazanzeni Episcopi & Theologi sermo. Eiusdem ad virginem admonitorius. Eiusdem laudes Maccabaeorum. Interprete Io. Oecolampadio concionatore Augustensi."]

"Some learned and noteworthy sermons of the divine Gregory Nazianzus on Passover according to Matthew, 'when Jesus had taken up these words....' Chapter 19. Praises of Cyprian the Martyr. Oecolampadius translator. A Speech of Oecolampadius given to the clergy at Augsburg on Christ's exhortation to Peter when he refused the foot washing." ["Divi Gregorii Nazanzeni eruditi aliquot et miraefrugis sermones In Pascha In dictum Matthaei, cum consummasset Ihesus sermones hos etc. Cap. xix Laudes Cypriani martyris. Oecolampadio interprete. Oratio Oecolampadij habita ad Clerum Augustensem, de expostulatione Christi cum Petro ablutionem pedum recusante."]

"The letters of famous men in Hebrew, Greek, and Latin to John Reuchlin Phorcensis, the most learned man of our age, sent at various times, to which is added a second book never previously published." ["Illustrium virorum epistolae, Hebraicae, Graecae et Latinae, ad Ioannem Reuchlin Phorcensem virum nostra aetate doctissimum diversis temporibus missae, quibus iam pridem additus est liber secundus nunquam antea editus."]

"A new collection of letters of Des. Erasmus Rotterdam to various men, and of others to him: some things are included which he wrote while yet a youth." ["Farrago nova epistolarum Des. Erasmi Roterodami ad alios, & aliorum adhunc: admixtis quibusdam, quas scripsit etiam adolescens."]

"Of the fruitful and also harmful winds of the garden of the soul. A useful sermon for wise virgins who would be like St. Katherine. A rule for true Christian virgins translated out of the Greek into German." ["Von den fruchtbarlichen auch von den schödlichen winden des gartens der Seele. Ain nutzlicher Sermon von den weysen Junckfrawen dero sancta Katherina aine gewesen ist. Ain Regiment der waren Christenlichen junckfrawen auss greckischer sprach in teutsch gepracht."]

1519/1520 "The 'unlearned' Lutheran Canons. ([Also called:] "Part II of the works R.P.D. Martin Luther, Augustinian Wittenberg.)" ["Canonici indocti Lutherani. ([Also called:] Secunda Pars operum R.P.D. Martini Lutherii, Augustiniani Wittenbergensis.") Also found in German as: "Die verdeutscht antwort der die Doctor Eck in seinem Sendbrieff an den Bischoff zu Meyssen hat die ungelarten Lutherischen Thumhern genandt."]

1520 "On charity: self-control and governing the soul, four hecatombs of Thalassius, translated by J. Oecolampadius. Here, reader, you will find 400 truly divine sayings which will lend guidance to your soul if you be a godly person." Aug. 1520. ["De charitate: continentia et regimine mentis Thalassii Hecatontades quattuor Io. Oecolampadio interprete. Habes hic lector Sententias quadringentas vere divinas, animaeque tuae conducibiles, modo adsis pius. Aug. 1520."] See also: "Thalasii Hecatontades quatuor, ex graeco in latinum. Aug. 1520."

"The Confession of Christian Penitence, from ten principles, teaching on all sorts of duties and errors in human morals, by Jodux Windesheim, public speaker at the famous French city Herbipolim Hagensium." ["Christiani Poenitentis confessio e decem praeceptis, humanorum morum et officia et errata quamlibet multa per stringens; per Ioducum Vuindshemium apud inclytam Francorum Herbipolim Hagensium concionatorem."]

"How much do the good works of the living benefit the dead. A sermon of John of Damascus. Translated by Johannes Oecolampadius." ["Quantum defunctis prosint viventium bona opera sermo Ioannis Damasceni, Ioanne Oecolampadio interprete."]

"An index to all the volumes of the divine Jerome, with translation of the Greek and Hebrew names, arranged in order by Johan. Oecolampadius theologian." ["Index in tomos omnes, operum Divi Hieronymi cum interpretatione nominum Graecorum et Hebraeorum, per Ioan. Oecolampadium, Theologum in ordinem digestus."]

"By Johan. Oecolampadius, a Sermon on the Sacrament of the Eucharist." ["Ioan+ Oecolampadii sermo de sacramento eucharistiae."] Also called in German: "Ain Predig und ermanung Joannis Oecolampadij von wirdiger erennbietung dem Sacrament des fronleichnam Christi. Mit Rö. Kan. Ma. Frenhait."

"A paraphrase of the divine Gregory, Bishop of Neocaesarea, of Solomon's Ecclesiastes, translated by Oecolampadius." This booklet is indeed short but very profitable, as the divine Jerome says. ["In ecclesiastem Solomonis metaphrasis divi Gregorii Neocaesariensis episcopi. Interprete Oecolampadio." Libellus hic breuis qdem est sed valde utilis, ut ait divus Hieronymus.] Hess lists it separately at the end of his bibliography under translations of the Greek Fathers, "Of Gregory of Neocaesarea, a Paraphrase on Solomon's Ecclesiastes and the Canticles." ["Gregorii, Neocaesariensis, Metaphrasis in Ecclesiast: Salomonis et Cant."]

"A Sermon on the Sacrament of the Eucharist." ["Concio de Sacramento Eucharistiae."] In German: "Predig vom Sacrament der Danksagung."

"On the Sacred Meal." Tübingen. 1520. ["De Sacra Coena." Tubingae. 1520.]

"On praising God in Mary, a sermon of Johannes Oecolampadius, doctor of theology." ["De laudando in Maria Deo Doctoris. Io. Oecolampadii theologi sermo."] Also called in German: "Ain Sermon des hochgelerten Doctors der hayligen geschrift Joannis Oecolampadij wie wir gott in Maria loben sollen."

"A registry or arrangement [bibliography?] of everything written by the holy Basil and translated into German by Oecolampadius." ["Ain Regiment oder ordnung der ganstlichen beschriben durch den hayligen Basilium und in teutsch gebracht durch Oecolampadium."]

1520/1521 "A judgment of Oecolampadius on Doctor Martin Luther." ["Oecolampadii iudicium de Doctore Martino Luthero."] Also called in German: "Oecolampadii der heyligen schrifft Doctor

Sant Brigitten ordens zu Alltenmünster urteyl und maynung auch andere reden antwurten von handlung Doctor Martin Luther belangend auss dem latein in Teütsch gebracht."

1521 "'That confession of a Christian is not burdensome, by Johannes Oecolampadius.' Discover, reader, how light is the Lord's burden, and how carefully He cares for His Church lest He burden them. You will find here rare, learned, pleasing, and needful things. Buy and take joy! Basel: 1521." [" 'Quod non sit onerosa Christianis confessio, paradoxon Ioannis Oecolampadii.' Experire Lector quam leve sit onus Domini, quam ubique diligenter curet Ecclesia, ne suos oneret, Rara, erudita, grata et necessaria reperies. Eme et Laetaberis. Basel: 1521."] Also called in German: "Ein lere von bewerung das die beicht ainen Christen menschen nitt burdlich oder schwer sen beschriben durch Jo. Hauszschein sust genant Oecolampadius sant Brigitten ordens." See also: "Dass die Beicht einem Christem nich beschwerlich sey. Basel. 1521. 4. auch lateinisch, eben daselbst 'quod non sit onerosa Christianis confessio.'"

"By Oecolampadius, a sermon on the joy of the resurrection, in which [he deals with] the mystery of the three days, against the sophists. Another of the same, on the words of Thomas, 'My Lord and my God,' in which [he deals with] true poverty." Basel: 1521. ["Io. Oecolampa. De gaudio resurrectionis sermo, in quo de mysterio tridui contra sophistas. Eiusdem alius. In verba Thomae Dominus meus, et Deus meus. In quo de vera paupertate." Basel: 1521.] In German: "Sermones de gaudio resurrectionis et mysterio tridui." Bas. 1521. 4.

"A sermon of Johannes Oecolampadius on the sacrament of the eucharist." ["Ioan. Oecolampadii sermo de sacramento eucharistiae."]

"By Oecolampadius, Doctor of Holy Scripture, of the order of Saint Brigitte at Altomünster, judgment and meaning and other speeches, answers, and action concerning Doctor Martin Luther, translated from Latin to German. 1521." ["Oecolampadii der heyligen schrifft Doctor Sant Brigitten ordens zu Altemmünster urteyl und maynung auch andere reden antwurten unn handlung Doctor Martin Luther belangend auss dem latein in Teütsch gebracht. M.D.XXI."]

"A most salutary small book about whether the obligation of confession is divine or human, and how far it binds Christians. By Doctor Johannes Oecolampadius, a professor most learned in true and pure theology, in Greek, in Hebrew, and in Latin. May the reader find that the burden of the Lord is light, and that where the church diligently looks after its people, it does not burden them. May you obtain things rare, learned, pleasing, and necessary." Eme and Loetaberis. 1521. ["De Confessionis obligatione, divina ne sit, an humana, et quatenus Christianos arctet, Libellus saluberrimus, D. Joannis Oecolampadij vere pureque theologie professoris, Grecece, Hebraice, Latineque doctissimi. Experire lector quod leve sit onus Domini, q ubi que diligenter curet Ecclesia, ne suos oneret, Rara, erudita, grata et necessaria reperies Eme et Loetaberis. Anno. xxi."]

"A sermon and exhortation of Johannes Oecolampadius about the valuable calling to remembrance of the body of Christ in the sacrament." ["Ain Predig und ermanung Joannis Oecolampadij von wirdiger erennbietung dem Sacrament des fronleichnam Christi. Mit Rö. Kay. Ma. Freyhait."]

1521/22 "A sermon by Johannes Oecolampadius from the verse in the Magnificat, 'My spirit exulted in God my Salvation.'" ["Ain Sermon Jo. Oecolampadij, von dem vers im Magnificat. 'Exultavit spiritus meus in Deo Salutari meo.'"]

"A most wise sermon of Gregory of Nanzianzus on the moderating of disputes. Johan. Oecolampadius translator." ["De moderandis disputationibus Gregorij Nazanzeni sapientissimus sermo. Ioan. Oecolampadio interprete."] Hess also lists this at the end under translations from the Greek Fathers: "Of Gregory Nazianzus, a Talk on Moderating Debates; On the Praises of Cyprian; On Loving the Poor; On the Praises of the Maccabees." ["Gregorii, Nazianzeni, Sermo de moderandis disputationibus; de laudibus Cypriani; de amandis pauperibus; de laudibus Machabaeorum."]

1522 "A Sermon about Simeon's Prayer in Luke 2 (Nunc dimittis), preached by Doctor Johannes Oecolampadius, on our Women's Candlemas Day." ["Ain Predig uber das Nunc dimittis, gepredigt von Doctor Jo. Oecolampadius, an unserer Frauen Lichtmesstag."] Also called: "Trostlich den Sterbenden."

"'Against the Usurer, and How Harmful It Is To Take up the Spirit of a Usurer,' a Sermon by Saint Basil, recently translated into German by Oecolampadius, to the Thumherren of Augsburg, dedicated to Bernhardt Udelmann von Udelmannsfelden. Augsburg." ["'Wider die Wucherer, und wie schädlich es sey, Wuchergelt auf sich zu nehmen,' ain Predig des heil. Basilii, neulich verteütschet dürch Oekolampadium, dem Thumherren zu Augsburg, Bernhardt Udelmann von Udelmannsfelden gewidmet. Augs."]

"An Epistle to Casp[ar] Hedio, with his response, That it is useful for the common people to promulgate the reading of the Gospel in the Mass in the vernacular speech." ["Epistola ad Casp: Hedionem, cum ejus responso: quod expediat Evangelii lectionem in missa vernaculo sermone plebi promulgari."]

"The Life of John of Damascus written by John the Patriarch of Jerusalem, recently put into Latin verse by Oecolampadius." ["*Ioannis Damasceni Vita*, a Ioanne Patriarcha Hierosolymitano conscripta, nuperque ab Oecolampadio in Latinum versa."]

"On the Apostle's saying to the Corinthians, 'when all things shall be subjected to Him, then also the Son Himself will be subjected, etc;' On the cleansing of leprosy; On the mystery of the Trinity and the horn of oil. A sermon of John Chrysostom, Bishop of Constantinople, translated by J. Oecolampadius, of Moguntia in his twenty-second year." ["In dictum Apostoli ad Corinthios. 'Cum autem subiecta fuerint illi omnia, tunc et filius ipse subijcietur ei etc.' De mundatonne leprosi, de mysterio ternarij, et cornu olei." Sermo B. Ioannis Chrysostomi interprete Io. Oecolampadio. Moguntiae an. XXII.] Also called: "The fifth book of the works of the divine John Chrysostom, Bishop of Constantinople, containing forty-five homilies." ["Tomus quintus operum divi Ioannis Chrysostomi episcopi Constantinopolitani, Continens Homilias XLV."]

"Fifth volume of the works of the divine John Chrysostom, Bishop of Constantinople, containing 45 sermons. Six books on the priestly dignity. Two books on the pricking of the heart. A single book on the recovery of the lapsed. Three books on the providence of God. Thirty-six sermons, the summaries of which you will find on the following page. They especially treat the incomprehensible nature of God. Five homilies against

the Antinomians. Translated by [from?] Theodore the Thessa-
lonican of Gaza. The first exhortation is to Theodore." ["De
dignitate sacerdotali, Lib. VI. De compunctione cordis, Lib.
II. De reparatione lapsi, Lib. unicum. De providentia Dei, Lib.
III. Sermones XXXVI. Quorum omnium argumenta comper-
ies pagina sequenti. Praeterea accesserunt De incomprehensibili
dei natura. Contra Anomaeos, Homiliae V. Theodoro Gaza
Thessalonicens i interprete. Ad Theodorum Paraenesis prior."]

"A homily on the Apostle's saying, 'If only you had endured a
little of my foolishness,' translated by Wolfgang Fabritius Capito. A homily on the Apostle's saying to the Corinthians, 'When
all things shall be subjected to Him, then also the Son Himself
will be subjected to Him.' On the saying of the Apostle, 'There
must be heresies, etc.' A homily translated by Johannes Oecolampadius." ["De eo quod dixit Apostolus: 'Utinam tolerassetis
paululum quiddam insipientiae meae,' Homilia, Guolphango
Fabritio Capitoni interprete. In dictum Apostoli ad Corinthios:
'Cumsubiecta fuerint illi omnia, tunc et filius ipse subiicietur
ei,' Homilia. In dictum Apostoli: 'Oportet haereses esse, etc.'
Homilia Ioanne Oecolampadio interprete."]

"A sermon of the divine John Chrysostom concerning alms and
the collection for the saints; on the words of Paul from his first
epistle to the Corinthians, not previously published in Latin.
Translated by Joh. Oecolampadius. Aug.: Vindel." ["Divi Ioannis Chrysostomi Sermo de Eleemosyna et collatione in Sanctos,
in verba Pauli ex priore ad Corinthios epl'a, Hactenun latine
non aeditus. Io. Oecolamp. Interprete. Aug.: Vindel."] Also
called in German: "Ain Sermon: Sancti Johannis Chrysostomi
vonn dem Almusen über die wort Pauli in der ersten Epistel
deren von Corinth. in Latin vonn Oecolampad. anzangt und
durch Joann. Dieboldt zu Ulm verteütscht."

*The Text of the Book of Genesis according to the Septuagint Transla-
tors.* Basel. [*Textus libri Geneseos secundum LXX. interpretes.* Basel.]

1523   "Epistle on not having collection for the poor, a most useful letter by Joh. Oecolampadius. Basel." ["Epistola de non habendo
pauperum delectu, Io. Oecolampadii Epistola utilissima.
Basel."] Also called in German: "Von usstenlung des Almu-
sens erstmals von Joanne Oecolampadio in Latin beschribben

und netz durch doctorn Thunradum Peutingern von Augspurb vertütschet. Vast nutzlich allen christen menschen zulesen."

"On the Passion of Christ; On the Veneration and Praise of God in Mary; On the Invocation of the Saints against Faber. Basel." ["De passione Christi; de venerando et laudando in Maria Deo; de invocaione Divorum contra Fabrum. Basel."]

Handbook of Greek Literature. In the same year. [*Enchiridion graecae litteraturae.* ib. eod.]

"Some censures of John Chrysostom, recently rendered into Latin verse for the first time by Johannes Oecolampadius with notes by the same. The next page provides an index to them." ["Divi Ioannis Chrysostomi Psegmata quaedam, nuperrime à Ioanne Oecolampadio in latinum primò versa: cum adnotationibus eiusdem. Quorum omnium indicem proxima pagella indicabit."]

Theses for a disputation with the opening line: "Johannes Oecolampadius: Grace and peace from Christ to the Christian brothers." ["Ioannes Oecolampadius Christianis Fratribus gratiam et pacem á Christo."]

"Sixty-six homilies on the whole book of Genesis by the divine Chrysostom, Archbishop of Constantinople, translated this year by Johannes Oecolampadius. It contains also the text of Genesis according to the Septuagint edition, which practically all the early authors used. Oecolampadius also translated this." ["Divi Ioannis Chrysostomi, Archiepiscopi Constantinopolitani, in totum Geneseωs librum Homiliae sexagintasex, à Ioanne Oecolampadio hoc anno versae. Habes praeterea textum Geneseωs, iuxta septuaginta interpretum aeditionem, qua authores prisci fermè omnes usi sunt, eodem interprete."] See also the 1532 entry.

"A comparison between a king and a monk, by the divine John Chrysostom Recently translated by Johannes Oecolampadius." ["Comparatio. Regis et Monachi, Authore Divo. Io. Chrysostomo, nuper à Ioanne Oecolampadio versa."]

"A litany to God the Father. [How] to speak and pray comfortingly to all fearful miseries and the miseries of those who are about to die. Preached at the old Munster [Cathedral]." ["Ain Lettanen zü Gott dem vatter. Inn allen angsten unnd den sterbenden in todes nöten trostlich vor zusprechen unnd zu beten. Ausgangen zu alten Münster."]

"The testimony of Jesus Christ that one until now has called the Mass, translated into German by Johannes Oecolampadius cleric of Adelnburg to all Evangelicals." ["Das Testament Jesu Christi das man bisher genent hat die Mess verteutscht durch Joannem Oecōlampadiō Ecclesiasten zu Adelnburg zu heyl allen Ewangelischen."]

1523/24 "A short daily prayer to God and of the knowledge of his [man's] own false ground and the old Adam, preached at the Altomunster [monastery], communicated to the nuns there on a blessed new year of 1524." ["Ain Kurtze tägliche Beicht zu Gott und von Erkentnis sein selbst falschen Grundts und des alten Adams zu Altenmünster aussgangen, den Closterfrauen daselbst zu einem säligen neuen Jahr des 1524 mittaylt."]

"Oecolampadius's Sermon on the Sunday after the Observance of the Three Holy Kings Day." ["Oecolampadii Sermon am Sontag nach dem Achteden der hailigen drey Künig tag."]

"Notes on the Epistle of the blessed Apostle Paul to the Romans, read by Johannes Oecolampadius at Basel, with index." ["In Epistolam B. Pauli Apost. ad Rhomanos Adnotationes à Ioanne Oecolampadio Basileae praelectae. Cum Indice."] Also called: "Annotations on the Epistle to the Romans, given in lecture and revised by Jo. Oecolampadius." 1525 and 1526. Basel." ["Annotationes in epistolam ad Romanos, à Jo.Oecolampadio praelectae et denuo recognitae,1525 et 1526, Basel."]

"Concerning Secret Confession, by Jacob Latomus, professor of theology. Johannes Oecolampadius's cure for the same, to Jacob Latomus." ["Iacobi Latomi Theologiae Professoris de Confessione Secreta. Ioannis Oecolampadii Elleboron, pro eodem Iacobo Latomo."] Also in 1525: "*Elaborum* on behalf of Jacob Latomus." Basel. ["Eleborum pro Jacobo Latomo," Basel.]

"A conversation of some preachers held at Basel with some advocates of rebaptism." ["Ein gesprech etlicher predicanten zu Basel gehalten mitt etlichen bekennern des widertouffs."] Staehelin lists this as: "A conversation of some preachers held at Basel with some advocates of rebaptism. Basel, 1525 by

Valentin Curio, in 4 [volumes?], and in Augsburg, 1525, in 4 [volumes?] by Silvanus Ottomar. Also, in Simmler's *Collection for the Elucidation of the Church History of Switzerland.* T.I. P. II, 492–517; and in *The Most Interesting [Writings] of Switzerland,* IV. 105–130." ["Ein Gesprech etlicher Predicanten zu Basel, gehalten mitt etlichen Bekennern des Wiedertauffs. Basel. 1525. Durch Valentin Curio, in 4, und zu Augspurg 1525. in 4. durch Silvanus Ottomar, auch in Simmlers *Sammi, zur Beleuchtung der Kirchengesch: des Schweizeri.* T.I.P.II. 492–517. und im *Interessantesten der Schweiz.* IV. 105–130."]

"The form and manner to be used and practiced at Basel for the Lord's Supper, infant baptism and visiting the sick (at home). The truth remains forever." ["Form und gestalt Wie das Herren Nachtmal der kinder Tauff Der Krancken haymsuchung zu Basel gebraucht und gehalten werden. Die warhait bleybt Ewig."] See also entry below under 1526.

Summary of Divine Writings. [*Summa der Godliker Scrifturen.*] This publication appeared in the Netherlands between 1523 and 1526, later appearing in German at the hands of a Stuttgart publisher in 1526. Staehelin lists in Dutch: "Summary of the divine Scriptures, or a Dutch theology: teaching and instructing all people, what the Christian faith is, whereby we all as members [?] become holy, and what baptism means, according to the teachings of the holy Evangelists and Saint Paul's Epistles. Now again very carefully corrected [edited]." ["Summa der godliker scrifturen Oft een Duytsche Theologie; leerende ende onderwijsende alle menschen, wat het Christen gheloove is, waer doer wi alle gader salich worden, ende wat het doopsel bediedt, na de leeringe des heylighen Evangelijs ende sinte Pauwels Epistelen. Nu weder om seer neerstelick ghecorrigeert."] Staehelin also lists it in 1557 as, "Summa der godliker scripfturen oft een duytsche Theologie leerende enn onderwiisende alle menschen wat dat Christen ghelooue is waer duer wi alle gader salich worden enn wat dat doopsel bediet nae die leeringhe des heyligen Euangeliis ende sinte Pauwels Epistelen. Nu wederom seer neerstelijk ghecorrigeert."

1524   "On free will, very learned short works of the divines Prosperus, Augustine, and Ambrose..." ["De Libero Arbitrio, Divorum Prosperi, Augustini et Ambrosii opuscula perquam erudita,..."]

"'On the Giving of Alms,'—the same book, translated into German by D. Conrad Peutinger. Basel, 1524. ["'De erogatione elecmosynarium'—idem lib: germ: per D. Conr: Peutingerum. Bas., 1524."]

"Public Speeches: that is, Twenty-one Addresses on the First Epistle of John. Neocaesarea." ["Demegoriae. i.e. Conciones XXI in epistolam Johannis I. Neoc.] Also called, "Public speeches (that is twenty-one homilies) of Johannes Oecolampadius on the First Catholic epistle of John the Apostle." ["In Epistolam Ioannis Apostoli Catholicam primam, Ioannis Oecolampadij demegoriae, hoc est homiliae una et XX."]

"A Detailed Exposition by Theophylact on the four Gospels, rendered from Greek into Latin. Ibid in the same [year?]" [Theophylacti in quatuor Evangelia ennarrationes, ex Graeco in lat, versa. ibid eod.] Also in 1528: "Lectures on the four Gospels by Theophylact, Archbishop of Bulgaria, translated by Johannes Oecolampadius." ["Theophylacti Archiepiscopi Bulgariae, in quatuor Euangelia enarrationes, Ioanne Oecolampadio interprete."] Also 1525, 1527, 1528, 1531, 1532, 1534. Staehelin lists it in 1527 as, "Theophylacti Archiepiscopi Bulgariae, in Quatuor Evangelia Enarrationes, Diligenter Recognitae. Basileae, Apus Andream Cratandrum, anno MDXXVII." Staehelin also lists it around 1530 as "Theophylacti Archiepiscopi Bulgariae in quatuor Euangelia enarrationes, iam nunc multo diligentius, tum exactius, q antea, reuisae atq recognitae Ioanne Oecolampadio interprete"; and in 1534 as "Theophylacti Archiepiscopi Bulgariae in Quatuor Evangelia enarrationes Luculentissime diligenter iam tandem et adamussim recognite, cum indice copioso et utili."

"Disputation of Priests Ee [geographic designation?] by Stephen Stör of Diessenhoffen, dwelling at Liechstal, and many other Christian brothers in honorable gathering at Basel in council, on the 16th day of February in 1524." ["Von der Priester Ee disputation durch Stephanum Stör von Diessenhoffen wonhafft zu Liechstal und andern vyl Christlicher brüdern in eerlicher versamlung zu Basel im Collegio am xvj. tag Februarij im xxiiij. jar gehalten."]

"Sermons on the First Epistle of John, translated from Latin by Caspar Hedio, it. Hedio's Message to those from Mainz, 12,

1524." ["Predigten über die I, Epistel Johannis, aus dem latein-
ischen übersesst, durch Caps. Hedio, it. Hedionis Missiv an die
von Mainz. 12. 1524."]

1525   "Johannes Oecolampadius's *On the Genuine Words of the Lord*,
'This is My body': a book in expositing according to the most
ancient authors. Basel, 1525." ["Ioannis Oecolampadii *De
Genuina Verborum Domini*, Hoc est corpus meum, iuxta vetustissimos authores, expositione liber. Basel, 1525."]

"An Epistle to the Brothers preaching Christ throughout Swabia.
Ibid." ["Epistola ad Frates per Sueviam Christum annunciantes.
Ibid."]

"*A Commentary on the Prophet Isaiah* in six books, by Johannes
Oecolampadius." ["*In Iesaiam Prophetam Hypomnematon*, hoc
est, commentariorum, Ioannis Oecolampadii Libri VI."] Basel:
Cratander. Staehelin lists an enlarged edition with notes on Genesis and the Psalms published in 1564 as "Esaiae prophetia cum
catholica expositione ecclesistice, quan augustinus marloraus,
Verbi Dei minister in sacris literis exeercitatissimus, es theologis omnium huius seculi praestantissimis excerpsit suumque in
eam symbolum contulit. Adiectus est inces locuples et artifici-
ose digestus, huic Expositioni communi cum eiusdem generis
expositionibus in Genesin et in Psalmos, antehac ab eodem
marlorato editis."

1525/1526 "Antitreatise to the Swabian churches, along with a treatise of theirs. Published together in Basel. 1525. 8.N.2. Also
separately published in Zurich. 1526." ["Antisyngramma ad
Ecclesiastes Suevos, una cum horum Syngrammate. Gensam-
mengedruckt zu Basel, 1525. 8.N.2. auch zu Zurich besonders
gedruckt, 1526."]

1526   "Concerning the Lord's Supper, evidence from the Gospel writings, where the account is, that the Lordss Supper is understood
and interpreted incorrectly,...by Johannes Oecolampadius,
translated for Christian common use by Ludwig Hätzer. 1526."
["Vom Nachtmal, Beweisung auss evangelischen Schrifften,
wer die seyen, so des Herren Nachtmals wort unrecht verstan-
den und ausslegen,...durch Ioan. Ecolampadium Christlicher
gemein zu nutz verdeutscht durch Ludwig Hätzer—O Gott
erlöss die Gefangnen. 1526."]

"Concerning the Sacrament of the Eucharist, about the true natural understanding of Christ's words 'This is My Body' according to the explanation of very old doctrines. Written in Latin by Johannes Oecolampadius, translated into German by Ludwig Haetzer. (1526 Zurich by Froschauer to the House of Wyngarten.) With Haetzer's peculiar preface, why he translated this writing without Oecolampadius's knowledge, and that he was drawn away from the doctrine of rebaptism by Zwingli in Zurich, also that the rebaptizers stood entirely indifferent and without scriptural basis before Zwingli." ["Vom Sacrament der Danksagung, von dem waren natürlichen Verstand der Worten Christi 'das ist mein Leib' nach der gar alten Lehrern Erklaerung, in latein beschrieben durch D. Joh. Oekolampadium, verdeutscht durch Ludwig Haetzer. (1526 Zurich by Froschower im Huss zum Wyngarten.) mit Haetzers merkwürdiger Borrede, warum er diese Schrift ohne Oekolampads Wissen übersesst, und dass er von Zwinglin zu Zürich, von der Lehr des Widertaufs sen abgebracht worden, auch dass die Widertaüfer ganz lau und Schriftlos vor Zwingli bestanden.] Staehelin's listing adds the following phrase after Haetzer's name: "O Gott erlöss die gefangenen."

"A speech given in 1526 before the Senate of Basel on the Restoration of Apostolic Excommunication; a synodical speech." ["Oratio habita 1526. coram senatu Bas: de reducenda excommunicatione apostolica; oratio synodica."] Staehelin lists it in 1528 as, "Repulsio Apologiae Sacrificii Eucharistiae quam Pelargus Factionis s. Dominici, Senatui Basilien. Obtulit." Per Ioannem Oecolampadium.

"The form and manner how infant baptism, the Lord's Supper, and visiting the sick at home is practiced in Basel by some preachers, 1526, in 8. Under this title there are two writings available, an earlier one without date, which must have been printed in the first years of the Reformation.—The old customs: the power which those priests grant by the absolution, the deliverance for the sick: the Lord's Supper offered at the death bed, and still standing burning candles on the altar, is still in it maintained and the later one from its above title and date. Haller calls it, in his critical index, an extremely rare church order, yet which was already to some extent purified of Catholicism, although the Reformation was still not completely inaugurated. Oecolampadius is the author, he has also written the introduction. Other new and amended editions are Basel 1537.8. Mullhausen, 1565.8. Basel 1591.8. Basel 1602.12. Basel 1634.8. Basel 1666.8. Basel 1701.8. Basel 1752.8." ["Form und Gestalt, wie der Kindertauf, des herrn Nachtmal, der Kranken Heimzuchung ist zu Basel von etlichen Predikanten gehalten werden. 1526. In 8. Unter diesem Titel find zwey Schriften vorhanden; eine fruhere, ohne Jahrzal, welche in den ersten Jahren der Reformation gebrukt senn muss.—Die alten Gewohnheiten, kraft deren die Priester die Absolution ertheilen, den Kranken das heil: Nachtmal auf dem Todbett reichen, und noch auf dem Altar brennende Kerzen stehen, find darinn noch beybehalten—und die spatere von obigem Titel und Dato. Haller nennt sie, in seinem critischen Verzeichnitz, eine hochst seitene Kirchenordnung, die doch schon einigermassen vom Catholicismus gereinigt sen, obgleich die Reformation noch nich ganzlich eingefuhrt war. Oekolampad ist der Verfasser, hat auch die Vorrede geschrieben. Andere neue und abgeanverte Ausgaben sind. Basel 1567.8. Muhlhausen 1565.8. Basel 1590.8. Basel 1602, 12. Basel 1634.8. Basel 1666. 8. Basel 1701.8. Basel 1752,8.] Staehelin lists it as apparently included in a larger compendium in 1590 as "Das Geistliche und herzliche Kleinot der Kirchen Gottes in Statt und Landtschafft Basel: Nemlichen I. Die confession oder Bekanntdnutz des heiligen Christlichen Glaubens. II. Der Catechismus oder Kinderberich für die jugendt. III Das Agendtbuch von Christlichen Kirchenbreuch und Ordnungen die in der Gemeine Gottes und bey den Kranken geübet werden. Auffs neüw Gott zu Lob under der Gemein Gottes zu heilsamer Lehre und Trost alles wol wider ubersehen wie in volgender Vorrede zu sehen: und mit fleiss getruckt: durch Sebastianum Henricpetri."

"Two apologetic talks on the dignity of the Eucharist, of which he gave the first on the day of Saint Thomas from the Gospel of John chapter 21, the latter on the eve of Christ's birth at Basel. Tig., 1526." ["De dignitae Eucharistiae, Sermones II, apologetici: quorum priorem in die S. Thomae, lecto Evangelio Joannis XXI, posteriorem in vigilia natalis Christi Basileae habuit. S. Tig. 1526."] Staehelin also lists it around 1550 as, "D. Ioannis Oecolampadii duo sermones apologetici de dignitate Eucharistiae quorum priorem in die S. Thomae lecto Euangelio Ioannis 21 posteriorem in vigilia natalis Christi, Basileae habuit. Tiguri excudebat Froschouerus."

Apologetics [Apologetica]:

1) "Two sermons on the dignity of the Eucharist." [1. "De dignitate Eucharistae Serm. II."]

2) "To Theob[ald] Billicanus, a preacher at Nordlingsanensis, on the question of who may import a foreign sense in the words of the Supper. etc." ["ad Theob: billicanum, Nordlingsanensem concionatorem, quinam in verbis coenae alienum sensum inferant, etc."] Staehelin adds to this listing "Ad Ecclesiastes Suevos Antisyngramma."

"To Willib[ald] Pirckhaimer, A letter and response on the matter of the Eucharist, earlier. 8 Basel." ["Ad Billib; Pyrkaimerum Epistola et responsio de re Eucharistica, prior. 8 Basel."] Staehelin lists it as, "Ioannis Oecolampadii ad Billibaldum Pyrkaimerum de re Eucharistiae responsio. Tiguri in aedibus Christophori Froschouer, Anno 1526."

"Sermons on the words of Thomas, 'My Lord and my God.' Tiguri. 1526.8." ["Sermones in Verba Thomae 'Dominus meus et Deus meus.' Tiguri, 1526,8."]

"'About the invocation of the saints,' Johannes Oecolampadius on some opponents, and above all Doctor Fabri, whose opposition was done uselessly. Answer preached publicly, November 1st, on All Saints Day. 8. Basel Adam Petri, 1526." ["Von Unruffung der Heylgen, Joannis Oecolampadii uff ettlicher Widersecher, und zuvorab Doctor Fabri, Annuss gegenwurfflish tandt, andtwort, offentlich gepredigt. I. Nov. an aller heylgen tag. 8 Basel 1526. durch Adam Petri."] Also published as: "Concerning the appeal of the holy Johannes Oecolampadius about some opponents and a small answer previously given unnecessarily by Doctor Faber, openly preached on All Saints Day." ["Von Anruffung der heylgen Joannis Ecolampadij uff ettlicher widersecher und zuvorab Doctor Fabri unnutz gegenwurfflich tandt andtwort Offenlich gepredigt an aller heylgen tag."]

"A modest response to Martin Luther's institution concerning the Eucharist, to which is added a response to the treatise, from the German into Latin, the translator being Ludovicus Lavaterus Tigurinus." ["Modesta responsio ad Mart: Lutheri institutionem de Eucharistia, cui adjecta responsio ad Syngramma, ex Ger. in Lat: vers: Ludov: Lavatero Tigur: Interprete."]

"Johannes Oecolampadius's reasonable answer to D. Martin Luther's report, partly on the sacrament, together with a short perception of some preachers in Swabian writing, concerning the Word of the Lord's Supper.—I request an interrogation. 4. Basel by Thomas Wolf. Also in Zurich. 4. In the same year by Froschauer." ["Billiche Antwort Joann Oekolampadii, auff D. Martin Luthers bericht, des Sacraments halb, sampt einem kurzen Begriff auff etlicher Prediger in Schwaben Schrifft, dieWort des Herrn Nachtmals antressend.—Ich bitt um Verhor.4. Basel den Thomas Wolf. Auch in Zurich.4.Ain gleichen Jahr bey Froschauer."]

"Refutation of the wrong reasons of Augustinus Marius, preacher at Thum [church] in Basel, to misunderstand that the Mass is a sacrifice," a respectful council entrusted [with] the same, by Johannes Oecolampadius 1528. 8. Basel by Thomas Wolff.—It is a letter from December 4, 1526, signed by five pastors in Basel, attached, wherein they admonish the priest at the cathedral to peace. ["Widerlegung der falschen Grunden, so Augustin Marius, Thumprediger zu Basel, zu verkennen, dass die Mess ein Opfer sey," einem ehrsamen Rath dofelbig uberantworter hat, durch Johann Oekolampadium 1528. 8. Basel bey Thomas Wolf.—Es ist ein Brief vom 4ten Decemb: 1526. von funf Pfarrern zu Basel unterschrieben, angehangt, worinn sie den Dommpriester zum Frieden ermahnen.]

"*The Prophet Malachi, with an interpretation by Johannes Oecolampadius*, delineated by him in Latin, translated with diligence into German by Ludwig Haetzer.—Oh God, redeem the captives—4. Basel by Thomas Wolff. 1526." ["Der Prophet Maleachi, mit ausslegung Joan: Ecolampadii, durch in im latein beschriben, mit Fleyss verdeutscht, durch Ludwig Haetzer.—O Gott erlöss die gefangnen.—4. Basel durch Thomas Wolff. 1526."]

"A new time and secret wonderful revelation of certain facts and deeds that were held, reported, and set out on the day of meeting at Baden in Ergöw before the envoys of the twelve parts of the honorable Swiss Confederation on the twenty-sixth day of June in the year 1526. 'The Word of the Lord remains and is fixed forever,' Psalm 118 [Ps. 119:89 in other than LXX]. Matthew 10, Mark 4, Luke 8: 'Nothing is covered that will not be revealed, or hidden that will not be known.'" ["Neüwe zeitung und heimliche wunderbarliche offenbarung etlicher sachen und handlungen so sich uff dem tag der zu Baden in Ergöw vor den Sandtbotten der Zwölf örter der loblichen Eydgnosschaft uff den Sechssundzweintzigsten tag des Brachmonats. Im jar Tausent Fünfhundert un XXVI. gehalten worden zugetragen und begeben hat. Psalmo 118. 'Das wort des Herren beleybt und wirt beston in ewig zeyt.' Matthei 10. Marci 4. Luce 8. 'Nihil opertum qd' non reveletur: et ocultum qd' non sciatur.'"]

"The tenth Psalm, preached in 1525 by Johannes Oecolampadius, preacher at St. Martin in Basel. Put together with exposition of the manner of singing." ["Der zehend psalm geprediget im fünff und zwentzigsten iar durch Joan. Oecolampadium Predicant by sant Martin zu Basel. Mit sampt der Ausslegung inn gsangssweyss begriffen."]

"The 36th and 37th chapters of *Isaiah* the Prophet, expounded by Johannes Oecolampadius, Preacher at Basel. Herein you find a beautiful example of a true trust in God, applied to distressed, troubled hearts in a wonderfully consoling way. O God, deliver the captives. Translated by L. Haetzer. Published in Augsburg by Silvanum Ottmar, 1526." ["Das Sechszt und Syben und dreyssigest Capitel Iesaia des Propheten Aussgelegt durch Joann. Ecolampadium Predicanten zu Basel. Hierin findest du ain schön beyspil ains waren vertruwens in Got Betrübten angefochten hertzen wunder trostlich zelesen. O Gott erlöss die gefanngen. Durch L. Haetzer ubersezt. Getrukt zu Augsburg durch Silvanum Ottmar. L. M.D. XXVI."]

"Two beautiful sermons: that one should not cut up brotherly love on account of the Lord's Supper. Also concerning the efficacy of the sacrament, with short rejections of many objections from opponents, preached by Johannes Oecolampadius at Basel, himself the principal priest of St. Martin's cathedral. O God, deliver the captives." ["Zwen Schön Sermon: inhaltende das man von wegen des Herren Nachtmals Brüderliche Liebe nit soll zertrennen. Auch von der wirdigkait des Sacraments mit kurtzen ablaynungen viler einreden den der widersächern durch Iohan. Ocolampadiu zu Basel geprediget Pfarrherren zu Sant Martin daselbst. O Gott erloss die gefangnen."]

1527   "To Willibald Pirckhaimer a second response on the matter of the Eucharist. 8 Basel at the [press] of Cratander, in the month of March, 1527." ["Ad Billib: Pyrkaimerum de re Eucharist:

responsio posterior. 8 Base. ap. Cratandr: mense Martio. 1527."]
Staehelin lists it printed in the same year in Latin with a different publisher as "Ad Bilibaldum Pyraimerum de Eucharistia,"
Ioannis Husschin, cui ab aequalibus a prima adolescenia Oecolampadio nomen obvenit, Responsio posterior. Nescitis, cuius
spiritus sitis. Lucae 9.

"An instruction concerning Anabaptisms, the magistrate, and
the taking of oath[s], against articles of Karlin N. Basel, 1527."
["Institutio de anabaptismo, magistratu, et jure. jurando contra
Caroli N. articulos, Bas. 1527."] See also: "Instruction regarding rebaptism, and the government, and the oath, against an
article of Karlin N., rebaptizer.—Answer to Balthasar Hub-
meier's booklet against the preacher's conversation in Basel,
concerning infant baptism, by Oecolampadius. 1527. 4to.—[It]
can contribute much to the explanation of the Basler's religious
conversation with the rebaptizers." ["Unterrichtung von dem
Wiedertauff von der Oberkeit und von dem Eyd auff Carlins
N. widertauffers artickel.—Antwort auff Balthasar Hubmeiers büchlein wider der Predicanten gespräch zu Basel von dem
kinder tauff. Durch Jo. Ecolampadiu." Basel: Cratander, 1527.]

"The lament of the holy prophet Jeremiah over the destruction
of the city of Jerusalem. Printed in Basel by Thomas Wolff.
1527" ["Die klag des heyligen propheten Jeremia über die zer-
störung der statt Hierusalem. Bedruckt zu Basel by Thoman
Wolff. MDXXVII."]

"*A commentary of Jo. Oecolampadius on the last three Prophets: Haggai,
Zechariah and Malachi*, with the favor and privilege of Caes[ar].
Basel, at the [press] of Cratander. 4. 1527." ["In postremos tres
Prophetas, nempe Haggaeum, Zachariam et Malachiam, com-
mentarius J. Oecol: cum gratia et privil: Caes; Bas: ap: Cratandr:
4.1527."] Staehelin adds to it in his listing, "cum indice."

"That the misunderstanding of D. Martin Luther regarding the
everlasting Word: 'This is My body,' cannot stand. The other
reasonable answer by Johannes Oecolampadius. 4 Basel, by
Cratander. 1527. On the 8th of June." ["Das der Miszverstand D.
Martin Luthers, off die ewig bstendige Wort, das ist mein Leib,
nit beston mag. Die ander billich antwort Joannis Ecolampadii.
4 Basel, bey Cratander. MDXXVII. am sten Brachmonat."]

"The first chapter of *Ezekiel* interpreted by Johannes Oecolampadius, concerning the office of the high society and the masses. (Translated by Ludwig Haetzer. 4) Dedicated to the country Earl Philip of Hess by Oecolampadius." ["Das Erst Capitel des propheten Jeheskiels, ussgelegt durch Johannem Oekolampadium, Von dem ampt der oberen und der underthonen. (durch Ludw: Haetzer, ubersezt. 4) dem Landgrafen Philipp in Hessen durch Oekolampad bedicirt."]

"The disputation before the twelve parts of an honorable Swiss Confederacy, namely Bern, Lucern, and the free Swiss Brotherhood, whether and how deeply a governmental process should take place with all the official participants, Glaris, Basel, Freiburg, Solathorn, Schaffhausen and Appenzell, for the sake of unity in Christian belief in their lands and in particular the four bishoprics Constance, Basel, Lausanne, and Thur. Heard and conducted and concluded in the year of Christ our Savior 1526, on the 16th day of May, at Baden in Ergöw and Mary completes." [Die disputacion vor den xij orten einer loblichen eidtgnoschafft namlich Bern Lutzern Vry Schvuytz Undervualden ob unnd nidt dem kern walt Zug mitt den sampt ufferen ampt Glaris Basel Friburg Solathorn Schaffhusen und Appenzell von wegen der einigkeit in christlichen glauben in iren landen und undterthonen der fier bistumb Costentz Basel Losanen und Thur beschehen und in dem iar Christi unsers erlösers Mccccc und xxvj uff den xvj tag des Meyes erhöret und zu Baden im ergöw irer statt gehalten unnd vollendet Maria.

"Concerning the way of the word of God, a letter of Caspar Schwenckfeld. Published in Basel, in the buildings of Thomas Wolf. 1527." ["De cursu verbi dei, Casparis Schwenckfeldii, epistola. Impressum Basileae, in aedibus Thomae Wolfii. M.D.XXVII."] This includes a one page introduction by Oecolampadius to the work.

"Misuse in the public office of bishop. Printed in Basel by Thomas Wolff." ["Was Miszbreuch im ruychbischofflichem ampt. Gedruckt zu Basel bey Thoman Wolff."]

1528   "A Rejection of the 'Apology of the Sacrifice of the Eucharist,' which Ambrose Pelargus offered to the Rulers of the Senate. Basel. 1528." ["Repulsio 'Apologiae Sacrificii Eucharistiae,' quam Ambros. Pelargus dominis Senatui obtulit. Bas: 1528."]

"*The Latin works of Cyril*, translated by Jo. Oecolampadius and George Trapezunt. Three volumes, Basel, 1528, Fol[io]." ["Cyrilli opera latina Jo. Oecolamp. et Georg: Trapezunt: Interpretibus, III. Tom: Basel. 1528. Fol.] Staehelin lists the three volumes separately with their individual titles: [1] Divi Cyrilli Archiepiscopi Alexandrini Opera; in tres partita Tomos: in quibus habes non pau ca antehac Latinis non exhibita. Hoc Primo Tomo Insunt, In Euangelium Ioannis commentariorum Libri XII. In leuiticum Libri XVI. [2] Secoundus Tomus habet, Divi Cyrilli Archiepiscopi Alexandrini Opus insigne quod Thesaurus inscribitur, de sonsubstantialitate filii et spiritus sanct cum Deo patre, aduer sus haereticos. Georgio Trapezontio interprete. Dialogorum cum Hermia de Trinitate libri septem cum appendice argumentorum, quod spiritus sanctus est Deus. De adoratione et cultu in spiritu et ueritate liber unus, Ioanne Oecolampadio interprete. [3] Tertius Tomus Habet Divi Cyrilli Archiepiscopi Alexandrini. contra Iulianum apostatem pro religione Christiana libros X. De rect fide in Christum ad Theodosium, et Reginas, libros III.]

"A hortatory Epistle to the Parisians, that they should follow purity of life and doctrine in all things. 8. Basel." ["Epistola exhortatoria ad Parisienses, ut vitae doctrinaeque puritatem in omnibus sectentur. 8. Bas."]

"A hortatory Epistle by Johannes Oecolampadius to the brothers who declare the Gospel of Christ in the territory of Basel, that they should follow purity of life and doctrine and ceremonies in all things. At Basel at the [press] of Valent[inus] Curio. 1528. The same is extant in the *Epistles of Zwingli and Oecolampadius*, p. 181–184." ["Joannis Oecolampadii ad Fratres, qui Evangelium Christi in agro Basileensi annunciant, epistola paraenetica, ut vitae doctrinaeque ac ceremoniarum puritatem in omnibus sectentur. Basileae ap: Valent: Curionem. 1528. Eadem extat in Zw: et Oecol: Ep. p. 181–184."] Staehelin lists it as apparently included in a larger compendium of 1590 as "Das Geistlich und herzliche kleinot der Kirchen Gottes in Statt und Landtischafft Basel: Remlichen I. Die confession oder Bekanntdnutz des heiligen Christliche Glaubesn. II. Der Catechismus oder Kinderberich fur die jugendt. III Das Agendbuch von Christlichen Kirchenbreuch un Ordnungen die in der Gemeine Gottes und bey den Kranken geubet werden. Auffs neuw Gott zu Lob under der Gemein Gottes zu heilsamer lehne und Trost alles wol wider ubersehen wie in volgender Borrede zu sehen: und mit fleiss getruckt: durch Sebastianum Henricpetri."

"About D. Martin Luther's book, named *Confessions*, two answers by Oecolampadius and Zwingli. Eod. 8." ["Ueber D. Martin Luthers Buch, Bekenntnis genannt, zwo Antworten Oekolampadii und Zwinglii. eod. 8."] Also listed as"Two answers by Johannes Oecolampadius and Huldrich Zwingli concerning Doctor Martin Luther's book called *Confession*. In 1528. Printed in Zürich by Christoffel Froschouer." ["Uber D Martin Luters Büch Bekentnuss genant zwo antwurten Joannis Ecolampadij und Huldrychen Zwinglis. Im M.D. XXVIII. jar. Getruckt zu Zürich by Christoffel Froschouer."]

"Sermon about the love of God for His Church. Ibid." ["Predig von der Liebe Gottes zu seiner Gemeind. Ibid."]

"Whether the Mass is a sacrifice, an answer to both preachers in Basel. Filed for investigation by a respectful council. S.l.e.a.8." ["Ob die Mess ein Opfer sey, beyder partheyen Predikanten zu Basel Antwurt. Uff Erforschung eins ersamen Radts eyngelegt. S l.e.a.8."]

"A Christian and earnest answer to the preacher of the Gospel in Basel, why they denounced the Mass as a horror. An investigation and determination of the respectful council to give in that very place. 8.S.l.e.a." ["Ein christliche und ernstlich Antwurt der Prediger des Evangelii zu Basel, warum sie die Mess einen Grüwel gescholten haben. Uff Erforschung und gheyss des Ersamen Radts daselbst geben. 8.S.l.e.a."]

"A circular letter of Johannes Oecolampadius to several brothers, so that the Gospel of Christ will be preached in the territory of Basel, admonishing, this is the purity, life, doctrine, and the customs that should be followed everywhere. Year 1528." ["Ain Sendbrieve Johannis Oekolampadii, an ettliche Brüder, so das Evangelium Christi in Basler Landschafft predigen, Ermanende, das sy der rainigkeit, lebens, leere unnd der gebreüche allenthalben nachvolgen sollen. Anno MCXXVIII."]

"The preachers' conversation with the rebaptizers in Basel. 4. Basel. 1528. Zurich. 1558." ["Der Predikanten zu Basel Gesprach mit den Wiedertaufern. 4. Basel. 1528. Zurich. 1558."]

"Sermon held at the Colloquy at Bern. 8 Zurich 1528." ["Predigt gehalten auf dem Gesprach zu Bern. 8 Zurich, 1528."] Staehelin lists it as "Die predigen so vonn frömbden Predicanten die allenthalb här zu Bernn uff dem Gespräch oder disputation gewesen beschehen sind. Berwerffen der articklenn und stucken so die Widertöuffer uff dem gespräch zu Bernn forersamen grossem Radt fürgewendt habend. durch Cunraden Schmid Commenthür zu Küssnacht an Zürich See. Getruckt zu Zürich durch Christophorum Froschouer im M.D.XXVIII."

"A refutation of the false basis that Augustinus Marius, Thumb Preacher at Basel, has used to say that the mass is a sacrifice, to a gathered council where he delivered himself up. By Johannes Oecolampadius. 1528." ["Widerlegung der falschen gründt so Augustinus Marius Thumb predicant zu Basel zu verwenen das die Mess ein Opffer sey eynem Ersamen Radt do selbig überantwort hat. Durch Joannem Oecolampadium. An. M.D.XXVIII."]

"Acts and proceedings of a disputation held at Bern in Uchtland." ["Handlung oder Acta gehaltner Disputation zu Bernn in üchtland."]

"Expositions of Theophylact Archbishop of Bulgaria on the four Gospels, carefully examined. Various marginal notations are added, and all the places in the Scriptures, now at length for the first time richly added. 1528." ["Theophylacti Archiepiscopi Bulgariae in Quatuor Euangelia Enarrationes, diligenter recognitae. Superadditae sunt variae ad marginem adnotationes, omniaque scripturarum loca, longe nunc primum adiecta locupletius. Anno MDXXVIII."] It was also published in 1530 and 1534.

1529 "True judgment that the body of Christ is not in the bread as a created thing but is in the Lord's Supper and in the hearts of believers through the word of God, in all praise and thanksgiving. Drawn up summarily in approximately three hundred arguments. September 1529." ["Warhafftig ursach das der leib Christi nitt in der creatur des brots aber durchs wort gots im nachtmal und hertzen der glaubigen sei on alle schumpffierung und zanckreden. Ungeferlich in dreihundert argument kürtzlich verfasset. Anno 1529. Mense Septembri."]

1530   "*Two books of Commentaries on the Prophet Daniel*, Basel 1530, along with *Explanations on the Book of Job*, printed again at Geneva. 1567. Folio." ["Commentariorum in Proph. Danielem Lib:II. Basil. 1530. una cum Exegematibus in librum Job. iterum impressa Genevae. 1567. Fol."] Staehelin lists it as "In Danielem Prophetam Ioannis Oecolampadii libri duo, omnigena et abstrusiore cum Hebraeorum tum Graecorum scriptorum doctrina referti."

"Confession of our Salvation. Christian Faith, how the churches of Basel hold it, written at Basel 1530, edited 1534 finally by Myconius, from the authority of the Senate; German. Folio with marginal notes." ["Bekanntniss unsers heil. Christi. Glaubens, wie es die Kil[r]chen zu Basel haltet. Bas. 1530 scripta. 1534 tandem a Myconio, ex autoritate Senatus, edita; germ: Fol: cum notis margin."] It is perhaps also included in Staehelin's publication listed 1590 as "Das Geistliche und herzliche Kleinot der Kirchen Gottes in Statt und Landtschafft Basel: Nemlichen I. Die confession oder Bekanntdnuss des heiligen Christlichen Glaubens. II. der Catechismus oder Kinderbericht für die jugendt. III das Agendtbuch von Christlichen Kirchenbreuch unnd Ordnungen die in der Gemeine Gottes unnd bey den Krancken geübet werden. Auffs neüw Gott zu Lob und der Gemein Gottes zu heilsamer Lehre unnd Trost alles wol wider ubersehen wie in volgender Vorrede zu sehen: und mit fleiss getruckt: durch Sebstianum Hericpetri."

"*A Dialogue*, [concerning] what the Ancient Greeks and Latins felt about the Eucharist; to which has been inserted a letter of Philip Melanchthon, which was sent to Oecolampadius from Spira, together with an Epistle of reply." ["Dialogus, quid de Eucharistia Veteres graeci et latini senserint; cui inserta est epistola Phil. Melanchth: quam e Spira Oecolampadio misit, una cum Epist: responsoria."] Staehelin lists it as "Quid de Eucharistia Veteres Tum Graeci, tum latini senserint, Dialogus in quo Epistolae Philippi melanchthonis et Ioannis Oecolampadii insertae. Autore Ioanne Oecolampadio, Anno M.D.XXX." Also 1572.

"The final volume of the works of the divine John Chrysostom, Archbishop of Constantinople, containing 66 homilies on

Genesis and certain other things that you may see in the catalog on the reverse page." ["Ultimus Tomus Operum Divi Ioannis Chrysostomi Archiepiscopi Constantinopolitani, continens homilias in Genesin LXVI & alia quaedam quorum catalogum versa pagina videre licet."]

Posthumous Publications

"Index of the writings of Oecolampadius which had been published first only after his death." ["Bezeichniss verjenigen Schriften Oekolampads, welche erst nach seinem Tod herausgekommen."]

1531 "*55 Commentaries on the Acts of the Apostles*, by the divine John Chrysostom." ["Divi Ioannis Chrysostomi Commentariorum in Acta Apostolorum Quinquagintaquinque."]

1532 "*Exegesis of the book of Job*. Basel. 4." ["Exegemata in librum Job. Bas. 4."] Staehelin lists it as "Ioannis Oecolampadii, Doctoris Undecunque Doctissimi in Librum Iob Exegemata: Eruditum Saneopus Ac Omnibus Divinae Scripturae Studiosis Utile." Staehelin lists it also as being printed in France after 1558 as, "Exposition de M. Jean Oecolampade, sur le livre de Iob. Traduit de latin en François. Edition premiere. Geneva," also 1550. Staehelin also lists an enlarged edition that includes *Daniel,* published in 1567 as "Io. Oecolampadii viri doctis. in librum Iob exegemata opus admondum eruditum, ac omnibus diuinae Scripturae studiosis utile. Eiusdem in Danielem prophetam libri duo. In huius tomi editione quantum elaboratum et quid effectum sit, praeposita ad lectorem epistola indicabit. Geneva."

"A beautiful common book of prayer in which are the principal prayers for various states and circumstances of the world. Also pious confession of sins together with beautiful explanations of the Lord's Prayer, etc. Faithfully written by many godly men and here brought together by D. Michaeln Weinmar, servant of the Gospel at Augsburg. 1532." ["Ein schön gemain Bettbüchlein darinnen die fürnemsten gebet für allerley stende unnd mengel der welt. Auch andechtige bekantnuss der sünden sampt schönen erklerungen de Vater unsers rc. Von vilen Gotseligen mennern getrewlich beschriben und hie alle zusamen bracht durch D. Michaeln Weinmar diener des Euangelions zu Augspurg. M.D.XXXII."] Also 1535.

1533   "Sixty-six Homilies of Chrysostom on *Genesis*.; Annotations on the Acts of the Apostles; Comments on the *First Epistle to the Corinthians*; A sermon on the giving of alms, etc. Rendered in Latin, in the works of Chrysostom, together with annotations on various smaller works of Chrysostom. Rendered into Latin by Oecolampadius." ["Christomi Homiliae LXVI. in Genesin; Annotationes in Acts Apost., Psegmata in Epist: I, ad Corinth, Sermon de Eleemosyna. etc, latine versus, in operibus Chrisost. una cum annotat. in varia Chrysostomi opuscula ab Oecolamp. in latinum versa."] Staehelin lists it in 1530 as "D. Ioannis Chrysostomi Archiepiscopi Constantinopolitani Opera, quae hactenus versa sunt omnia, ad Graecorum codicum collationem multis in locis per utriusque linguae peritos emendata. Accessere non pauca hactenus non vulgata, velut commentarii in utranque ad Corinthios Epistolam, et aliquot Homiliae in Acta apostolorum: nihil autem admixtum est usquam, quod quenquam offen dat novitate dogmatum. Neque nostra conquiescet industria, donec universum Chrysostomum latinis auribus dederimus." Staehelin lists the book of *Acts* again separately as "Divi Ioannis Chrysostomi Commentariorum in Acta Apostolorum Quinquagintaquinque."

"*Annotations on the Gospel of John*. Tig. 1533. 8. The same [at] Basel, 1535. 8." ["Annotationes in Evangelium Johannis. Tig. 1533. 8. item: Basil. 1535. 4."] Staehelin lists it as "*Annotationes piae ac Doctae in Euangelium* Ioannis, D. Ioanne Oecolampadio autore."

"*Commentary on the Prophet Jeremiah in three volumes and Detailed Exposition on the Lamentations of Jeremiah*. Argentor. 1533. 4." ["Commentariorum in Prophetam Jeremiam Libr. III. et ennarrationes in Threnos Jeremiae,. Argentor: 1533."] Staehelin lists it as "*In Hieremiam Prophetam Commentariorum* libri tres Ioannis Oecolampadii. Eiusdem in threnos hieremiae enarrationes. Argentinae anno MDXXXIII." Also 1558.

1534   "*A Commentary on Ezekiel*. Argent: at [the press] of Matthew Apiarius. 1534. In the preface [there is a] Life of Jo. Oecolampadius, described by Jo. Faber Capito." ["Commentarius in Ezechielem. Argent: ap. Math. Apiarium. 1534. In praes: Jo. Oecol. vita, per Jo. Fabr. Capitonem descripta extat.] Staehlin lists it as "*In Prophetam Ezechielem Commentarius* D. Ioan. Oecolampadii, per Wolfgangum Capitonem aeditus. De obitu

Oecolamp. Epist. Grynaei. De vita eius Wolfgan. Capito. Apiarius." Also 1558.

"*An Explanation of the Epistle to the Hebrews,* ibid. 1534." ["Expla-
natio in epist: ad. Hebraeos ibid.1534."] Staehelin lists it as, "*In
epistolam ad hebraeos,* Ioannis Oecolampadii, explanationes, ut
ex ore prelegentis excepte per quosdam ex auditoribus digeste
sunt. Argentorati Apud Mathiam Apriarium Mense Augusto,
Anno MDXXXIIII."

"Confession of our holy Christian faith, how the church of
Basel holds it. Folio. 10. pages. Also, it says it in the *Treasure
of the Churches of God in the City and Territory of Basel.* 1666 in
8. pages 15–30. In Latin in Laurent: *Syntagm: confessionum.*
1654, in 4, 72–75. In Alting. *Method [of] Theological Catechism*
Basel: 1666. 8, pages 29–38. And translated into French by
[Abraham?] Ruchat, *Réformation* V., pages 510–526.—This
confession is approved in the name of the council of the city
of Basel, under Adelberg Meyers consulate/mayor, the 21st
of January, 1529, and was signed by Heinrich Ryhiner, town
clerk of Basel, names of the registry. Oecolampadius has written it and Oswald Myconius edited it after his death. Leo Jud
translated it into German.—It is short, and consists only of
twelve articles: It differs occasionally from the Helvetic Confession, and is also incomplete and less extensive.—S. Haller's
Bibl: *Switzerland. History* III. Th.n.382." ["Bekanthnuss unsers
heyligen Christenlichen Glaubens, wie es die Kilch zu Basel hal-
ter. Fol. 10 S.Stecht auch im Kleinod der Kirchen Gottes in der
Stadt und Landschaft Basel. 1666 in 8. S.15–30. Lateinisch in
Laurent: Syntagm: confessionum, 1654. in 4. 72–25. In Alting.
Method. Theolog. Catechet. Bas. 1666. 8. S.29–38. u. franz. in
Ruchat. Réform.V.S.510–526.-Diese Confession ist im Namen
des Raths der Stadt Basel, unter Adelberg Meyers Consulat,
den 21sten Jenner 1529, genehmigt, und von Heinrich Ryhiner,
Rathschreiber zu Basel, Rainens des Standes, unterschrieben
worden. Oekolampad hat sie verfasset, und Oswald Myconius
nach seinem Tode herausgegeben. Leo Jude hat sie ins Deutsche
ubersezt.-Sie ist kurz, und besteht nur aus 12 Artikeln: Weicht
hin und wieder von der helvetischen Confession ab, und ist auch
unvollstandiger und weniger ausgedehnt.-S.Hallers Bibl: der
Schweiz. Gesch. III.Th.n.382."]

"Seven books by John Cassian, a most eloquent man, concerning the incarnation of the Lord. Now newly edited. Also
a sermon of the blessed Cyril, about why the Word of God
was made man." ["Ioannis Cassiani viri disertissimi, de incar-
natione Domini libri VII. iam recens aediti. Item Beati Cyrilli
sermo, de eo quod verbum Dei factum sit homo."]

1535   "*Annotations on Hosea, Joel, Amos, Obadiah, Jonah, and two chapters
of Micah*. Basel. 1525. Geneva 1578." ["Annotationes in Hoseam,
Joelem, Amos, Abdiam, Jonam et duo Capita Micheae. Bas:
1525. Genev. 1578."] Staehelin lists it as "Annotationes piissimae doctissimaeque in Ioseam Ioëlem Amos Abdiam, etc. D.
Ioanne Oecolampadio autore."

"The works of John of Damascus, a man who in his own
time held the preeminent place in divine things—all the works
that up to the present have been obtained, either by us or by
others, collated and emended according to the older Greek
manuscripts. They are these: About the orthodox faith, translated by Jacob Faber Stapulensis [Jacques Lefèvre d'Étaples],
four books. A sermon, How much the good works of the living
are of benefit to the dead, translated by Johannes Oecolampadius. In addition, the history of Jehoshaphat and Barlaam [sic],
which was translated by Trapezunt [Georgio Trapezontio]. The
life of John of Damascus, translated by Johannes Oecolampadius." [Ioan Damasceni viri suo tempore in divinis primatum
tenentis, omnia quae hactenus et à nobis & ab alijs haberi
potuerunt opera, ad vetustiora Graecorum exemplaria collata
atque emendata. Sunt autem haec. De orthodoxa fide, Iacobo
Fabro Stapulense interprete, Lib IIII. Quantum bona opera
viventium defunctis prosint, Ioanne Oecolampadio interprete,
Sermo. Praeterea historia Iosaphat et Barlaam, quam ferunt
Trapezontium transtulisse. Eiusdem Damasceni vita, Ioanne
Oecolampadio interprete."]

1536   "*Annotations on Genesis*. 1536. Basel. ["*Annotationes in Genesin*.
1536. Bas."] Staehelin lists it as "D. Io. Oecolampadii in Gen-
esim enarratio." Stahelein also lists it as published after 1558 as
"Genesis cum catholica expositione Ecclesiastica id est, ex uni-
versis probatis theologis (quos Dominus diversis suis Ecclesiis
dedit) excerpta, à quodam verbi Dei ministro, diumultúmque
in theologia versato. Sive Bibliotheca Expositionum Geneseως,
Id est, expositio ex probatis theologis (quotquot in Genesin

aliquid scripserunt) collecta, et in unum corpus singulari artificio conflata: quae instar bibliothecae multis expositorum libris refertae esse possit."

"Detailed Exposition on the Gospel of Matthew with popular addresses on certain passages of the New Testament. Ib." [Ennarationes in Evang: Mathaei cum Concionibus popularibus in aliquot loca Novi Test: Ib:"] Staehelin lists as, "Enarratio in euangelium Matthaei D. Io. Oecolampadio autore: et alia nonnulla quae sequens pagella indicabit."

"Four Books of Letters by Oecolampadius and Zwingli. But also— A Selected Sermon on not holding a collection for paupers; A Speech to the Augustinian Clergy, on Christ's expostulation with Peter, when he was excusing himself from the washing of feet. Ib. Folio." [Epistolarum Oecolampadii et Zwinglii Libri IV. Daben auch—Sermo de non habendo pauperum Selectu; Oratio ad Clerum Augustanum, de expostulatione Christi cum Petro, ablutionem pedum excusante. ib. Fol."]

"The entire title of this most odd letter collection is:" ["Der ganze Title diser hochst merkwurdigen Briefsammlung ist:"]

"Four books of the Letters of Doctors Johannes Oecolampadius and Huldrich Zwingli. Dealing thoroughly with the principal things, not only the headings of the religion handed down to us by Christ, but also the duties of Church administration, particularly as they pertain to our age, troubled as it is thus far by errors. A work learned and pious, and especially necessary for those who are zealous for the reborn Gospel now finally brought to light for the first time. To these has been appended a defense of the Authors Oecolampadius and Huldrich Zwingli, by Theodore Bibliander, professor of Sacred Letters of the Tigurine Church. A life and obituary of each, by authors Simon Grynaeus, Wolfgang Capito, and Oswald Myconius. Hebrew, Greek and Latin epigrams on the same. Lastly, a very full index of memorable things. At Basel. 1536. Folio. The reverse page contains an exposition of those things which are contained in the books of the four Gospels." ["DD Ioannis Oecolampadii et Huldrichi Zvinglii epistolarum libri quatuor, praecipua cum religionis à Christo nobis traditae capita, tum Ecclesiasticae administrationis officia, nostro maxime seculo, tot hactenus erroribus perturbato, convenientia, ad amussim experimentes.

Opus cumprimis eruditum ac pium, renatique, evangelii studiosis apprime necessarium, nunc denique primum in lucem editum. ad haec scriptorum Io. Oecolampadii et Huldrichi Zvinglii Purgatio, per Theodorum Bibliandrum, sacrarum literarum Tigurinae Ecclesiae professorem, conscripta. Utriusque vita & obitus, Simone Grynaeo, Wolfgango Capitone, & Osvaldo Myconio autoribus. Epigrammata Hebraica, Graeca, Latina, in eosdem. Rerum denique memorabilium locupletissimus index. Basileae. 1536. Fol. Versa pagin continet Elenchum eorum, quae quatuor epistolaerum libris continentur."]

"Namely:" ["Scilicet:"]

[1] "The Epistles of the first book explain various passages of Scripture, and some more difficult questions of the Christian religion." ["Primi libri Epistolae, diversa Scripturae loca et religionis Christianae difficiliores quaestiones explicant."]

[2] "The second book has epistles on true and false baptism, in which the various errors of the Catabaptists are most thoroughly refuted." ["Secundus liber veri et falsi baptismi epistolas habet, quibus varii Catabaptistarum errores solidissime confutantur."]

[3] "The third book embraces those things which pertain to the business of the Eucharist." ["Tertius liber, ea, quae ad Eucharistias negotium pertinent, complectitur."]

[4] "The fourth and final contains epistles of the hortatory sort, having as much to do with the rule of the Church as of importance to civil tranquility." ["Quartus ac ultimus, Paraenetici generis Epistolas, pluriumum tam ad Ecclesiae regimen, quan civilem tranquilitatem momenti habentes, continet."]

"This letter collection is also even again reprinted. Basel 1529.4. under the title: 'Monument of the commencement of the kingdom of Christ [or in memory of?] and the reborn Gospel,' in memory of the fathers throughout Switzerland. This edition is very rare." ["Eben diese Briefsammlung ist auch wieder abgebruckt. Basil. 1529.4. unter dem Titel: Monumentum instaurati, patrum memoria, per Helvetiam regni Christi et renascentis Evangelii.—Diese Ausgabe ist sehr rar."] Staehelin lists it in 1546 as "Epistolae Doctorum uiroru, quibus cum Eucharistiae et Anabaptismi negotium, tum alia religionis capita, et Ecclesiasticae administrationis officia, nostro seculo perturbatissimo iiprimis obseruatu utilia continentur. Opus cumprimis eruditum ac pium, renaticz Euangelii studiosis apprime necessarium, Reip. Christianae ergo in lucem editum. Rerum et vuerborum in his omnibus memorabilium. index. lege et iudica."

"Most learned writings of Olympiodorus on Ecclesiastes. Learned things, new and put into translation unaccustomed to Latin ears, by Aquila, Theodotion, and the LXX. Zenobius Acciaiolus-Florentinus translator. By the divine Gregory of Neocaesaria paraphrase of the same, or, as the Swiss have it, the entirely wonderful word: Johannes Oecolampadius translator...." ["Olympiodori doctissima in Ecclesiast. scholia, nova & latinis auribus insueta translatione inserta, Aquilae videlicet, Theodotionis, & LXX. Zenobio Acciaiolo-Florentino interprete. Divi Gregorii Neocaesariensis in eundem metaphrasis, vel, ut Suidae placet, πάνυ θαυμαστός λόγος, Ioanne Oecolampadio interprete...."]

1537 "Form for the Sacraments as it is used at Basel, together with a short account for children. Published at Basel by Lur Schouber. 1537." ["Form der Sacramenten bruch wie sy zu Basel gebrucht werden mit sampt eynem kurtzen kinder bericht. Zu Basel by Lur Schouber. M.D. XXXVII."]

1538 "A short preparation for confirmation of young people, concerning the Lord's Prayer, faith, baptism, the Lord's Supper, the Ten Commandments, and other daily and particular prayers that are almost necessary for growth. Christoffel Wyssgärber teacher at S. Martin's in Basel. Printed at Basel by Wolffgang Friess near Spital spring. 1538." ["Ein Kurtze Underwissung der Jugent im Vatter unser Glouben Touff Herzen nachtmal Zehen gebotten und anderer täglicher unnd besonderer gebätten den alten auch fast nutzlich Christoffel Wyssgärber Lehrmeister zu Basel bey. S. Martin. Getruckt zu Basel bey Wolffgang Friess am sprung by dem Spital brunnen. 1538."]

1544 "Certain sermons on the Psalms, namely: 73, 77 and 137." ["Conciones in Psalmos aliquot. Scil: 73.77. et 137."] Staehelin lists it as "In Psalmos LXXIII, LXXIIII, etc conciones Ioannis Oecolampadii piissimae, per Ioannem Gastium Brisacensem exceptae, nuncque primum latinitate donatae, et in lucem divulgatae. Sequens pagella, quae in libello isto continentur, indicabit."

"*A Christian Education, or A Catechism of children,* together with certain pious small prayers, added for the use of the same." At Basel, through [the press] of Jo. Oporinum. 1544. In the Month of November. 8. In the preface: written on October 9, Myconius mentions that he made this Latin Catechism of Doctor Oecolampadius, with some explanations added, only so that boy students of the Latin language might not be compelled to be foreigners in the schools and public examination, as up until this point, except for reason of their studies." ["Institutio Christiana, sive Catechismus puororum, una cum preculis aliquot piis, in eorundem quoque usum adjectis." Basileae. per Jo. Oporinum. 1544. Mense Nov.8.-In praefat: die 9. Oct.scripta, Myconius refert, se hunc D. Oecolampadii Catechismum, fecisse latinum, quibusdam adjectis interpretationibus, nonnisi ut pueri latinae linguae studentes in ludis et publico examine non cogantur esse, ut hactenus, praeter studiorum suorum rationem barbari."] It is perhaps also included in Stahelin's 1544/50 and 1590 publication list as, respectively, "Frag und antwort in verhörung der kinder der kirken zu Basel kurtz gestelt durch doctor Johann Ecolampadium" and "Das Geistlich und herzliche kleinot der Kirchen Gottes in Statt und Landtischafft Basel: Remlichen I. Die confession oder Bekanntdnutz des heiligen Christliche Glaubesn. II. Der Catechismus oder Kinderberich fur die jugendt. III Das Agendbuch von Christlichen Kirchenbreuch un Ordnungen die in der Gemeine Gottes und bey den Kranken geubet werden. Auffs neuw Gott zu Lob under der Gemein Gottes zu heilsamer lehne und Trost alles wol wider ubersehen wie in volgender Borrede zu sehen: und mit fleiss getruckt: durch Sebastianum Henricpetri." Also 1591.

"Concerning the beginning of anabaptism, along with the errors, abominable histories, and refutations. Two books, by Johannes Gastius Brisacensus. Now first published and brought into the light." ["Anabaptismi exordio, erroribus, historiis abominandis, Confutationibus adiectis. Libri duo, autore Ioanne Gastio Brisacensi. Nunc primum in lucem editi."]

1545   "A beautiful exposition of the lamentation of Jeremiah the holy prophet by Johannes Oecolampadius, preached in the church at Basel and never before put in print." ["Inn die Clag Hieremie des heiligen propheten ein schöne usslegung durch Joannem

Oecolampadium in der kirchen zu Basel geprediget vorhin nie im Truck ussgangen."]

"The exposicion of Daniel the Prophete gather oute of Philip Melanchton, Johan Ecolampadius, Chonrade Pellicane, and out of Johan Draconite, etc. By G. Joye. A. Prophecye diligently to be noted of all Emprowrs and kinges in these last dayes." [A British press?]

1546   *"A life of John of Damascus, by John, Patriarch of Jerusalem,* Latin. Colon [Koln?]. 1546. Basel. 1548. Folio." ["Joannis, Patriarch: Hieros: Vita, Joannis Damasceni lat: Colon: 1546. Bas. 1548. fol."]

"Several pious and learned discourses on the Epistle of St. Paul to the Colossians, very much suitable for our times, now first brought to light in publication. Author Johannes Oecolampadius." ["In Epistolam D. Pauli ad Colossenses. Conciones aliquot piae ac doctae ad tempora nostra valde accomodae, nunc primum in lucem aeditae. Authore Ioanne Oecolampadio."]

1544–1550 "Small book of church order in Basel." ["Agendbüchlin der Kirchen zu Basel.]

1550 (ca.) "A Sarmon of J. Oecolampadius to yong men and maydens. [Translated by J. Foxe] H. Powell,…sould by H. Syngleton: London."

"*Micropresbytikon* [a small group of elders], a small book reviewing some old small theologians, whether bishops or elders, or of other holy order, who lived either in the time of the Apostles or not long after, whose names (as you see) follow here." ["MIKRO-PRESBYTIKON Veterum Quorundam brevium Theologorum, sive Episcoporum sive Presbyterorum, aut sacri ordinis aliorum qui aut tempore Apostolorum, aut non multò post vixerunt, elenchus: Quorum hinc nomina (ut vides) sequuntur:"]

1553   *"Commentaries on Job, Daniel, Hosea, Joel, Amos, Obadiah, Jonah, Micah, Haggai, Zechariah & Malachi.* Geneva. 1553. Also Basel, 1533. Folio." ["Commentarii in Jobum, Danielem, Hoseam, Joel, Amos, Abdiam, Jonam, Micheam, Haggaeum, Zachariam et Malachiam. Genev. 1553. et. Bas: 1533. fol."]

1558   *"Commentaries on Isaiah, Jeremiah, Lamentations & Ezekiel.* Geneva. 1558. Folio. The works of Franciscus Gaius, with a preface by

Bullinger, in which Oecolampadius's teaching is vindicated." ["Comment: in Esaj: Jerem: Threnos et Ezech: Gen: 1558. fol: Opera Francisci Gaji, cum praes: Bullingeri, in qua doctrina Oecol: vindicatur."] Staehelin lists an abbreviated but similar volume in 1558 as "Ioannis Oecolampadii viri piissimi et doctiss. commentarii omnes in libros prophetarum, Tam insigni doctrinae magnitudine atque varietate referti, ut ad praestantem verae Theologiae cognitionem maximo usui omnibus piis sint futuri. Librorum inscriptiones sequens pagina ordine commemorat." It is also listed by Staehelin as "Ioannis Oecolampadii viri piissimi et doctissimi commentariorum in prophetas tomus posterior. Librorum inscriptiones sequens pagina ordine commemorat."

"Notes on the prophets, which they call minor, by Johannes Oecolampadius, a most pious and learned man, edited by him and after his death made collectively and publicly available from his lectures. Geneva." ["In Minores, quos vocant, prophetas, Ioannis Oecolampadii, viri piissimi et eruditissimi lucubrationes quaecunque ab ipso editae, et post decessum ex ipsius praelectionibus colecte et publice factae extant. Geneva."]

1562 "Exposition by Johannes Oecolampadius on the Book of *Job*. Translated from Latin into French. First edition. Geneva." [Exposition de M. Jean Oecolampade, sur le livre de Iob. Traduit de Latin en François. Edition premiere. Geneva.]

"Book of the Psalms of David, with catholic ecclesiastical exposition. Songs from diverse places in the Bible, with the same exposition." ["Liber psalmorum Davidis, cum catholica expositione Ecclesiastica. Cantica ex diversis Bibliorum locis, cum eadem expositione."]

1564 "Small book of order of the church in Basel. Here one finds first how one should bless marriage [?] before the congregation. Then the form and order of the holy high sacraments of baptism and the Lord's Supper, with instruction about visitation of the sick and about 15 statements for children." ["Agend Büchlin der Kirchen zu Basel. Hierin find man erstlich wie man die Eelüt vor der gemein ynsägnen soll. Demnach die form und ordnung der H. hochwirdigen Sacramenten dess Touffs und dess Herren Nachtmals mit zu gethoner heimsuchung der kranken und angehencktem 15 kinderbericht."]

1569 "Book of order or Christian church use and usage as it is practiced in the church at Basel under God. Following it is a page
statement." ["Agendbuch oder Christliche kirchenbrüch und
übung wie die zu Basel under Gottes gemein gehalten werden
darvon volgends blat bericht gibt."] Also published in 1572,
1578, and 1584.

1590 *"Dialogue on the Lord's Supper. 8. Basel."* ["Dialogus de Coena
Domini. 8. Bas."] Staehelin lists it as "Ioh. Oecolampadii Dialo-
gus, quo Patrum sententiam de Coena Domini bonafide explanat.
Huldrichi Zvinglii confession fidei ad Carolum V. Imp. Philippi
Melanchthonis iudicium de controuersia Coene Domini, ad
illustriass. Electorem, Fridericum III. pium, Comitem Palati-
num, etc. Ioh. Iacobi Grynaei Exomologessis ad Deum Opt.
Max. Basila=eae Typis Conradi Waldkirchii. MDXC."

Undated Publications

The following undated publications or writings of Oecolampadius
were listed by Salomon Hess in his bibliographic index of 1793.

"Exhortation to the Reading of Sacred Literature." ["Exhortatio ad
sacrarum litter: lectionem."]

"On the Difference between the Internal and External Word." ["De
Discrimine verbi interni et externi."]

"Sermons to Girls, with an Exposition of the Apostles Creed; Given in a
Debate at Bern; On the Song of Simeon." ["Conciones ad puel-
los, cum expositione simboli apostolici: Bernae in disput: habitae;
de Cantico Simeonis."] Staehelin lists this as published around
1550. It may may be the same sermons as published in English as
"A Sarmon of J. Oecolampadius to Young Men and Maydens."

"Discussion on how little sacrifices should be restored into the [liturgical?]
order" ["Consilium quomodo in ordinem redigendi sacrificuli."]

"A protest on the sacrifice of the Mass, against Aug[ustine] Marius."
["De sacrificio missae contentio, contra Aug: Marium."]

"Themes 114 argued at Basel in the auditorium of the Theologians.—
Acts of the Baden Debate." [Themata 114. Basileae disputata in
auditorio Theologorum.—*Acta Disputationis Badensis."*]

"Further Oecolampadius has also prepared the following translations from the Greek Church Fathers." ["Ferner hat Oekolampad noch folgende Ubersetzungen aus griechischen Kirchenvatern verfertigt."]

"Of Gregory of Nyssa, a Speech on the Life of Moses." ["Gregorii Misseni Oratio de Vita Mosis."]

*"Of Nicephorus Cartophylax, a Letter on the Power of Binding and Loosing." ["Nicephori Cartophylacis Epistola de ligandi et solvendi potestate."]

"The following individual letters by Oecolampadius are found in:" [Folgende einzelne Briefe von Oekolampad:]

"Gerdesius Dan[iel], *Introduction to the Evangelical History*, renewed in the 16th Century. Groningen. 4. 4 Volumes 1744–1752. Particularly printed." ["Gerdesii Dan. Introduct: in Hist: Evangelii—Sec. XVI. renovati. Groningae. 4. 4 Vol. 1744–1752. besonders abgebrukt."]

"An Epistle to W. F. Capito on Reformation. Basel. P. 139 Volume II, from the *Annals of Scultetius*. December. II. 136 and following." ["Epistola ad W. Capitonem de Reformatione. Basil: p.139. T.II. ex *Sculteti annal*: Dec:II. 136.sq.]

"An Epistle to the Same on the Church at Solodurensis. P. 142 ibid." ["Epistola ad eundem de Ecclesia Solodurensi. p.142. ibid."]

"Amoeboean [i.e. antiphonal] Epistles of Oecolampadius and S. Grynaeus. p. 144 ibid." ["Oecolampadii et S: Grynaei epistolae. Amoeboeae. p. 144. Ibid."]

Oecolampadius's Commentary on Isaiah 36–37

[As far as I know, none of Oecolampadius's works have been translated into English. A few exceptions would include translations done in the sixteenth century. What follows is the only translation into English of any of his commentaries. It is hoped that the riches observed below might encourage others to translate remaining buried treasures from his commentaries on Genesis, Job, Psalms, Isaiah, Jeremiah, Ezekiel, Daniel, Hosea, Joel, Amos, Obadiah, Jonah, Micah (chapters 1–2), Haggai, Zechariah, Malachi, Matthew, Romans, Colossians, Hebrews, and 1 John. Please forgive any imperfections in my translation.]

Isaiah 36:1–3

And it came to pass, in the fourteenth year of King Hezekiah, Sennacherib King of Assyria went up against all the fortified cities of Judah and conquered them.

And the King of Assyria sent Rabshakeh himself from Lachish to Jerusalem to King Hezekiah in the midst of a great army, and he stood in the channel of the upper pool in the way of the fullers' fields.

And there went out to him Eliakim the son of Hilkiah who was in charge of the palace and Shebna the scribe, and Joah the son of Asaph from the recorders.

And it came to pass.) What earlier was obscured in many wrappings of figures and prophecies is unfolded now under two headings.

We have moreover an outstanding example of faith by which in all adversities we can be consoled [in the fact that] we will not be left destitute of divine help, provided that our faith abides healthy. Otherwise there was no need to lay it forth in so many figures nor to call to mind the miracle with such careful narration. And although now history clearly is being narrated, it is nevertheless itself also a type pregnant with great mysteries, just as the history of the bronze serpent which Moses lifted up is true, and we are not able to confess but that the serpent itself also was no less a figure of Christ.

Thus also here our Jerusalem is, I say, the true church of God of which we are made citizens through true faith in Christ; and it has its own Sennacherib and its own Rabshakeh, whom you may take as the antichrist, who takes care of the business of the king. They, in fact, scheme to conquer the church by various methods, and they try to drive us away from the true worship of God, which is in faith, into servitude to them. However, God through His own Messenger Jesus Christ wore away the adversarial powers (without our death) by His own power in the cross. It remains that first we have faith in Christ and in us He will triumph over demons and his servants. And finally He will triumph completely when He will have abolished death and when all things will be subjected to Him.

And it came to pass.) I have predicted wonders, but that I am not a false prophet, those things which I spoke of earlier are being proven true by the outcome while I yet live.

In the fourteenth year.) The carefulness of the number shows the certainty of the history: let us abandon allegory as somewhat too superstitious to those who would play games.

King Hezekiah.) Consider also that even under those ruling justly the tempests of war arise; indeed such [rulers] especially are tempted both so that their faith may be tried and so that the impiety of the common people may be corrected; this impiety is more grievous under a good ruler and is less excusable than under impious [rulers], under whom the people are able to excuse themselves because they have been led astray by an evil example.

Sennacherib went up.) Concerning this he foretells above in Chapter 7 where he [Sennacherib] and the Assyrians are called the "bees resting in the valley"; chapter 8, "flowing water"; chapter 10, "rod of rage"; chapter 17, "multitude and roaring of nations"; chapter 20, Sargon's capture of Ashdod; chapter 25 [sic? chapter 28:22], appearance of a connected chain; chapter 33, the "devastator devastating." He seizes, moreover, and conquers all the cities of Judah except Jerusalem, that is the true church of God, which trusts solely in the Word of God. Moreover, the fact that he is said to ascend is partly due to the physical location of the place, and partly it points out his overconfidence that he will be victorious, for the spiritual Sennacherib also has said: "into Heaven I will ascend, above the stars of God I will put my throne." [Isa. 14:13]

And the king of Assyria sent.) He does not immediately besiege Jerusalem, but first he attacks through deceptions, and he sends Rabshakeh.

From Lachish.) This is in the tribe of Benjamin, not far from Jerusalem, for having captured it Sennacherib started out into Egypt for the siege of Pelusium, as Josephus reports. The prophet calls that city which he [Sennacherib] besieged, "Lobna."

To Jerusalem.) Rabshakeh had received from the king a part of the army for the capture of Jerusalem and so that he might be that much more fearsome. He stands, therefore, in the aqueduct of the pool in order that he might appear more conspicuous and frightful to all men. And while standing he declares himself invincible and confident.

He is, moreover, a type of the antichrist who is a servant of the Devil, fortified by deceits and frauds, who not only stands, but also confidently sits in the temple of God and is raised up against everything which is said to be God [2 Thess. 2:4]; he prefers indeed his own mandates to the divine mandates, and he makes divine things [mandates] to serve his own profit.

And there went out to him Eliakim.) Concerning Eliakim and Shebna,
see what I said above, in chapter 22. They went out, moreover, at
the command of the king in order to discuss conditions of peace.
Although earlier Hezekiah had yielded a great amount of money to
Sennacherib, nevertheless even now also, he rejects nothing in order
that he might turn him away from the city.

And behold how patient they were, bearing all the things which
pertained to peace. They had offered whatever gold was in the temple,
now they go out and they decline none of the conditions of peace,
that they might only not be subservient to the Assyrians, so that they
might be able to serve the one God in Jerusalem. And we also must
put aside and lose the body and all substance so that we may find the
pearl of faith, and once it has been found we may keep it.

This man is mentioned among the recorders which we are
accustomed to call a stenographer.

Isaiah 36:4–10

*And Rabshakeh said to them: "Go tell Hezekiah: thus says the king,
the great king of Assyria, 'What is this confidence in which you have
trusted?*

*I have said: How [is it that] by a word of the lips, by strategy and
by strength[1] [you prepare] for war: now in whom were you trusting
that you have rebelled against me?*

*'Behold, you have trusted in the strength of that reed, on Egypt,
on the one who indeed will go into and pierce the hand of every one
who leans upon him. Thus [is] Pharaoh, king of Egypt, to all those
trusting in him.*

*'And if he will say to me, we have hoped in the Lord our God,
is it not that Hezekiah himself, you who are removing his high places
and his altars, and said to Judah and Jerusalem you will worship
before this altar?'*

*"And come now, discuss war with my lord the King of Assyria:
and I will give to you two thousand horses, if in fact you will be able
to provide for yourself men to ride on them.*

---

1. The word translated "strategy" may also be translated "wisdom." "Strength"
may be translated as "courage."

*"And how would you appease the face of one prince of the least
of the servants of my lord: and do you trust in Egypt and in [his]
cavalry and [his] horsemen?*

*"And now, did I come up to the land to devastate it apart from the
Lord? The Lord said to me, 'Go up into that land and devastate it.'"*

And Rabshakeh said to them.) Behold here particularly that nothing is
of such concern to the enemy than that he lead us away from faith
in God and that he prune away all hope so that he might deliver us
to himself. But that wicked orator declares the words of the great
king, not the words of God. How endless is the skill of the impos-
ters that they may fawn upon their kings with grandiose titles, while
the name of God is kept silent and it is held in frozen speech. They
cry out: "The most holy high priest commands," "the most just king
enjoins," "the church observes this custom," "the authority of councils has it so." Thus it has seemed right to the leading schoolmasters
of the age. Nevertheless, we wait upon the words of God, from
which it is not permitted to deviate even if an angel from heaven
should order something. Why are the ghosts of these characters, the
shadows of shadows forced upon us?

I have said, "How [is it that] by a word of the lips?") In the books of the
Kings it reads "you said": But here, "I said." There he speaks to the
king, "You said," that is, "You thought in [your] heart that it would
go well for you on account of the words of [your] lips, that is on
account of [your] prayer to God. But I say to you that not by prayers
is a thing done, but by strategy and strength." Or perhaps, as others
expounded, "The strength and strategy which you have are nothing
but words." As for the rest as we read here, Rabshakeh says: "I have
said to myself, 'How is it that you plan to wish to be free by prayers,
and also how is it you consider them [prayers] to be your strategy
and strength; but you are mistaken; you need other protection.'"
Notice carefully, moreover, the things which in his speech the antichristian rhetorician sets forth.

For he introduces three matters in regard to which he strives to
persuade that hope must not be placed in any one of them, min-
gling true things with false things. And he speaks truly about the

first two things, for neither is it permitted to trust in ourselves nor in any creature, but in God. But the enemy is thinking this especially, so that he may cut off hope in God. He says this first thing rightly, "How [is it that you are trusting] in the word of lips, [rather than] in strategy and strength." For prayers are indeed most powerful, and God denies nothing to tears. And yet we must not pray in such a way as if we were trusting in our own prayers and making God indebted.[2] But we are heard through Christ alone who is a beloved Son of the Father in whom God is well pleased.

God has commanded to pray, but we receive [it] making requests in the name of Christ.[3] There are also helps in the mysteries of the church, but it is not permitted out of these to do works in which we may put hope, [hope] which must be placed only in God's mercy. In the same manner, it is not surprising that many [people] are not heard however much they may persist in prayers, for they attribute more to themselves than to divine mercy. And it happens to them just as [it happened] to the Jews who lost the victory along with the ark of God which had been led forth into battle. [1 Sam. 4] Therefore, nothing of our works suffices to free us, nay, rather all things.[4]

Therefore he says truly, "How will you put your hope in speeches or in strategy or in strength?" Our enemy knows that there is nothing found in our strength, and do we still continue to boast in our attempts or in the power of [our] free will? Still do we sell merits and our works as if we even overflowed [enough] to help others, as if it were in us to dispense them?

You have rebelled against me.) However good peaceful people are, even if they do not yield in evil to the evil people, they are [then] called rebels and seditious, and Barabbas is discharged and Christ as [if He were] seditious is dragged away to the cross.

---

2. The phrase "we must not pray in such a way" may be translated "not so must it be prayed."

3. Possibly a textual error that should read "accipimur," which would mean "we are received asking in the name of Christ."

4. This sentence may also be translated, "All our efforts together do not suffice," as the German text states it.

Behold you have trusted.) Secondly, and rightly, he says that when we are in danger, hope is not to be put in externals, that is in men or any other creature. Every man is a liar as the psalmist said. [Ps. 116:11] Therefore, they act foolishly who, abandoning Christ, trust in the prayers[5] of the saints. For just as Rabshakeh reproaches [Hezekiah] concerning the Egyptians, just so do the demons [use this as a reproach] concerning creaturely things against those who are destitute of hope in God. For indeed nobody is able to give us any assistance without God. This appears most truly in death: for then most bitterly Satan torments anxious people. Or would he spare us who did not fear even to attack Christ?

And if he will say to me.) Here appear the tricks of the enemy. For he makes danger where there is no danger, and he turns the highest justice into injustice. For what is more admirable than the zeal of Hezekiah in his removing the high places and grinding up the bronze serpent? And behold here the enemy tries his hardest to cast down his hope, as if he were such a great sinner who is unworthy to be heard. And also, he manifestly wishes to lead him into despair and to hold him forth before the people as impious. In fact there had been high places erected in the honor of God, but not according to the law, and consequently abominable in His eyes, but pleasing to the people, and seeming worthy of highest honor.

No king previously was able to destroy them, even those who were very righteous, such as Asa, Jehoshaphat, Joash, Amaziah, and Jotham. However, only Hezekiah demolished the high places, smashed the statues, cut down the sacred groves, and shattered the bronze serpent, to which the sons of Israel had even begun to burn incense against the command of God. Whence this Rabshakeh says, "How will you put hope in God, since your king has destroyed the altars which were erected in the honor of God? Would He whose altars you demolish assist you?" But the evil enemy kept silent

---

5. This is put somewhat sarcastically, as if the saints could vote or lobby for you. In fact, it could be translated "trust in the lobbying or voting of the saints."

because those things were not raised up by the precept of God, and they were not pleasing to God.

Today we have heard of similar things happening in regard to the sacraments, images, and other things, which thus far in the eyes of the common people appear impressive, but in reality, on account of the abuses, are held to be harmful. While, therefore, some things are being corrected according to the Word of God, the enemies of piety say, "What hope do you have since you are demolishing those things which have been instituted in the honor of God?" But they who will be circumspect, as Hezekiah was, will not be frightened by threats of this sort, since they know that there is no other zeal more pleasing to God than to live according to His Word. Also there is no peril in exhorting the people to worship before the one and only altar, that is according to the commandment of God and as it is prescribed in the canonical Scriptures.

And come now, discuss.) This passage is explained in two ways. First, so that they might cut off their hope, if they were in fact putting [hope] in their own power, whence according to Josephus the sense is: "Promise that you will come out to us, and we will deliver to you two thousand horses; but see your poverty, for you will not even have that many horsemen to mount the horses and oppose us. Behold you could not even come out against the least servant of my lord." And we also confess freely our weakness so that God's mercy may be greater. And no less bitter a taunt does he throw out, that is his hope in the Egyptians, as if the impotence of the Egyptians and the Jews were the same.

Others explain for "condicas" [that is, "you discuss"] to mean, "Make a pleasant thing for [that is "be on good terms with"] the king of Assyria," because it is the Hebrew word התערב [that is, "to mingle"] [which has] many meanings[.] And giving this sense: "If you behold such kindness from him, why do you not subject yourself to my king, who will willingly supply you with more horses than you would be able to supply horsemen for? Furthermore, he would deal with you more faithfully than the Egyptian king." More-over, it is not the least of the skills and devices of the antichrist to ensnare by gifts, and today the antichrist seeks various ways in order to betray the truth; for he ensnares some with sacerdotal offices, and others with privileges, and others with gold coin, so that those whom he cannot conquer by threats he may conquer by gifts. And what is strange about this? For he dared to say even to the Lord, "I will give you all the kingdoms, if you fall down and worship me." Furthermore, even this which Rabshakeh promises is against the law of God, which forbade the Jews from raising horses so that they might have greater hope in the Lord.

And now [is it that] apart from the Lord.) He puts the weightiest temptation in the last place. This moreover is the belief that God is angry with him. For just as when [we are] assured of God's grace we are gladdened in conscience, so when we believe God is angry with us are we most greatly terrified; indeed, this is hell itself.

Hence the Jews would say to Christ that He should free Himself now if He wishes, wishing to declare Him [to be] an enemy of God. And Rabshakeh does this too in order to weaken all the hope of the Jews, trying to make them hateful to God but himself claiming to be at the command of God. And indeed it was true that the prophets had predicted of Sennacherib that he would lay waste the land of Israel, for he was the rod of God's wrath: but it was not granted to him to harm the city of God. And the demon can boast about his power because there is nothing like it on earth, but it is unfit for war against the City of God and the truly faithful. Behold among these sure trials how often the Devil suggests that your faith is in vain and that you are among the number of the damned.

Many divine promises ought to enliven us sufficiently. And notice that the enemy says he can do nothing without the approval of God, since he says he has gone up not apart from the Lord.

Isaiah 36:11–21

And Eliakim, and Shebna, and Joah said to Rabshakeh, "Please speak to your servants in Syrian, because we hear; and may you not speak to us in Hebrew in the ears of the people who are upon the walls."

And Rabshakeh said, "Is it to your lord and to you that my master has sent me to speak those words? Is it not to the men who dwell upon the wall, they that shall eat their filth and drink the waters of their feet[6] with you?"

And Rabshakeh stood, and cried out with a loud voice in Hebrew, and he said, "Hear the words of the king, the great king of Assyria.

Thus said the king, 'Do not let Hezekiah impose upon you for he will not be able to deliver you.

'And do not let Hezekiah make you trust in the Lord saying, "Delivering the Lord will deliver you; He will not surrender that city into the hand of the king of Assyria."

'Heed not Hezekiah,' for thus said the king of Assyria, 'Make peace with me, and come out to me, and eat each one from his own vine and each one from his own fig tree, and drink each one from his own well water.

'Until I shall come and take you to a land just like your land, a land of grain and new wine, a land of bread and of vines.

'By no means let Hezekiah tempt you saying, "The Lord will free you." Did it happen that the gods of the nations delivered each one his land from the hand of the king of Assyria?

'Where are the gods of Hamath and Arpad? Where are the gods of Sepharvaim? And did they deliver Samaria from my hand?[7]

'What god is there in all of those lands who delivered his land from my hand so that the Lord should deliver Jerusalem from my hand?'"

And they kept silent and they did not answer him a word, for the command of the king that he spoke was "You shall not respond to him."

And Eliakim said.) Hezekiah's ambassadors, knowing the strategy of Rabshakeh, who is trying to stir up a disturbance among the people, beseech him to speak no more in the Hebrew language. For the people, hearing of the destruction of the high places and the altars, which they had believed were erected in God's honor, were able to vacillate. But the leaders were aware of this and so would not have paid attention.[8] For these men knew that the deed not only would not be detrimental to the health of the commonwealth but

---

6. The phrase "waters of their feet" means "urine."

7. These are rhetorical questions that expect an implied negative response.

8. Another way of translating this sentence is, "But not so the princes would have worried who were informed."

even would be beneficial. It appears from this that Rabshakeh was from among the Jewish deserters and the friends of Shebna, partly because he knew the prophets, partly because he spoke Hebrew, but this is a tenuous conjecture.

And even now the antichrist goes out from us, and he is not one of us, not being ignorant of the same tricks that he learned from his father the Devil, who first seduced Eve as the weaker one.

And Rabshakeh said.) See also in this place how in a sheep's clothing hides a wolf, for cunning Rabshakeh disguises himself as the friend of the people of Jerusalem, saying that he is not sent to have mercy on the king or on the leaders, who are unworthy of mercy, but rather on the people who were seduced by the leaders. And this is a trick of the antichrist, namely to make odious the true shepherds and those who are purely teaching the Word of God, so that he may more freely tear in pieces the sheep left behind by them: hence he especially defames them and he makes them suspect, as if they were infidels and seducers who by false counsels draw the people to their ultimate ruin, which he holds forth in tragic terms. For he sets forth two dreadful things, namely that for fear they will both defecate and urinate, and that for hunger they will be forced to eat filth of this sort. And so for this reason the apostle reminds Timothy not easily to accept an accusation against a presbyter except by two or three witnesses. Observe moreover this also: that the world considers as dung all the glorious things of the Christians, such as the Word of God, the cross, and the sacraments. On the other hand, Paul and the Christians for the sake of Christ no less despise all the glories of the world. Thus the pious are crucified to the world and the world to the pious.

And Rabshakeh stood.) From this speech of Rabshakeh it appears how great is the vanity of those in whom there is no knowledge of God, for they say nothing sound, but seek to prevail only with clamor and commotion and the din of empty eloquence. For Rabshakeh cries with a loud voice and in Hebrew, since he realized that already it was going badly for the common people. And although he boasts that he is there not without God's [leading], still he does not speak

the words of God, but rather he magnifies his own king, who also
is a man himself and a mortal. So also do many, who, forsaking the
Word of God, make a lot of noise and they call upon "the fathers,
the fathers" and "those most holy and upright men."

Then again he is zealous to slander Hezekiah as a seducer and
a liar, although he should have been *proving* him to be a liar. Surely
that would be easy even for any prostitute, but to disprove it is not
the same. He [Rabshakeh] says that it [Scripture] says that "God will
not deliver you." Where does he prove this lie? He will not be able to
prove that even one [person] out of all those who trust in God has
been abandoned. Moreover, it is no less foolish than impious of him
to compare the true God with idols. He knew the prophets, he knew
Hebrew, and does he dare so impiously to blaspheme? He passes
over innumerable miracles of God, he only taunts [them] with the
momentary abandonment that is before their eyes.[9]

For the rest, no more prudently today do all the antichristian
rhetoricians defend themselves and strive to whitewash a collapsing
wall. And truly they themselves are drunk with the wine of error of
which Rabshakeh is the cupbearer according to the interpretation
of his name.

Make peace with me.) Can it really be a blessing to enter upon a
covenant with the king who is tearing away [people] from Jerusalem, as if somehow it were a favor to daily await fetters, captivity,
and death? He offers fields, vineyards, and other no less cultivated
estates. But what exchange will a man be able to accept for his own
soul? It is not the same to live in a contaminated nation as [to live]
in a city in which God is praised daily. Is this your generosity, that
you would lead us into a kingdom where no one is not leprous? You
promise such things in order to steal greater things.

Who could trust you? Thus do you taunt God, whose city you
have not yet captured? What then will you do if she should come
into your power? They wish Hemath to be the Antioch mentioned

---

9. The phrase "which is before their eyes" may be translated "which they have
immediately in view."

by the ancients. Sepharvaim is in the region of the Assyrians, whence colonists came to Samaria. Jerome attests that Arpad was a city in Damascus.

And they kept silent and they did not answer.) They do not deserve the Word of proclamation who are accustomed to blaspheme the name of the Lord. For they are the swine and dogs before whom it is not fitting to throw pearls and the holy things. More merciful are those who remove the Word from them lest they become occasions of some even greater [guilt] and [lest] they burst forth into more serious blasphemies.

Isaiah 36:22–37:7

And Eliakim came, the son of Hilkiah who was over the household, and Shebna the scribe, and Joah the son of Asaph from the recorders to Hezekiah with rent clothes; and they announced to him Rabshakeh's words.

And it came to pass after King Hezekiah heard, he also rent his clothes; and he made himself to be covered with sackcloth and came to the house of the Lord.

And he sent Eliakim who was over the household, and Shebna the scribe, and the elder priests[10] covered with sackcloth to Isaiah son of Amoz, the prophet.

And they said to him, "Thus has said Hezekiah, 'The day of tribulation and of reproach and of blasphemy [is] this day; because the sons have come all the way to birth, and there is no strength for birthing.

'O that the Lord your God would hear the words of Rabshakeh whom his lord the king of Assyria sent to blaspheme the living God and to reproach his speech which the Lord your God has heard; and you will lift up a prayer on behalf of the remaining ones which have been found.'"

And the servants of King Hezekiah went in to Isaiah.

And Isaiah spoke to them, "Thus you will say to your master: thus spoke the Lord, 'Do not be frightened by the face of words which you heard with which the slaves of the king of Assyria blasphemed Me.

---

10. The phrase "elder priests" could also be translated "the chiefs of the priests."

*'Behold I give a spirit into him, and he will hear a message, and
he will return into his land, and I will overthrow him by sword in
his land.'"*

And Eliakim came.) You will now behold what should be done in
dangers and trials, and you will see, above all, the holy and truly
devout people in Jerusalem. For previously, however much a siege
was threatening and famine was oppressing, they were not in
mourning; but when they heard the blasphemy against God, they
rent clothes and they put on sackcloth. For thus our own disgraces
are to be despised and zeal for the glory of God [is to be shown].

The rending of the clothes bears witness to the extreme indigna-
tion and to the grief over the glory of God's despised name; and it
was fitting for every man to lose everything before he was willing, so
that he might yield something to the divine glory.

And it came to pass.) No lesser piety appears in the king. And learn
[this; that] however much we may have the most certain promises
of God and [however much] we may be fully aware of them, still it
is necessary that we not be lazy and complacent about them, especially in the midst of perils; but rather penitence must be observed
and God must be importuned with prayers.

Hezekiah was just and he had heard many promises, yet he did
not judge it to be beneath his kingly dignity to be dressed in hair-
cloth, or to be an example to others of humility and frugality, nor
was he simply clothed in plain sackcloth. But even when he was
covered he did not wish to be seen by the people, fulfilling by the
sackcloth that which Christ commanded, that when we are fasting
we are to anoint our face with oil. Moreover, by the term "sackcloth," fasting is also understood and the other things that pertain
to the disciplining of the body. And likewise, prayer also in trials is
necessary for us. For Christ then commanded His disciples: "Watch
and pray lest you enter into temptation." And He Himself also as
an example to us three times besought the Father when He was
approaching His passion.

Observe, moreover, how Belteshazzar, king of Babylon, and
Babylon itself, and Sodom and other cities perished almost in the

midst of luxurious pleasure. But Nineveh and Jerusalem were saved observing penitence.

And he sent Eliakim.) It did not seem enough for a pious king to pray on his own, for he also sends to Isaiah that he might intercede, either because [he believes] the prayers of many people will be heard more easily or because the prophet prays with greater assurance. You have here an example of seeking the intercessions of holy people living in this life. *But* we do not have in the same way examples in Scripture that we should take refuge in the saints who have *departed* this life.

On the other hand, so that the intercession of others might benefit us, we also by the example of Hezekiah ought to pray at the same time. Moreover, see here how great was the sanctity of our prophet, in whose prayers alone the welfare of the city seemed to be founded. See likewise in what great esteem he was held. [See] furthermore what he bears as the type of Christ, just as his name indicated. For through Christ we offer our prayers to the Father, who is our only mediator, advocate, and high priest in the presence of God. Moreover, the king sends to Isaiah also for another reason, namely that he himself and others may be strengthened by a new prophecy.

And they said to him.) At first he mentions the greatness of their danger saying: "the day of tribulation," that is, by which we are afflicted; "the day of reproach," by which we are reproached because of our sins; [and] "the day of blasphemy," on which the name of God hears evil. For the first two things in one way or another [are] endurable; this last thing for the faithful is hell and the pain is compared to those in labor, who, on account of their feebleness, are unable to give birth. Holy men burn with zeal and they grieve that they are unable to vindicate the glory of God's name. He next commands that the prophet be advised to intercede for them.

O that He would hear. [sic in Latin]) It is permitted to see how just was the prayer of those men. Nor indeed do they pray for their own advantage, but for the glory of God, and thus almost always do the saints pray. Thus the psalmist [says], "Help us, God our Savior, for

the sake of the glory of Your name, etc." And Moses [Ex.] 32 prays
on behalf of the people, that their slaughter might not overflow to
the disgrace of the divine name, for he says, "Lest the Egyptians
hear and say 'He could not lead them into the land,' etc." Also in
this passage, he begs that God be prayed to and that the blasphemy
of Rabshakeh might cease. In fact, this is truly praying in Jesus'
name so that the name of God might be hallowed.

Moreover, it is clear that the Assyrians would blaspheme even
more; for since they blasphemed so much when Jerusalem was not
yet captured, how much more would they do so once she were
made desolate.

On behalf of the remaining ones.) He says that the people of God have
been reduced to a small number so that God might be provoked to
greater mercy. On the other hand, the small number of people has
been mentioned earlier in many places: chapter one [verse 9], the
forsaken seed is mentioned; chapter 8 [verse 18], children for signs
and portents; chapter 13 [verse 12], a man more precious than gold;
chapter 18, consummation completed on earth,[11] chapter 17 [verse 6],
a cluster of olives and the harvesting[12] of olives; chapter 20 [verse 6],
an island; chapter 30 [verse 17], a mast[13] on the top of a mountain.

And the servants went.) We do not read what the king's ambassadors
said to the prophet. From which there is a close similarity to what is
written of Elisha in 4 Kingdoms 6 [2 Kings 6], in that, knowing of
their arrival through the prophetic spirit, Isaiah spoke first to them
in the words of the following prophecy in order to strengthen them.

Thus you will say to your master.) He says "to your" not "to our,"
either in the sense "you have been sent by him" or because, on

---

11. This reference is not so clear, in part because it occurs out of numerical
order, giving rise to suspicion. It is probably referring to chapter 18:5–6, although
other possibilities present themselves, such as 18:3 or 7, 15:9, or 16:4.

12. The word used specifically refers to the method of harvesting where there
is a shaking down with some remaining on the tree.

13. The word "mast" could also be translated as "tree" or "pole."

account of his eminent regard for the prophetic office, he would not recognize a lord other than God, [Isaiah himself] being above laws and kings as the Apostle says, "Shall we not judge even the angels?" In other matters, he was a debtor, so that he [Isaiah] was obeying every ordinance and power, as is read in the Apostle Peter [1 Peter 2:13]. But because he possessed nothing earthly, he did not have money pertaining to an earthly king. He says, "by the appearance of the words," that is, by the words themselves, which are nothing except ghosts and empty little terrors.

Behold I give into him.) Understand "spirit" as "desire" according to the Hebrew, also as we soon come to it below; "I could put a ring in the nostrils and a bridle in the lips," that is, I will make him withdraw with such easy strength as if he had a ring in his nose or as if the wind were driving the dust.

He will hear a message.) Who this might be will follow presently.

His land.) Namely, that of the Assyrians. There are some who explain "the land" as "Israel,"[14] for those returning from Egypt. And we also in our trials have this certain promise in which we may trust. For He says, "Behold I am with you always even to the consummation of the age."

Isaiah 37:8–13

And Rabshakeh returned and he discovered that the king of Assyria was fighting against Libna, since he had heard that he had set out from Lachish.

And he had heard that it was said about Tirhakah king of Cush, "He has gone up to fight with you"; and he heard and he sent messengers to Hezekiah saying:

"You will speak to Hezekiah the king of Judah saying: 'Let not your God in whom you trust deceive you saying, "Jerusalem will not be handed over into the hand of the king of Assyria."

---

14. The word "Israel" could also be understood to be only the Northern Kingdom.

> *'Behold you have heard what the kings of Assyria have done to all the lands, laying them waste, and will you be delivered?*
>
> *'Have the gods of the nations delivered them whom my fathers laid waste, Gozan and Haran, and Rezeph and the sons of Eden who [are] in Telassar?*
>
> *'Where [is] the king of Hemath, and the king of Arpad, and the king of Sepharvaim; has he not gone away and been bowed down?'"*

And Rabshakeh returned.) [For] how it is that Sennacherib left from Libna, which is Pelusium, a distinguished city of Egypt near Judah, see Josephus, *Antiquities*, book 10, chapter 1, where he cites Herodotus and Berosus as witnesses that the kings of the Assyrians waged war in Ethiopia and Egypt.

Moreover, the report that the king of the Assyrians had heard, according to Josephus, was a certain message that announced the arrival of the king of Ethiopia, and it forced him to lift the siege. Therefore, he turns against Hezekiah as the weaker one, and again by deceitfulness he tries to call back the king from faith in God. And see how an end to the trials is not given immediately, for although Rabshakeh had been confounded, still Sennacherib pursued the same blasphemies and he sent a letter full of no lesser blasphemy.

And he heard and he sent.) Here it means that he heard the response of Hezekiah through Rabshakeh, and Hezekiah will not acknowledge his tyranny, and so he has sent a letter that would have more authority.

You will speak to Hezekiah.) It is apparent that Isaiah's prophecy had been revealed to the Assyrians by the betrayal of Shebna, in that King Hezekiah did not fear the Assyrians for himself, having been strengthened by a divine oracle. So then he does this one thing through a letter in order to call the king away from his faith in God and in order to weaken the truth of the prophetic response. For the rest, just like above, so also now, "you fool and you impious person" [to Sennacherib], for indeed the truth itself cannot deceive, nor can the Highest Good not benefit those who trust in it.

Behold you have heard what they have done. [sic Latin]) All of the historians record that the kingdom of the Assyrians was most powerful and most ancient. Whence King Sennacherib, setting himself above his parents, argues: If the other kingdoms could not resist my parents, neither can you resist me. The impious king did not perceive [what] a distinction [there was] between the sons of God and the other nations, between the true God and demons.

Concerning Gozan, you have 4 Kingdoms 17 [2 Kings 17]; it might be in Media. Ptolemy, if his chart is not mistaken at Tablet 4, Asia 74.37, puts [it] in Mesopotamia near the River Chabora, which flows out of Mount Casio into the Euphrates; moreover, he says "Gauzam" for "Gozan." It is not far from Haran, which he calls Carre, to which Jacob had fled for help (Gen. 28), and whence Abraham departed when his father, Terah, had died there, (Gen. 12 and Acts 7). And among the historians it is famous for the massacre of Crassus, whom Surena the commander of the Parthians slew when he had captured him by trickery.

Strabo (Book 16) calls the river "Aborra." They called Reseph "the rock of Arabia." In Ptolemy you will find [it is] in the Palmyrian region, in the same chart 74.35. Furthermore, the sons of Eden are Eastern people who live in Telassar. These certainly, unless I am mistaken in my inference, are inhabitants of the Tigris in the Macedonian region of Babylon, along [that part of] the Tigris whose chief city he calls "Thalata," chart 4, 33.80. Concerning Hemath, it has often been said to be Antiochia Epiphania. Arpad, moreover, is said to be in Syria of Damascus. It is not clear where Sepharvaim is unless, as we read in 4 Kingdoms 17 [2 Kings 17], from there colonists were deported into Samaria. It is less certain concerning Ana and Ava, which the LXX calls one city.

I am following the [Targum of] Jonathan, which says: טלטילינון ואגליאונון הלא. "Have they not been transported and have they not departed?" In fact, they were transported into Damascus and Samaria.

Isaiah 37:14–20

And Hezekiah received the letter from the hand of the couriers, and he read it; and he went up into the house of the Lord, and Hezekiah laid it out in the presence of the Lord.

And Hezekiah prayed to the Lord saying,

"O Lord, God of the armies of Israel, sitting above the cherubim, You that [are] God alone over all the kingdoms of the earth; You have made the heavens and the earth.[15]

"Incline, O Lord, Your ear and hear; open, O Lord, Your eyes and see; and hear all the words of Sennacherib by which he has sent to curse the living God.

"Truly Lord, the kings of Assyria have desolated all the lands and the ground of them.

"And he has handed over their gods into the fire, for they are not gods themselves, but the work of human hands, wood and stone, which will perish.

"And now, O Lord, our Lord, save us from his hand that all the kingdoms of the earth may know that You are the Lord alone."

And Hezekiah received.) At one time, the Jews had the certain promise that their prayers in the temple would be heard. For so the Lord had said to Solomon, 4 Kingdoms 7 [*sic*; 2 Chronicles 7]: "My eyes will be open, and My ears attentive to the prayer of those who shall pray in that place."

Therefore, in whatever place they were, they would pray turned toward the temple. And so Daniel in Babylon prayed facing toward the temple. And Hezekiah in bed turns his face toward the wall of the temple when praying. But with the destruction of the temple at Jerusalem and with the glory of God shining forth in the whole world, Paul teaches in 1 Timothy 2 that we should turn toward the spiritual temple, namely Christ. "I wish," he says, "that men everywhere lift their hands to God." Then Hezekiah prudently did not read the blasphemies of the letter before the people lest he diminish their faith, but rather he read it before God, whom he knew to be his people's shield.

And Hezekiah prayed.) You have here the form of a holy and pious prayer, seeing that here many words occur that strengthen our faith. First he begins from the unutterable tetragrammaton name that we

---

15. In the commentary, a different verb is used that means "created," and "heavens" is singular.

express as "Adonai" [Lord]. The Hebrews write יהוה [Yahweh] with four letters, in which name [are] many mysteries that now we pass over. Nevertheless, it is a matter of special favor that God wished this name to be familiar to the people of the Jews, and He gave it to them in a particular covenant. Whence they were accustomed to invoke Him thus peculiarly, just as we also by our Lord's teaching call God our Father, which name itself is a reminder of no small covenant.

Moreover, the Lord testifies that at one time the name "Adonai" was not used, when He says in Exodus 6, "I am the Lord who appeared to Abraham, Isaac, and Jacob as God omnipotent, and I did not manifest My name 'Adonai' to them." Furthermore, that it is the name of a treaty and covenant, He adds, "I will take you for a people to Me and I will be your Lord, and you will know that I am the Lord God your Adonai." Then also the name "Sabaoth," which we also employ in [connection with] worship,[16] that name strengthens faith, for it signifies just as much the physical armies as the spiritual ones that fight against us, and which He is able to destroy in one moment; or that all armies are His servants, the heavenly as much as the earthly, and He can send them for the aid of His own people.

The Hebrew says אלהי ישראל [Elohe Israel], concerning which also we have noted earlier; for the most part, when it is connected with the tetragrammaton, it signifies God as judge and liberator. Earlier, when he says, "who sits above the cherubim," likewise he strengthens our faith just as when we spoke about his entering the temple. Moreover, the cherubim were certain small winged likenesses for covering the mercy seat, as in 3 Kingdoms 6 [1 Kings 6] and Exodus 25. And since God had promised that He would be the propitiator of those entering the temple, much more He was believed to be present at the ark and the mercy seat.[17] And truly God has wished always for there to be certain signs by which He might keep His people in faith lest they be led away by idolatries.

---

16. The word "worship" could also be translated as "holy matters."

17. The phrase "mercy seat" could be translated more literally as "propitiation place."

But our mercy seat is Christ, just as at Romans 3, "whom God has displayed," and at Hebrews 9. His two cherubim are two testaments, that is, the law and the gospel. Moreover, our faith is strengthened through the promises, whether in the old or the new law.

You that are God alone.)[18] Again he uses the name אלהים [Elohim], which has reference to judgment, as if to say, "You who are contained by neither heaven nor earth but who have founded them and have promised that You will be found to be propitiable in this place. However much You may scarcely seem to be 'our' God, still You are the God and Judge of all kingdoms."

You have created heaven and earth.)[19] These words also strengthen hope and faith, in that for Him who has created all things, it is a slight matter also to aid or assist us. For what are we compared with the heaven and the earth?

Incline, O Lord, Your ear.) You see that he reminds God of the words which He had spoken to Solomon.

Hear all the words of Sennacherib.) Again, he does not pray except on behalf of the glory of God's name. Indeed, the end of all of our prayer ought to be that God be glorified and that it be known that He Himself alone is God.

Isaiah 37:21–35

> And Isaiah son of Amoz sent to Hezekiah saying, "Thus has spoken the Lord the God of Israel, 'In that you have prayed to Me concerning Sennacherib, King of Assyria.'
>
> "This is the word which the Lord has spoken against him: 'She has despised you, she has mocked you, the virgin daughter of Zion; she has shaken [her] head after you, the daughter of Jerusalem.

---

18. The word "are" is missing in the Latin scriptural portion.

19. The Latin scriptural portion uses the word "made" instead of "created" and the word "heavens" instead of "heaven."

'For whom have you taunted and whom have you blasphemed, and over whom have you lifted up your voice and have you raised up the pride of your eyes, against the Holy One of Israel.

'In the hand of your servants, you have reproached my Lord, and you have said, "In the multitude of my cavalry I have gone up [to] the summit of the mountains the sides of Lebanon; and I have cut down the tallness of her cedars her chosen fir trees, and I have come to the highest point of her borders and to the forest of her cultivated field.

"I have dug and I have drunk water and with the sole of my footstep I have dried up all the rivers of the siege mounds."

'Or have you not heard from afar, I did it and I formed it from the ancient days; now I have brought it forth and it has happened for devastation and for laying in wasted heaps the fortified cities.

'And their inhabitants have feared and been confounded as cripples. They have become the grass of the field and the green grass and the hay of the roofs[20] and have been burned up before they sprouted.

'I have known your habitation and your going out and your going in, and I have known the tumult of your assembly against me.

'Inasmuch as the raging of your assembly against me and your extravagance have come up in my ears, I will both put a bridle in your nostrils and a muzzle in your lips and I will make you return[21] on the way which you came.

'And this will be the sign for you: Eat in this year what falls down, and in the second year what springs forth on its own; and in the third year sow and reap and plant vineyards and eat their fruit.

'And the redemption of the sons of Judah will be gathered together, that is the remainder of the root which is below, and it will form fruit above.

'For the remnant will go out from Jerusalem and salvation from Mount Zion; the zeal of the Lord of the hosts will do it.'

"Therefore thus said the Lord to the King of Assyria, 'He will not come to this city,[22] and he will not hurl an arrow there; and a shield will not seize her, and he will not throw against her a rampart.

'On the road by which he came on it he will return, and he will not come to this city,' said the Lord.

---

20. The phrase "hay of the roofs" could be translated as "thatch" or "hay of plasterers."

21. The word order is changed in the commentary quote, but not the meaning.

22. The word order is different in the commentary, but not the meaning.

'And I will be a shield over that city, that I may save her for my sake and for the sake of David my servant.'"

And Isaiah sent.) God their merciful guard does not allow them to be tempted further than what they can bear, nor does He scorn their prayers. And thus, here also, Hezekiah is answered through the prophet. And learn in how much honor He holds His elect ones, and learn also with what great mercy He pursues [His elect ones], likewise with what great severity He punishes those who treat His servants unworthily.

This [is the] word which he has spoken.) This prophecy is full of expressions of fondness, as are all. For He addresses His people by the name of Zion and Jerusalem like a boy and a tender little daughter whom a father wishes not to be despised, as if He were saying: "I consider well how the injury of the enemy has affected you my beloved and tender daughter. This only I have allowed: that he despise and mock you." Meanwhile, by the name Zion and Jerusalem, understand also that "the church" (which also is called "the virgin" by the apostle, since he says "I espoused you to one man") in this world has been despised and has been the offscouring of all. And yet the Redeemer and Savior will not forget her forever. Nor must all the injuries of this life be considered in any other way than as if a weakling, who must by all means be condemned, were to make slight ridicule of us, who afterward are to be crowned with endless joys.

For whom have you taunted.) He turns his speech to Sennacherib, whose crime He makes clear according to the common usage of Scripture, intending next to add the penalty, and all of this for the consolation of Jerusalem. Now, moreover, He says that it is no small injury by which His sons have been offended. For whoever will strike one of the least servants of God, strikes God Himself. Thus also Christ speaks to Paul when he is persecuting the church, "Saul why do you persecute Me?" and Zechariah 2, "Whoever touches you touches the pupil of My eye." Therefore, every person who has been despised [in this world] is made full in regard to the Holy One of Israel, that is

God Himself, who has sanctified Israel to Himself and has chosen Israel for a peculiar people and is sanctified in Israel. Furthermore, Sennacherib's sin is greater in that not only did he himself sin but he also sent his servants to blaspheme. For "in the hand of your servants" [means] "through [the agency] of your servants."

In the multitude of my cavalry.) Sennacherib asserts in his boastful bragging that he has laid waste the entire holy land that begins from Mount Lebanon and extends all the way to Egypt. By the "height of the mountains" understand the region around Dan and where the Jordan originates. There, close by Damascus, whatever was lifted up and tall I took away: princes and distinguished leaders (who are signified by cedars and fir trees), destroying them and leading them into captivity.

And so laying waste he has crossed over to the height or to the utmost part of his territory, and he has even gone to the forest of a field planted with fruit-bearing trees, that is, he has come to Jerusalem, which is the chief city of the whole land. Whence he says arrogantly, "Since I have laid waste the other lands, nothing prevents me from also laying waste Jerusalem, and so I will be the lord of the whole land." Then he boasts that he even has arrived at Egypt and at the mouths of the Nile, which he has dried up by the multitude of his men.[23] Or again understand [that he speaks here] by another metaphor concerning Jerusalem.

"I have dried up all of the streams of the ramparts," that is, "all of the land I have subjected to myself; I will seize the fount itself, namely Jerusalem." His arrogance is like that of the Devil, who spares neither Christ nor His elect, but tempts them [with the claim that] he has previously subdued the whole human race to his tyranny. For Christ and His church might be called "the height of the summit."

Or have you not heard from afar.) This passage is explained in two ways. First, Sennacherib is warned, lest he be ignorant, that whatever he has done he has done by divine ordination; and thus it convicts him of boasting just as above in chapter 10, "Will the ax

---

23. This is a reference to classical literature concerning an incident with Xerxes.

boast over against him who does the cutting?" And "I made it and I have formed it and I have brought it about" is explained [by] 'understanding "it" to be the dispensation of all things.

"And since I^{24} have done [it], what are you presuming to claim for yourself? And My will has come about that you should lay waste cities and make of them molehills fighting among each other, (that is according to the Hebrew "demolished heaps") and that the inhabitants of the cities should be crippled and weak and those who were strong like the grass of the field and green vegetation should become dry like roof grass, which dries before it is fully grown." Others explain it as follows: "Do you not know that I have chosen Jerusalem and her people, and I have wished them especially to be Mine, and on account of them I have also in time past laid kingdoms waste and I have turned fortified cities into ruined heaps; wherefore, O Sennacherib, you should more rightly fear them than they you...."

Thus also the church has been chosen by God, as in Romans 8: "I have chosen you."[cf.] John 3; and against the apostles all of the heretics, philosophers, and kings prevailed not at all, and all the princes of the world were crippled ones and as the grass of the rooftops in which no vigor appears.

And your habitation.) The sense [is]: "Just as I have done all things through your fathers, so you also have done nothing without Me. Indeed I have known your habitation and going out. Through Me it has come about that you were occupying those lands; I was ignorant of none of these things which you have attempted up to now, however much I may have feigned that appearance.[25]

'That you may see this, behold, you will not be able to go any further except as much as it pleases Me. And My will will be for Me as a muzzle and a bridle with which to restrain you according to My desire." From this it is also clear enough that Sennacherib served the divine will as an instrument and nonetheless was culpable by his

---

24. The "I" here is emphatic.

25. The meaning here is that God has in some ways disguised His providential hand so that He is left unnoticed as a primary cause, especially by the unbeliever.

sin. Therefore, "free will" has no dignity as long as we are looking to the divine things, by which everything subsists by sure laws. And from this it is manifest [that] our opponents are not able to do more against us than God has permitted them.

I will make you return.)[26] In fact, the king did return to his people in dishonor, and he was made a witness of what great things God had done, as below.

And this [will be] the sign for you.) He strengthens the faith of Hezekiah and the Jerusalemites by a new and extraordinary sign, that he might know that Sennacherib will not prevail. The sign moreover was as follows: Sennacherib had devastated all the land of Judea [while] crossing over into Egypt, whence arose the famine that was dealt with earlier. "I will give you bread in short supply." But God so blessed the fields that the things that fell when trampled by the enemy in the first year still sufficed for the Jerusalemites. In the second year, moreover, those things that sprang up from the trampled parts were sufficient for harvest, and finally in the third year they again began to sow. And this sign truly was given to them, but no less to us, namely, Christ in Himself, if only we will believe.

Indeed, since by His flesh He satisfies us far more happily than once did the manna satisfy those who were in the desert, clearly also by feeding He will preserve us secure for the future life more than the fallen and renewed crop once fed the Jerusalemites. The third year has reference to the mystery of the resurrection, which carries within itself full peace and the abundance of all fruits.

And the redemption [of the sons] will be gathered together.) By the "deliverance" and the "remnants" and "delivered ones" understand those who had been shut up in Jerusalem and later were saved from capture by Sennacherib.

---

26. The word order is different in the Latin scriptural portion, but not the meaning.

And the remainder of her, whose.)[27] The saints of God are compared to a tree that has been cut down, whose root and trunk are still below ground, from which it draws moisture; although it is despised among men, nevertheless, again it sprouts and brings forth fruits upward. For those who are despised in this world bring forth before God fruit that is both copious and heavenly, and although they die, nevertheless they will live forever. Wherefore also the apostle says he wishes us to be rooted by faith in the land of the living ones.

For from Jerusalem.) He promises here two things, that those who have been shut up and straitened in dire straits by the siege of the enemy will go out again without fear of the enemy. Especially also the church of Christ must first be gathered by the apostles in Jerusalem and then it must be spread abroad in the whole world.

Therefore thus said the Lord.) He promises the deliverance more clearly because Sennacherib is not going to harm them saying, "He will not come"; that is, "He will not conquer" and "He will not shoot an arrow," even more he will not have the power of harming or defending. The power of attacking is signified by "arrows" but defending [is signified] by the "shield."

"He will not come into this city.")[28] For his army was extinguished on that night before the day in which he was preparing to attack.

"And I will be a shield over [that] city.") And just as also earlier He compared Himself to a hen who offered herself for her chicks. Moreover, He says, "for My own sake" because His name had been blasphemed, He works all things for His own sake, as below in chapter 48, "For my Name's sake I will make my rage to be far off," and chapter 42, "I will not give my glory to another." Therefore, vengeance must be left to God, Deuteronomy 20, "Vengeance is mine and I will repay."

---

27. This is a summary reference rather than an exact quote from the Latin scriptural portion.

28. The word order is different in the Latin scriptural portion, but not the meaning.

However, He adds, "for the sake of David [My] servant" so that He may recall to memory the promise given to David, whereby they may be more strengthened in their faith. Nor is it what someone might construe as homage of the deceased saints either here or in similar passages. For here he is mentioned that we might be mindful of the covenant of God and trust Him. Thus, for David's sake the kingdom of Solomon will not be removed, 3 Kingdoms 11 [1 Kings 11]. See, moreover, that nothing is ascribed to the sanctity of Isaiah or Hezekiah or others; but God says, "I will do it for My sake." Finally, what is permitted to happen here is temporary, but what is promised to the church is eternal. The church, which is safe from every hostile attack and against which the gates of hell do not prevail. From this we can learn that the enemy is not coming or shooting an arrow. We have, moreover, the stronger promise given to us in Christ, who was God's beloved, and He Himself is that poor and wise one through whom God delivered the city [Eccl. 9:15].

Isaiah 37:36–38

> *And the anger of the Lord went out and struck in the camp of Assyria 185,000 and they awoke in the morning and behold, they [were] all dead bodies.*
>
> *And Sennacherib, King of Assyria, set out and departed*[29] *and returned and lived in Nineveh.*
>
> *And it came to pass, he himself was worshiping in the temple of his god Nisroch, and Adrammelech and Sharezer, his sons, struck with the sword, and they themselves escaped into the land of Ararat; and Esarhaddon his son reigned in his place.*

And the angel of the Lord went out.) This is that remarkable miracle that has been touched upon frequently throughout this book, that Jerusalem will be freed from her cruelest enemies, not by a human but by a divine hand, as [mentioned] in chapter 9, when the scepter of the overseer is overcome as in the day of Midian.

---

29. The commentary adds a preposition lacking in the Latin scriptural portion, but this does not change the meaning.

- Chapter 10. A scourge like the ruin of Midian and a rod above the sea. And in the same place the small flask is broken in fright.

- Chapter 16. The dust is limited and let the wretched man be consumed.

- Chapter 17. Just as the dust of the mountains is carried away by the face of the wind, just as a whirlwind before a storm, this is the lot of those who have devastated us.

- Chapter 25. The Lord is become the strength of the poor, [our] hope in the midst of whirlwind, a shade from the heat, and He has a banquet of fat things.

- Chapter 28. Just as the Lord stands in Mount Perazim and in the valley of Gibeon.

- Chapter 29. The multitude of those troubling you will be as fine dust and in the same place [there will be] a punishment in thunder and earthquake.

- Chapter 31. The Lord will do battle as a lion over Mount Zion.

- Chapter 33. The plunderer is become the plunder and the one laying waste is laid waste. And the people will be like ash from a conflagration. These things, moreover, happened in Nob not far from Jerusalem, as [is mentioned] above in chapter 10. The day is yet [coming] when one will take a stand at Nob.

They [the Jews] hand down, furthermore, that these things were done on the night of the Passover, in which the army of the Egyptians was submerged. We have often had to do with the allegory because these things were fulfilled by Christ, who by His own death conquered the world and delivered us from the Devil's bondage, things that are typified for us by the submerging of the Egyptians in the mystery of our baptism.

And he set out and he departed.)[30] Here is fulfilled what was said earlier in chapter 30.[31] "Behold I will give to him a spirit" [37:7]. And later, "I

---

30. The commentary adds a preposition lacking in the Latin scriptural portion, which does not change the meaning.
31. This probably refers to 30:28.

will lead you back on the way in which you came" [37:34]. Moreover, he does not perish before Jerusalem, so that by his dishonor he may be a witness of the glorious works of God; and so that he who was seeking to slay the sons of God may be slain by his own sons, otherwise, they who were the most powerful and the flower of the whole nobility of the East would have perished. Thus, truly, 2 Chron. 33 [sic 32:21], the angel has struck every strong man and warrior and the leader of the army. For this leanness or plague has been sent against the fat, as above in chapter 10. Whence it can be exclaimed against them, "Where is the learned, where is the scribe, where [is] the prosecutor? [1 Cor. 1:20]."

And it came to pass.) The tradition of the Hebrews is that Sennacherib asked his priests for what reason he was not able to conquer the Jews, and the response was that Abraham was willing to sacrifice his son Isaac to God.

Wherefore the king, wishing by way of imitation to oblige his god to himself, attempted to slay his two sons Adrammelech and Sharezer. [They] however, having slain their father escaped into Ararat, which is in Armenia situated to the north of Assyria.

And Esarhaddon reigned.) This is the glorious mutability of earthly things, even in the things that appear most blessed and firm.

Latin	German	English
Et factum est, in quartodecimo anno regis Hizkiiahu, ascendit Sanherib rex Assur contra omnes ciuitates Iehudah munitas, & expugnauit eas.	Es begab sich im Vierzehenden Jar des Künigs Hizkiah daz der Sennacherib ain künig auß Assyrien hinauf wider alle vest stett Jehuda zoch uñ nam sy ein.	1. And it came to pass, in the fourteenth year of King Hezekiah, Sennacherib King of Assyria went up against all the fortified cities of Judah and conquered them.
Et misit rex Assur, ipsum Rabsake à Lachis ad Ierusalã, ad regem Hizkiiahu in exercitu magno: & stetit in aquaeductu piscinae superioris, in uia agri fullonis.	Unnd der Künig aus Assirien hat den Rabsake selbs von Lachis zů dem Künig Hizkiah gen Jerusalem mit grossem Hœre gesandt. Und er ist am strom des obern Teichs gestanden der da ligt an der Straß auf dem Acker des Walckmüllers.	2. And the king of Assyria sent Rabshakeh himself from Lachish to Jerusalem to King Hezekiah in the midst of a great army, and he stood in the channel of the upper pool in the way of the fullers' fields.
Et exiuit ad eũ Eliakim filius Hilkiiahu, qui domui praeerat: & Sebna scriba, & Ioah filius Asaph à commentariis.	Eliakin aber der Hofmaister ain Sun Hilkia und der Canzler Sebna auch Joah der Secretari ain Sun Asaph seind zů im hinausgangen.	3. And there went out to him Eliakim the son of Hilkiah who was in charge of the palace and Shebna the scribe, and Joah the son of Asaph from the recorders.

Bibliography

Alighieri, Dante. *Epistle to Can Grande della Scala*. James March-
     and, trans. In *Dante to Cangrande: English Version*. Accessed
     at http://ccat.sas.upenn.edu/jod/cangrande.english.html,
     Feb. 14, 2009.

Backus, Irena. "What Prayers for the Dead in the Tridentine
     Period?" In *Reformiertes Erbe*, 13–24. Zürich: Theologischer
     Verlag, 1993.

Baker, J. Wayne. "Church Discipline or Civil Punishment: On the
     Origins of the Reformed Schism, 1528–1531." *Andrews Uni-
     versity Seminary Studies* 23 (1985): 3–18.

———. "Covenant and Society: The *Respublica Christiana* in the
     Thought of Heinrich Bullinger." PhD diss., University of
     Iowa, 1970.

———. *Heinrich Bullinger and the Covenant: The Other Reformed Tradi-
     tion*. Athens, Ohio: Ohio University Press, 1980.

Bainton, Roland H. *Studies on the Reformation*. Boston: Beacon
     Press, 1963.

Bienert, Wolfgang A. "Marcion in Werk Martin Luthers." In *Rez-
     eption und Reform: Festschrift für Hans Schneider zu seinem 60
     Geburtstag*, Wolfgang Breul-Kunkel, Lothar Vogel, Hans
     Schneider, Donald F. Durnbaugh, eds., 19–34. Darmstadt,
     Germany: Verlag der Hessichen Kirchengeschichtlichen
     Vereinigung, 2001.

Bild, Guy. "Bild an Luther," *Zeitschrift des Historischen Vereins für Schwaben und Neuberg* 20, no. 160 (1893): 221–222. Accessed at http://periodika.digitale-sammlungen.de/schwaben/Band_bsb00010266.html, Aug. 19, 2010.

Bromiley, Geoffrey W., ed. and trans. *Zwingli and Bullinger: Selected Translations with Introductions and Notes*. Philadelphia: Westminster, 1953.

Bucer, Martin. *The Common Places of Martin Bucer*. D. F. Wright, trans. Appleford: Sutton Courtenay, 1972.

Cairns, Earle E. *Christianity Through the Centuries*. Grand Rapids: Zondervan, 1954.

Calvin, John. *Articles concernant l'organisation de l'église et du culte à Genève*. Submitted to the Genevan city council, January 16, 1537.

———. *Commentary on the Book of the Prophet Isaiah*. William Pringle, trans. Grand Rapids: Eerdmans, 1947.

———. *New Testament Commentaries*. Thomas H. L. Parker, ed. Grand Rapids: Eerdmans, 1959–65.

———. *Corpus Reformatorum* [CR]. Volume 39. William Baum, Edward Cunitz, Edward Reuss, eds. Brunsvigae: C. A. Schwetschke and Sons, 1863–1900.

———. *The Epistles of Paul the Apostle to the Romans and to the Thessalonians*. Ross McKenzie, trans. Grand Rapids: Eerdmans, 1980.

———. *Institutes of the Christian Religion*. Henry Beveridge, trans. 2 vols. Grand Rapids: Eerdmans, 1970.

———. *Johannes Calvini in Epistolam Pauli ad Romanos*. Thomas H. L. Parker, trans. Leiden: E.J. Brill, 1981.

———. "Partaking of the Flesh and Blood." In *Calvin: Theological Treatises*. J. K. S. Reid, trans., 292. Philadelphia: Westminster, 1954.

Chrysostom, John. *Patrologiae cursus completus....* J. P. Migne, ed., 55:126–127. Paris: Garnier Fratres, 1879.

———. *Saint John Chrysostom Homilies on Genesis 1–17*. Robert C. Hill, trans. Washington, D.C.: Catholic University of America Press, 1986.

Chung-Kim, Esther. "Consent of the Ancients: Role of the Fathers in Sixteenth Century Debates over the Lord's Supper." PhD diss., Duke University, 2005.

Cottrell, Jack W. "Covenant and Baptism in the Theology of Huldreich Zwingli." PhD diss., Princeton Theological Seminary, 1971.

d'Aubigné, Merle Jean-Henri. *History of the Reformation of the Sixteenth Century*, H. White, trans., vol. 4, book 16. New York: American Tract Society, 1836.

Demura, Akira. "Church Discipline According to Johannes Oecolampadius in the Setting of His Life and Thought." PhD diss., Princeton Theological Seminary, 1964.

———. "Two Commentaries on The Epistle to the Romans: Calvin and Oecolampadius." In *Calvinus sincerioris religionis vindex*. Wilhelm H. Neuser and Brian G. Armstrong, eds., 165–188. Kirksville, Missouri: Sixteenth Century Journal Pub., 1997.

English Standard Version Bible. Wheaton, Ill: Crossway, 2001.

Fairbairn, Donald. "Patristic Exegesis and Theology: The Cart and the Horse." *Westminster Theological Journal* 69, no. 1 (Spring 2007): 1–19.

Farmer, Craig S. "Changing Images of the Samaritan Woman in Early Reformed Commentaries on John." *Church History* 65, no. 3 (September 1996): 373.

Fraenkel, Peter. "Ten Questions Concerning Melanchthon, the Fathers, and the Eucharist." In *Luther and Melanchthon*, Vilmos Vajta, ed., 146–164. Philadephia: Muhlenberg, 1961.

Froude, James A. *Life and Letters of Erasmus*. New York: Scribners, 1895.

Fudge, T. A. "Icarus of Basel?" *The Journal of Religious History* 21, no. 3, 268–284.

Gauss, Julia. "Basels politisches dilemma in der Reformationzeit." *Zwingliana* 15 (1979–82): 509–548.

Gorday, Peter. *Principles of Patristic Exegesis, Romans 9–11 in Origen, John Chrysostom, and Augustine*. New York: Edwin Mellen, 1983.

Greschat, Katharina. "'Dann sind gottwilkommen Marcion und Marciönin': Marcion in den reformatorischen

Auseinandersetzungen um das Abendmahl." In *Marcion und seine kirchengeschichtliche Wirkung* 150:235–251. Gerhard May, Katharina Greschat, and Martin Meiser, eds. Berlin/New York: Walter de Gruyter, 2002. In series Texte und Untersuchungen zu Geschichte der altchristlichen Literatur. ["'Then Marcion and the Marcionites are acceptable to God': Marcion in the Reformation Disputations over the Lord's Supper." In *Marcion and His Impact on Church History*.]

Hammer, Karl. "Der Reformator Oekolampad (1482–1531)." In *Reformiertes Erbe*, 157–170. Zürich: Theologischer Verlag, 1993.

———. "Oecolampads Reformprogramm." *Theologische Zeitschrift* 37, no. 3 (May–June 1981): 149–163.

Herminjard, Aimé Louis, ed. *Correspondance des réformateurs dans les pays de langue française*. 9 vols. Reprint. Nieuwkoop: De Graaf, 1965–66.

Hess, Salomon. *Lebensgeschichte D. Johann Oekolampads, Reformators der Kirche in Basel*; nebst einem Anhang ungedruckter Briefe von Oekolampad an Zwingli. Zürich: Ziegler und Söhne, 1793.

Hoffman, Hermann Gottfried. "Sententia Patrum: Das Patristiche Argument in der Abendsmahlskontroverse zwischen Oekolampad, Zwingli, Luther und Melanchthon." PhD diss., Ruprecht-Karl Universität zu Heidelberg, 1971.

Horsch, John. "The Faith of the Swiss Brethren (2)." *Mennonite Quarterly Review* 5, no. 1 (January 1931): 17f. #115.

Kittelson, James M. *Wolfgang Capito: From Humanist to Reformer*. Leiden: E. J. Brill, 1975.

Köhler, Walther. "Das Marburger Religionsgespräch." *Schriften des Vereins für Reformationsgeschichte* 48 (1929).

———. *Das Marburger Religionsgespräch 1529: Versuch einer Rekonstruction*. Leipzig: M. Heinsius Nachfolger Eger & Sievers, 1929.

Kuhr, Olaf. "Calvin and Basel: The Significance of Oecolampadius and the Basel Discipline Ordinance for the Institution of Ecclesiastical Discipline in Geneva." *Scottish Bulletin of Evangelical Theology*, no. 16 (Spring 1998): 19–33.

———. *Die Macht des Bannes und der Busse: Kirchenzucht und Erneuerung der Kirche bei Johannes Oekolampad, 1482–1531.* Bern: Peter Lang, 1999.

Kweit, Jan J. "The Life of Hans Denck (ca. 1500–1527)." *Mennonite Quarterly Review* 31, no. 4 (October 1957): 227–259.

Law, David R. "Descent into Hell, Ascension, and Luther's Doctrine of Ubiquitarianism." *Theology* 107, no. 838 (July–August 2004): 250–256.

Lillback, Peter. *The Binding of God: Calvin's Role in the Development of Covenant Theology.* Grand Rapids: Baker, 2001.

Locher, Gottfried W. *Zwingli und die schweizerische Reformation.* Göttingen: Vandenhoeck & Ruprecht, 1982.

Luther, Martin. *D. Martin Luther's Werke.* Weimar: H. Böhlaus, 1912–30.

Maley, William J. "*Contra Julianum* of St. Cyril of Alexandria and St. Peter Canisius." *Theological Studies* 25, no. 1 (March 1964): 70–74.

Manschreck, Clyde Leonard. *Melanchthon: The Quiet Reformer.* New York: Abingdon, 1958.

McNeill, John T. *The History and Character of Calvinism.* New York: Oxford University Press, 1954.

Moeller, Bernd. *Imperial Cities and the Reformation.* Philadelphia: Fortress, 1972.

Northway, Eric W. "Patristic Reception and Eucharistic Theology in Johannes Oecolampadius (1482–1531), with Special Reference to the *Adversus Haereses* of Irenaeus of Lyons." PhD diss., University of Durham, 2009.

Oecolampadius, Johannes. *Annotationes piae ac doctae in Euangelium Ioannis.* Basel: Cratander, 1533. Also Basel: Cratander and Bibelium, 1535.

———. *Antisyngramma ad Ecclesiastes Suevos, una cum horum Syngrammate.* Gesammengedruckt zu Basel, 1525. 8.N.2.Basel: [unknown printer], 1525. Also in Zürich: Froschauer, 1526.

———. *Commentarii omnes in libros Prophetarum.* Basel: Crispinus, 1558.

———. *Das der miszverstand D. Martin Luthers uff die ewigbstendige wort Das ist mein leib nit beston mag.* Basel: Cratander, 1527.

———. and Oswald Mykonius. *Enarratio in euangelium Matthaei D. Io. Oecolampadio autore: et alia nonnulla quae sequens pagella indicabit.* Basel: Andreas Cratander and Johann Bebel, 1536.

———. *In Epistolam B. Pauli Apost. ad Rhomanos Adnotationes.* Basel: Cratander, 1525 and 1526.

———. *In Epistolam Ioannis apostoli Catholicam primam, Ioannis Oecolampadii demegoriae, hoc est homiliae una & XX.* Basel: Cratander, 1524.

———. *In Hieremiam prophetam commentariorum libri tres.* Basel: Apiarius, 1533.

———. *In Iesaiam Prophetam Hypomnematon, hoc est, commentariorum, Ioannis Oecolampadii Libri VI.* Basel: Cratander, 1525.

———. *In postremos tres Prophetas, nempe Haggaeum, Zachariam et Malachiam, commentarius.* J. Oecol: cum gratia et privil: Caes. Basel: Cratander, 1527.

———. *In prophetam Ezechielem commentarius.* Basel: Apiarius, 1534.

———. *In Psalmos LXXIII LXXIIII, etc. conciones.* Basel: Robert Winter, 1544.

———. *Ioannis Oecolampadii, doctoris undecunque doctissimi in librum Iob exegemata.* Basel: Henric Petris, 1532.

———. *Liber Psalmorum Dauidis.* Basel: Henricus Stephanus, 1562.

———. "Unterrichtung von dem Widertauff von der Oberkeit und von dem Eyd auff Carlins N. widertauffers artickel.— Antwort auff Balthasar Hubmeiers büchlein wider der Predicanten gespräch zu Basel von dem kinder tauff." Basel: Cratander, 1527.

Pelikan, Jaroslav. *The Christian Tradition: A History of the Development of Doctrine: vol. 4, Reformation of Church and Dogma (1300–1700).* Chicago: University of Chicago Press, 1984.

Pries, Edmund. "Anabaptist Oath Refusal: Basel, Bern and Strasbourg, 1525–1538." PhD diss., University of Waterloo, 1995.

Poythress, Diane. "Johannes Oecolampadius' Exposition of Isaiah, Chapters 36–37." 2 volumes. PhD diss., Westminster Theological Seminary, 1992.

Raitt, Jill. *The Eucharistic Theology of Theodore Beza.* Chambersburg, Pa.: American Academy of Religion, 1972.

Registers of the Consistory of Geneva in the Time of Calvin, 1542–1544, vol. 1. Robert M. Kingdon, ed. Grand Rapids: Eerdmans, 2000.

Roussel, Bernard. "De Strasbourg à Bâle et Zurich: une 'école Rhénane' d'exégèse (*ca* 1525–*ca* 1540)." *Revue d'Histoire et de Philosophie Religieuses* 68 (1988): 19–39.

Rupp, Ernest Gordon. *Six Makers of English Religion 1500–1700.* London: Hodder and Stoughton, 1957.

———. *Patterns of Reformation.* London: Epworth, 1969.

Staehelin, Ernst. *Das Buch der Basler Reformation: zu ihrem vierhundertjährigen Jubiläum im Namen der evangelischen Kirchen von Stadt und Landschaft Basel.* Basel: Helbing & Lichtenhahn, 1929.

———. *Briefe und Akten zum Leben Oekolampads.* Leipzig: M. Heinsius Nachfolger Eger & Sievers, 1927; New York: Johnson Reprint Corp., 1971.

———. *Frau Wibrandis: Eine Gestalt aus den Kämpfen der Reformationszeit.* Bern and Leipzig: Gotthelf-Verlag, n.d. [1934?].

———. *Oekolampad-Bibliographie.* 2. Aufl. Nieuwkoop: DeGraaf 1963.

Strohl, Henry. *La pensée de la Réforme.* Neuchatel/Paris: Delachaux et Niestlé, 1951.

van 't Spijker, Willem. "Des kirchengeschichtliche Kontext des Genfer Psalters." In *Genfer Psalter und seine Rezeption in Deutschland, der Schweiz und den Niederlanden*, Willem van 't Spijker, 45–60. Tübingen: Niemeyer, 2004.

Wackernagel, Rudolf. *Humanismus und Reformation in Basel.* Basel: Helbing & Lichtenhahn, 1924.

Walchenbach, John Robert. "John Calvin as Biblical Commentator: An Investigation into Calvin's Use of John Chrysostom as an Exegetical Tutor." PhD diss., University of Pittsburgh, 1974.

Wendel, François. *Calvin, sources et évolution de sa pensée religieuse.* Paris: Presses Universitaires de France, 1950.

Ziegler, Donald, ed. *Great Debates of the Reformation.* New York: Random House, 1969.

Zwingli, Huldreich. *Huldreich Zwinglis sämtliche Werke.* Vol. 8. Emil Egli *et al*, eds. Leipzig: M. Heinsius Nachfolger, 1914. [CR 95.] Also Vol. 14. Zurich: Verlag Bericht Haus, 1959. [CR 101.]

Scripture Index

Galatians
2:16   89
2:20   74
6:14   74

Ephesians
book of   6

Philippians
3:8   74

Colossians
book of   1, 32, 128, 133, 171
3:1   128

1 Thessalonians
2:13   63

2 Thessalonians
2:4   173

1 Timothy
1   89
2   190
4:8   109
5:19   181

Hebrews
book of   2, 105, 133, 171
1   104n64
9   89, 192

1 Peter
1   89
2:13   187

1 John
book of   2, 14, 132, 133, 171
1   72
1:1   87n7
2:16–17   74
2:18   86
4:1   87n6
5:24   88n10

Revelation
2   73
3:7   63
4   104n64
6   73
18:2   72

Index of Subjects